Annotations to Surplus Lines Statutes

SIXTH EDITION

RONNIE L. JOHNSON, EDITOR

AMERICAN BAR ASSOCIATION
Tort Trial and Insurance Practice Section

Cover design by Betsy Kulak/ABA Design

Printed in the United States of America.

27 26 25 24 23 5 4 3 2 1

ISBN 978-1-63905-295-0

A catalog record for this book is available from the Library of Congress.

Contents

Preface

This book will be very useful to insurance regulatory lawyers, surplus lines brokers, surplus lines insurers, state surplus lines associations, and stamping offices. Attendees at National Association of Insurance Commissioners meetings have expressed interest in an updated edition.

The surplus lines market segment has grown tremendously since the fifth edition of this book. Surplus lines carriers have been providing more coverage in hard-to-insure markets and when the insurance market becomes "hard"—meaning domestic insurance prices rise. As two examples, in Louisiana, 85 percent of property insurance on properties south of Interstate 10 is insured under surplus lines policies. In Texas, over the last few months, $1 billion in premiums was spent each month in the surplus lines market. And with more catastrophic losses, such as losses caused by wildfires, hurricanes, and other weather-related events, causing a hardening market, the amount of insurance written through the surplus lines market has and will continue to increase greatly. Industries such as construction that find getting coverage to be a difficult task are also turning to the surplus lines market. The U.S. surplus lines insurance market size was valued at $52.1 billion in 2019 and is projected to reach $125.9 billion by 2027.

Much of what was covered in the fifth edition of the book was affected or displaced by the Non-Admitted and Reinsurance Reform Act (NRRA), which was part of Dodd-Frank, and other changes to the law.

Some states are attempting to assert more regulatory control over surplus lines insurers to protect consumers, even though they are not admitted in the state and even though this was not done historically.

Timothy M. Thornton and Ronnie L. Johnson

Acknowledgments

During the fall of 2016, I was tasked by the Excess, Surplus Lines & Reinsurance Committee of the American Bar Association to update *Annotations to Surplus Lines Statutes*. The book, which was in its fifth edition, had not been updated since 2009.

Much had changed since the last publication. The Nonadmitted and Reinsurance Reform Act (NRRA, or "Act") was signed into law on July 21, 2010, by President Barack Obama as part of the larger Dodd-Frank Act. The NRRA, which went into effect a year later, made fundamental changes to surplus lines law. Most notably, the Act (1) limited regulation of the placement of each surplus lines risk to the home state of the insured; (2) limited taxation of the risk to the home state of the insured; and (3) prohibited states from imposing state-specific insurer eligibility requirements other than those set forth in the Act.

I reached out to a number of the people who had been involved with the last edition and asked if they would help with the update. David Childers, Dan Maher, and David Ocasek agreed to participate. Alex Gonzales, Ben McKay, Sabrina Miesowitz, and Steven Stephan also agreed to join in on the endeavor. Andrew McNichol assisted David Childers, Howard Greene assisted Dan Maher but went on to play a much more substantial role, and Joe Gunset filled in for Sabrina Miesowitz when he retired following an almost 20-year career with Lloyd's.

An early decision of the group was to start from scratch in preparing summaries of the laws of each state. The states were divided up among the group members and a template for providing information was developed. On December 18, 2017, Howard Greene, Dan Maher, Ben McKay, David Ocasek, Steven Stephan, and I met in Denver and worked on revising the draft template from 8:00 a.m. to 5:00 p.m. with only a one-hour lunch break. David Ocasek was kind enough to serve as the scribe for the new template, a service that would entitle him to many more hours of additional services as scribe.

Work continued on the state summaries, and the last of the state summaries was received in March 2020. A meeting of the group was scheduled for April 2, 2020, in Salt Lake City, Utah, in conjunction with another surplus lines meeting. The purpose of the meeting was to address the tone and wording of the state summaries so that it would appear as if the same person or group of persons wrote each state summary. Of course, the COVID-19 pandemic forced the cancellation of that meeting.

On June 10, 2020, the group had a call and a subgroup was established to edit the state summaries to ensure they were complete, consistent, and of one voice. The editorial group consisted of Joe Gunset, Howard Greene, Ben McKay, David Ocasek, and me. Three-hour working sessions were scheduled via Zoom for every Wednesday, commencing in June 2020 and ending in February 2021. Our illustrious scribe, David Ocasek, shared his screen and made all of the revisions that the editorial group felt necessary.

Everyone who worked on this book felt passionate about having the best and most useful product available on the market. We certainly hope you feel this way about the book.

It has been a pleasure working with each of the fine people who played a part, and I will miss the weekly three-hour Zoom meetings with my friends.

Ronnie L. Johnson

About the Editor

Ronnie L. Johnson, J.D., is a Member of McGlinchey Stafford, PLLC where he advises clients nationwide on insurance regulatory matters, governmental relations and issues management. He is the current Vice-Chair of the Federation of Regulatory Counsel, serves on the board of directors of State Law Resources, is active with Surplus Lines Law Group, and served as Chair of the ABA TIPS Insurance Regulation Committee for two years. Ronnie is ranked by Chambers USA, and is a *Martindale-Hubbell* AV Preeminent® Peer Review Rated Lawyer. Prior to joining McGlinchey Stafford, he served as Deputy Commissioner of Insurance, Office of Property and Casualty, for Louisiana.

About the Contributors

S. David Childers, JD, recently retired from Kutak Rock where he was chair of the firm's Insurance, Regulatory, and Governmental Affairs practice. Prior to joining Kutak Rock, David was director of insurance for the state of Arizona and later president of the firm Low & Childers, P.C. where he practiced law from 1990 to 2009. He obtained his juris doctor from Louisiana State University.

Alexander J. Gonzales, JD, is a partner at Duane Morris. Alex practices in the areas of corporate and insurance regulatory law. He serves as a team lead for the Duane Morris insurance/reinsurance industry group. For more than 30 years, he has represented insurance companies and other financial institutions in regulatory matters, including mergers and acquisitions; company formation and licensing; administrative and compliance proceedings in insurance, antitrust, market conduct, DTPA, and rate matters; as well as representation in legislative matters involving the creation and implementation of legislative and regulatory strategies. Alex is a former associate commissioner of insurance at the Texas Department of Insurance, and was acting commissioner in 1990. While at the department, he developed the concept for and drafted the initial legislation for the Insurance Fraud Bureau. Prior to entering private practice, Mr. Gonzales served as a trial attorney and command staff judge advocate in the U.S. Navy, Judge Advocate General's Corps.

Howard Greene is the director of government affairs & strategic initiatives for the Excess Line Association of New York (ELANY). Howard is an industry veteran of more than 30 years; he has been with ELANY since May 2017. He came to ELANY from TIAA, where he was vice president of state government relations and associate general counsel. Prior to that, Greene held similar positions with GRE Insurance Group and the Risk and Insurance Management Society in New York.

Joseph Gunset, JD, retired from Lloyd's after spending just under 20 years as Lloyd's first full-time U.S. general counsel. While at Lloyd's he built a high-quality legal team for Lloyd's; participated in the negotiations for a temporary suspension of U.S. regulatory deposits following the events of 9-11; worked with counsel for Berkshire Hathaway to insure regulatory approvals of the National Indemnity-Equitas reinsurance transaction; participated in the efforts to seek an amendment to the Dodd-Frank Act, which created the U.S. Federal Insurance Office; and coordinated with industry representatives on the creation of the Terrorism Risk Insurance Act. After retiring from Lloyd's, he joined McGlinchey Stafford to work with Ronnie Johnson and his team, focusing on state regulatory matters.

Ronnie L. Johnson, JD, is a member of McGlinchey Stafford, PLLC where he is on the firm's Policy Committee (governing body), leads the firm's insurance regulatory practice, and leads the firm's government relations and issues management practice. In addition to advising clients on a nationwide basis, he is the current vice chair of the Federation of Regulatory Counsel, serves on the board of directors of State Law Resources, and is active with Surplus Lines Law Group.

Dan Maher, JD, is the executive director and chief operating officer of the Excess Line Association of New York (ELANY). The Association is a statutorily created industry advisory association responsible for facilitating and encouraging compliance with New York's excess line law. He joined the association in 1997 and, as a registered lobbyist in New York state, has influenced a number of changes to the New York state insurance law. Prior to joining ELANY, Dan served as senior vice president and general counsel for Lancer Insurance Company from 1985 to 1997, where he was responsible for, among other things, the analysis of insurance policy coverage and commercial and insurance litigation. From 1982 to 1985, he was general counsel and secretary for DMT Financial Group, and, from 1981 to 1982, he was a litigation associate for Greenhill, Speyer & Thurm.

Benjamin J. McKay, JD, MPA, is the chief executive officer and executive director of The Surplus Line Association of California. He previously spent eight years with the Property Casualty Insurers Association of America (PCI) as senior vice president for federal government relations. In that role, Ben was named one of Washington, D.C.'s top lobbyists five times by *The Hill*, one of the city's leading political newspapers. Prior to his time at PCI, he served as chief of staff to a member of the U.S. Congress in Washington, D.C., and worked on financial services and international relations issues.

David Ocasek is the chief executive officer of the Surplus Line Association of Illinois, a nonprofit association created by public statute to act as a liaison between the Illinois Department of Insurance and surplus line producers, and to provide marketplace data, education, and compliance support. He joined the Association in 1991 as its assistant executive director, and became CEO in 1998. He is responsible for the development and implementation of the overall strategic goals of the Association with a focus on technology, education, and regulatory affairs. During his tenure, he has guided the Association through major business model and regulatory changes, as well as a 1,200 percent growth in volume. Prior to joining the Association, David held positions with Dallas-based Golf Corp, American Medical International in Los Angeles, the Chicago Sting Soccer Team, and Playboy Enterprises, where he began his career after attending Yale University.

Steve Stephan, JD, CPCU, ARe, ASLI, MCM, is a partner at Egan Nelson, LLP where his practice focuses on representing insurance agents and brokers, managing underwriters, surplus lines brokers, and insurance carriers. He previously served as general counsel for a surplus lines insurer, director of government relations for a surplus lines agent's and carrier's association, and regulatory counsel for a large surplus lines broker. He has broad insurance regulatory experience, having worked on insurance broker compliance in all 50 states, insurance broker compensation compliance, insurance electronic trading platforms, Insuretech, insurance agent and broker acquisitions, carrier-producer transactions, risk purchasing groups, master polices, and drafting policy forms. He previously served as a law clerk at the Missouri Supreme Court and the Kansas Federal District Court. He is active with the Surplus Lines Law Group, SILA Surplus Lines Subgroup, and has taught surplus lines classes for 15 years.

ALABAMA

Alabama Department of Insurance
201 Monroe Street, Suite 502
Montgomery, AL 36104
(334) 269-3550
www.aldoi.gov
Insdept@insurance.alabama.gov

Alternate Address:
P.O. Box 303351
Montgomery, AL 36130-3351
Producer Licensing: (334) 240-3282

Alabama does not have a stamping office.

Nonadmitted Insurer Eligibility

General Information

A certificate of authority is not required for surplus lines coverages that are lawfully written.

(ALA. CODE § 27-3-2(3))

Alabama has not instituted a formal approval process of foreign and alien insurers but rather must be in compliance with the following. It is the obligation of the surplus lines broker to verify compliance with the eligibility requirements.

(ALA. CODE § 27-10-26(b))

Foreign

Foreign insurers must be authorized in at least one state for the kind of insurance involved and have capital or surplus, or both, amounting to at least $5 million; or guaranteed trust fund amounting to at least $5 million. Further, a foreign insurer is not eligible if it has transacted insurance as an authorized insurer in its state or country of domicile for less than five years, unless it is a wholly owned subsidiary of an insurer authorized to transact insurance in this state, or unless it makes a deposit of cash or securities acceptable to the commissioner and with a market value of not less than $1 million.

(ALA. CODE § 27-10-26(b), (c))

Alien

Alien insurers must be authorized to transact insurance in at least one state of the United States, unless the insurer shall have established an effective trust fund of at least $2.5 million within the United States administered by a recognized financial institution and held for the benefit of all its policyholders or policyholders and creditors in the United States, and with capital or surplus, or both, amounting to at least $15 million. Further, an alien insurer is not eligible if it has transacted insurance as an authorized insurer in its state or country of domicile for less than five years, unless it is a wholly owned subsidiary of an insurer authorized to transact insurance in this state, or unless it makes a deposit of cash or securities acceptable to the commissioner and with a market value of not less than $1 million.

(ALA. CODE § 27-10-26(b), (c))

Nonadmitted Insurer Eligibility List

Alabama does not maintain a nonadmitted insurer eligibility list. *See* http://www.aldoi.gov/FAQ.aspx#SurplusLines (last visited July 15, 2020).

Types of Coverage Permitted or Prohibited

General Information

Alabama does not have an export list of coverages. However, the Alabama Department of Insurance through Bulletin No. 2010-01 has effectively exempted personal or commercial property insurance coverages for wind and/or hail for properties located within an area in Baldwin County or Mobile County south of the southern right-of-way line of Interstate 10 from diligent effort requirements.

(Alabama Department of Insurance Bulletin No. 2010-01)

Exempt Transactions

The Alabama surplus line insurance law does not apply to the following insurances when so placed by licensed agents or brokers of this state:

- Wet marine and transportation insurance;
- Insurance on subjects located, resident, or to be performed wholly outside of this state or on vehicles or aircraft owned and principally garaged outside this state;
- Insurance on property or operation of railroads engaged in interstate commerce;
- Insurance of aircraft owned or operated by manufacturers of aircraft or aircraft operated in scheduled interstate flight, or cargo of such aircraft or against liability, other than workmen's compensation and the employer's liability, arising out of the ownership, maintenance, or use of such aircraft; and
- The property and operations of the shipbuilding and ship repair industry engaged in interstate or foreign commerce and vessels, cargoes, watercraft, piers, wharves, graving docks, drydocks, marine railways, and building ways, commonly known as wet marine.

(Ala. Code § 27-10-34)

Service of Process

Insurers transacting under the surplus lines law shall be deemed thereby to have appointed the commissioner as its attorney upon whom may be served all lawful process in any action or proceeding against it in this state arising out of such insurance.

(Ala. Code § 27-10-33(a))

Licensed nonresident surplus lines brokers shall be considered to have appointed the commissioner as their attorney to receive service of legal process issued against the nonresident in this state upon causes of action arising within this state out of transactions under the nonresident's surplus line broker license. Service upon the commissioner as such attorney shall constitute effective legal service upon the nonresident.

(Ala. Code § 27-10-24(c)(1))

Limitations on Actions Involving Judicial Proceedings

"No unauthorized insurer shall institute or file, or cause to be instituted or filed, any action or proceeding in this state to enforce any right, claim, or demand arising out of any insurance transaction in this state until such insurer has obtained a certificate of authority to transact such insurance in this state." The prohibition of bringing action by unauthorized insurers in Alabama does not apply to transactions where a certificate of authority is not required, surplus line coverages written under the surplus lines law of Alabama, or coverages exempted from the surplus line law (see Ala. Code § 27-10-34 for list of coverages exempted).

(Ala. Code § 27-10-3(a), (b))

Domestic Surplus Lines Insurers

Alabama statutes have no provision allowing domestic surplus lines insurers.

Nonadmitted Insurer Filing Requirements

Alabama statutes do not set forth periodic filing requirements for nonadmitted insurers.

Surplus Lines Broker Licensing

Both individuals and business entities transacting as surplus lines brokers must maintain surplus lines licenses to conduct surplus lines business in Alabama.

Individuals licensed as resident property insurance producers may be licensed a surplus lines broker for the same lines they are authorized for as a resident producer with (1) application to the commissioner; (2) license fee paid to commissioner; and (3) a currently in force bond in the sum of at least $50,000 of aggregate liability in favor of the State of Alabama.

(ALA. CODE § 27-10-24(a)(1)–(3))

Business entities that act as surplus lines brokers must designate and pay a fee for each individual operating under that license.

(ALA. CODE § 27-10-24(b))

In order for nonresident individuals and business entities to obtain surplus lines broker licenses:

a. The person must submit to the commissioner a copy of the application for licensure that was submitted to the home state.
b. The person must submit form [AL-SLB-13] requesting licensure and pay the fees as set forth in section 27-4-2.
c. The person's home state must issue a nonresident surplus line broker license to persons from Alabama on the same basis.
d. The person is currently licensed as a resident surplus line broker and is in good standing in the applicant's home state.
e. The authority under the Alabama surplus line broker license will be coterminous with the person's home state authority as a surplus line broker.

(ALA. ADMIN. CODE 482-1-036-.03(2)(a)–(e))

Due Care in Selecting Nonadmitted Insurer

The commissioner may suspend or revoke a surplus lines broker's license if it finds that, among other things, a surplus lines broker has "willfully or without exercise of due care" placed a policy with an unauthorized insurer.

(ALA. CODE § 27-10-32(b))

Diligent Effort/Diligent Search

Surplus lines insurance may be procured from unauthorized insurers when the full amount of insurance required cannot be procured, after diligent effort, from insurers authorized to transact and actually transacting that kind and class of insurance in this state or has been procured to the full extent such insurers are willing to insure.

(ALA. CODE § 27-10-20(1)(b))

Export List

Alabama does not maintain a list of coverages that may be exported to the surplus lines market without first making a diligent search of licensed insurers.

Exempt Commercial Purchasers

Although the NRRA (15 U.S.C. § 8201) exempts a broker from any diligent search requirements when the insured is an exempt commercial purchaser, the Alabama Insurance Code does not address this topic.

Surplus Lines Broker Filing Requirements

Surplus lines brokers must file with the commissioner a written report indicating the surplus lines coverage has been lawfully placed. This report is due within 30 days after the effective date of such insurance.

(ALA. CODE § 27-10-21)

Surplus lines brokers are required to file with the commissioner a verified statement of all surplus lines transactions during the preceding calendar year on or before the first day of March each year (Ala. Code § 27-10-30(a)). The statement should be on forms prescribed by the commissioner and detail:

- Gross amount of each kind of insurance transacted;
- Aggregate gross premiums charged, exclusive of sums collected to cover state or federal taxes;
- Aggregate of returned premiums and taxes paid to insureds;
- Aggregate of net premiums; and
- Additional information as required by the commissioner.

(Ala. Code § 27-10-30(b))

Notices

All surplus lines coverages must "be initialed by, or bear the name and license number of, the surplus line broker who procured it and shall have stamped upon it the following: 'This contract is registered and delivered as a surplus line coverage under the Alabama Surplus Line Insurance Law.'"

(Ala. Code § 27-10-22)

Additionally, particular classes of personal lines coverages require an additional acknowledgment form to be signed by the insured.

See AL Department of Insurance Bulletin No. 2013-03 at https://www.aldoi.gov/Legal/Bulletins.aspx (last visited Nov. 11, 2020).

Taxes, Stamping Fees, and Other Government-Imposed Charges

Surplus lines tax is 6 percent on the direct premiums, less return premiums and exclusive of sums collected to cover state or federal taxes, payable by the broker to the state treasurer through the commissioner.

(Ala. Code § 27-10-31(a))

Producer, Policy, Inspection, and Other Fees

Alabama generally prohibits additional fees but allows the charging of administrative fees to process property and casualty insurance applications when the fees have been approved by the commissioner.

(Ala. Code § 27-12-17(b))

The commissioner approved certain fees with limits in a bulletin dated 12/21/2001, which was effective 1/1/2002, and is available at https://www.aldoi.gov/currentnewsitem.aspx?ID=173 (last visited Dec. 2, 2020).

Industrial Insured Exemption

When coverage cannot be obtained through authorized insurers, surplus lines coverages are available to industrial insureds, which are defined as insureds:

- That procure the insurance of any risk by use of services of a full-time employee acting as an insurance manager or buyer or the services of a regularly and continuously retained, qualified insurance consultant;
- Whose aggregate annual premiums for insurance on all risks other than workmen's compensation and group insurance total at least $25,000.00; and
- That have at least 25 employees.

(Ala. Code § 27-10-20(2))

Independent or Direct Procurement Law

Alabama allows for insureds to independently procure insurance coverages from unauthorized foreign insurers. Insureds who do so must file within 90 days of procuring such insurance a written report on a form designated by the commissioner detailing the information of the coverage. Independently procured coverage is subject to a tax of 4 percent of the gross premium. This tax is due within 30 days after the coverage was indecently procured. Should the insured fail to remit such tax to the commissioner, it is subject to a tax of 6 percent per annum, compounded annually.

(Ala. Code § 27-10-35)

ALASKA

Alaska Division of Insurance
Department of Commerce, Community,
and Economic Development
333 Willoughby Avenue, 9th Fl.
Juneau, AK 99801-1770
(907) 465-2816

https://www.commerce.alaska.gov/web/ins/SurplusLines/PremiumTaxAudits.aspx
insurance@alaska.gov

Alaska does not have a stamping office.

Nonadmitted Insurer Eligibility

General Information

Surplus line insurers must meet eligibility standards in order to underwrite risks presented by specially licensed surplus lines brokers. To be eligible, the nonadmitted insurer must establish satisfactory evidence of good repute and financial integrity and must meet one of the eligibility requirements.

(Alaska Stat. § 21.34.040)

In addition to meeting the requirements of AS 21.34.040, a nonadmitted insurer shall be considered an eligible surplus lines insurer if it appears on the most recent list of eligible surplus lines insurers published by the director.

(Alaska Stat. § 21.34.050)

If an insurer has less than the minimum capital and surplus otherwise required, the insurer may satisfy the requirements of this section upon an affirmative finding of acceptability by the director. The director's finding must be based on factors including quality of management, capital and surplus of any parent company, company underwriting profit and investment income trends, market availability, and company record and reputation within the industry. The director may not make an affirmative finding of acceptability when the nonadmitted insurer's capital and surplus is less than $4.5 million.

(ALASKA STAT. § 21.34.040(f))

Foreign

A foreign but nonalien insurer, mutual insurer, reciprocal insurer, or a mutual protection and indemnity association must either have the minimum unimpaired basic capital and additional surplus equal to that required in its domiciliary jurisdiction, or $15 million, whichever is greater.

Each syndicate or insurer belonging to an insurance exchange created by the laws of individual states may qualify if the insurance exchange maintains capital and surplus, or the substantial equivalent, of not less than $50 million in the aggregate; for insurance exchanges that maintain funds for the protection of all insurance exchange policyholders, each individual syndicate shall maintain minimum capital and surplus, or the substantial equivalent, of not less than $3 million.

(ALASKA STAT. § 21.34.040(e))

Alien

Alien insurers must be published on the NAIC International Insurer Department's most recent quarterly listing to be eligible.

(ALASKA STAT. § 21.34.040(e)(7))

A Lloyd's syndicate or an insurer belonging to a similar group, including incorporated and individual unincorporated insurers, may qualify if it maintains a trust fund jointly and severally with the other members of the group in an amount not less than $50 million, as security to the full amount, for the protection of all policyholders and creditors of each member of the group in the United States.

(ALASKA STAT. § 21.34.040(e)(4))

Nonadmitted Insurer Eligibility List

In addition to meeting the requirements of AS 21.34.040, a nonadmitted insurer is considered an eligible surplus lines insurer if it appears on the most recent list of eligible surplus lines insurers published by the director of the Division of Insurance. The list is to be published at least semiannually by:

1. Posting the list on the division's internet website at https://www.commerce.alaska.gov/web/ins/SurplusLines.aspx (last visited July 15, 2020); and
2. Providing a copy of the list to a person on request to the division.

A nonadmitted insurer shall be removed from the list of eligible surplus lines insurers if the nonadmitted insurer fails to meet the requirement under AS 21.34.040(d). However, the director may reinstate a nonadmitted insurer on the list of eligible surplus lines insurers if the nonadmitted insurer has remedied the reason for removal from the list.

(ALASKA STAT. § 21.34.050)

Types of Coverage Permitted or Prohibited

A surplus lines broker can procure insurance other than reinsurance, wet marine and transportation insurance, insurance independently procured, life insurance, health insurance except as provided in AS 21.34.035, and annuity contracts from nonadmitted insurer.

(ALASKA STAT. § 21.34.020(a))

Exempt Transactions

The surplus line tax does not apply to insurance of risks of state government or its political subdivisions, to an agency of state government or its political subdivisions, or to insurance of aircraft primarily engaged in interstate or foreign commerce.

(ALASKA STAT. § 21.34.180(i))

Service of Process

The transaction of insurance by an unauthorized person or nonadmitted insurer is deemed an irrevocable appointment of the director and the successors of the director in office to be the lawful attorney of that person or insurer upon whom may be served all legal process, except in an action, suit, or proceeding by the director or by the state.

(ALASKA STAT. § 21.33.021)

Limitations on Actions Involving Judicial Proceedings

Alaska statutes do not set forth any limitations on actions involving judicial proceedings that apply to the lawful transaction of surplus lines business.

Domestic Surplus Lines Insurers

Alaska statutes have no provision allowing domestic surplus lines insurers.

Nonadmitted Insurer Filing Requirements

Foreign Surplus Lines Insurers

In order to remain eligible as a surplus lines insurer, the following requirements must be met by June 30th each year:

- Maintain capital and surplus of $15 million and electronically file with the National Association of Insurance Commissioners (NAIC), the company's annual statement including all supplementary reports, exhibits, and schedules required by the NAIC.
- Provide a Certificate of Compliance from the company's domiciliary state showing the lines of authority it is authorized to write by July 1st of the current year.

Alien Surplus Lines Insurers (On the Quarterly Listing of Alien Insurers)

A non-U.S. insurer (alien) is considered eligible to write insurance in Alaska on an unauthorized basis in Alaska if it is listed on the Quarterly Listing of Alien Insurers maintained by the NAIC.

See https://www.commerce.alaska.gov/web/ins/SurplusLines.aspx (last visited Aug. 26, 2020). When accessing the site, scroll down to Surplus Line Insurers—Eligibility Continuation.

Alien Surplus Lines Insurers (Not on the Quarterly Listing of Alien Insurers)

Alien insurers that are not on the Quarterly Listing of Alien Insurers and who wish to write business in Alaska must apply for approval to be listed on the eligible surplus lines insurer list. The director needs to approve an alien insurer's request for eligibility.

The following renewal requirements are due by September 30th of each year:

- An audited financial statement
- Payment of $600 (a $500 renewal fee plus a $100 annual statement fee)
- Proof of a minimum of $2.5 million deposited in a U.S. financial institution (Trust statement only, please does not send a copy of the agreement.)

See https://www.commerce.alaska.gov/web/ins/SurplusLines.aspx (last visited Aug. 26, 2020). When accessing the site, scroll down to Surplus Line Insurers—Eligibility Continuation.

Surplus Lines Broker Licensing

In order for an applicant or licensee to qualify for a surplus lines broker license, one must first meet the general qualifications in the statute for insurance licensing.

(Alaska Stat. § 21.27.020)

In addition, the applicant must be licensed as either an insurance producer or managing general agent for property and casualty lines of authority, and, if required by the director by regulation, maintain a bond as described in the statute in an amount acceptable to the director that requires the surplus lines broker to conduct business under title 21.

(ALASKA STAT. § 21.27.190)

A surplus lines broker must promptly remit the taxes and fees required by law, return premiums promptly when due, and pay proper losses promptly. If the director requires, applicants must maintain an errors and omissions insurance policy acceptable to the director.

(ALASKA STAT. § 21.27.790)

Due Care in Selecting Nonadmitted Insurer

A surplus lines broker may procure insurance from a nonadmitted insurer only if the insurer is an eligible surplus lines insurer.

(ALASKA STAT. § 21.34.020(a))

Insurance may be procured through a surplus lines broker from a nonadmitted insurer that does not appear on the current published eligible list only if the portion to the risk cannot be obtained from a nonadmitted insurer that appears on the list under AS 21.34.050 or on the list described in AS 21.34.040(c)(7).

Diligent Effort/Diligent Search

A surplus lines broker or a producing broker must conduct a search of the licensed market to attempt to procure the coverage from a licensed insurer that the broker has reason to believe might consider writing the type of coverage or class of insurance. Diligent search efforts of the admitted market must be documented prior to binding with a surplus lines insurer. The documentation must be provided to the surplus lines broker no later than 15 days after binding. An affidavit is one acceptable method of documenting the search and needs to be maintained in the client's file.

(Section 3 AAC 25.010, ALASKA STAT. § 21.34.020)

See also https://www.commerce.alaska.gov/web/ins/SurplusLines.aspx (last visited Aug. 20, 2021).

Export List

Alaska maintains an export list. The list of coverages currently on the export list are set forth in AK Regulatory Order No. R 17-02, as amended. The order is updated periodically. The most recent update, as of October 1, 2020, was AK Regulatory Order No. R 20-01, which is available at https://aws.state.ak.us/OnlinePublicNotices/Notices/View.aspx?id=196655 (last visited Oct. 10, 2020). To see the full updated list when accessing the site, scroll down to the section titled Attachments, History, Details and click on the pdf attachment.

Exempt Commercial Purchasers

For any insured that meets the standards of an exempt commercial purchaser, insurance may be procured from a surplus lines broker even when such coverage may be available in the licensed market, if the broker has disclosed to the exempt commercial purchaser that the insurance may or may not be available from the admitted market that may provide greater protection with more regulatory oversight; and the exempt commercial purchaser has subsequently requested in writing that the broker procure or place the insurance from a nonadmitted insurer.

(Alaska Stat. § 21.34.020(b))

Alaska recognizes the Exempt Commercial Purchaser definition under NRRA.

(Alaska Stat. § 21.34.900(13) and Bulletin B 11-03 (July 22, 2011))

Surplus Lines Broker Filing Requirements

A surplus lines broker shall file with the director, on forms prescribed by the director, a report of all surplus lines insurance, by type of insurance as required to be reported in the annual statement that must be filed with the director by admitted insurers.

The report must include all surplus lines insurance transactions during the preceding period, showing the aggregate gross premiums written, the aggregate return premiums, the amount of aggregate tax remitted to this state, and the amount of aggregate tax remitted to each other state for which an allocation is made under AS 21.34.180. The forms shall be filed quarterly on March 1, June 1, September 1, and December 1 of each year.

(ALASKA STAT. § 21.34.170)

As of June 1, 2018, Alaska requires the quarterly reports be made through OPTins.

See Insurance Department reporting instructions, https://www.commerce.alaska.gov/web/ins/SurplusLines.aspx (last visited Oct. 14, 2020).

Notices

Every evidence of insurance negotiated, placed, or procured by a surplus lines broker must bear the name of the surplus lines broker, which may not be covered, concealed, or obscured by the producing broker, and the following legend in at least ten-point type:

> This is evidence of insurance procured and developed under the Alaska Surplus Lines Law, AS 21.34. It is not covered by the Alaska Insurance Guaranty Association Act, AS 21.80.

A surplus lines insurer must include with each policy, an Alaska Policyholder Notice. The approved form of the Alaska surplus lines policyholder notice required under 3 AAC 25.050 is:

> ALASKA POLICY HOLDER NOTICE
>
> This policy is issued by a nonadmitted or surplus lines insurer. Insurance may only be purchased from nonadmitted insurers if the full amount, kind, or class of insurance cannot be obtained from insurers who are admitted to do business in the State of Alaska. Your broker or the surplus lines broker has determined that this was true on the date the policy was placed. Before issuing a renewal policy or extending this policy, remarketing is

required. To avoid intentional or unintentional extension of coverage in the surplus lines market when an admitted market for that coverage exists, a nonadmitted insurer is prohibited from the automatic renewal or extension of a policy without remarketing by your broker or the surplus lines broker.

A surplus lines insurer may submit another format for review and possible approval by the director.

In order to comply with the Alaska Administrative Code, the following notice is also given:

> You are hereby notified that, under 3 AAC 25.050, your policy will terminate effective no later than the date and time of its expiration. We reserve the right to cancel this policy sooner than the expiration date by giving you notice of cancellation as required in AS 21.36.220. You may request through your broker that a new policy from the surplus lines broker be concurrent with the effective date of the termination of this policy. You are also notified that a new policy, if issued by us, is subject to rerating, which may result in a premium increase of more than ten percent (10%). As required by 3 AAC 25.050, you are hereby notified that any subsequent policy issued by us may be subject to a ten percent (10%) or more increase in premium. The actual premium will be based upon rates that apply at the time a subsequent policy, if any, is issued and will be made available to you before the effective date of the new policy, or the date subsequent coverage is bound, whichever occurs first.

Taxes, Stamping Fees, and Other Government-Imposed Charges

For insurance other than wet marine or transportation, a surplus lines broker must pay a tax of 2.7 percent plus 1 percent filing fee, on the net premium, which is the total gross premiums written, less any return premiums, when Alaska is the home state of the insured.

(Alaska Stat. § 21.34.180, § 21.34.190)

The tax is 0.75 percent for wet marine and transportation insurance.

(ALASKA STAT. § 21.34.180, § 21.33.055)

Where the home state of the insured is Alaska and the insurance covers properties, risks, or exposures located or to be performed both within and outside Alaska, the tax payable will be computed based on an amount equal to 2.7 percent on that portion of the net premiums allocated to Alaska, plus an amount equal to the portion of the premiums allocated to other states or territories based on the tax rates and fees applicable to other properties, risks, or exposures located or to be performed outside Alaska.

(ALASKA STAT. § 21.34.180)

Producer, Policy, Inspection, and Other Fees

Alaska permits brokers to charge broker's fees to the insured as long as the insured signs a written contract which must:

1. Contain an appointment by the client naming the insurance producer as their broker;
2. Set out the duties, functions, powers, and authority of the insurance producer as broker;
3. Disclose the amount of the broker's fee charged to the client, including amounts charged by surplus lines wholesalers to access their markets; and
4. Be kept in the insurance producer's permanent records and made available for the director's inspection.

The three permitted forms of compensation for brokers fees are:

1. Fee that requires the insurance producer to offset or reimburse the client for the full amount of a commission earned by the insurance producer;
2. Combination of a fee paid by a client and a commission paid by an insurer with which coverage is placed that may offset or reimburse a client for all or part of a commission earned by the insurance producer if the amount of the commission is disclosed to the client; or

3. Commission paid by an insurer with which coverage has been placed.

(ALASKA STAT. § 21.27.560)

Industrial Insured Exemption

Alaska statutes and regulations do not contain an industrial insured exemption with regard to surplus lines insurance.

Independent or Direct Procurement Law

Alaska allows individuals to procure, continue, or renew insurance from foreign insurers. The insured must file a report with the Director of Insurance within 30 days of the coverage date. The insured is subject to a 3.7 percent premium tax to the Director of Insurance on all insurance other than wet marine or transportation insurance. Wet marine and transportation is subject to a tax of 0.75 percent.

(ALASKA STAT. § 21.33.061)

ARIZONA

Arizona Department of Insurance
100 North 15th Avenue
Suite 102
Phoenix, AZ 85007
(602) 364-2499
https://insurance.az.gov/contact-us

Arizona has a stamping office.

Surplus Lines Association of Arizona
15849 N. 71st Street, Suite 100
Scottsdale, AZ 85254
(602) 279-6344
https://www.sla-az.org/

Nonadmitted Insurer Eligibility

General Information

An unauthorized Lloyd's association or similar association must maintain a trust fund in the United States of at least $100 million as joint and several security.

(Ariz. Rev. Stat. § 20-413(D))

An unauthorized insurance exchange authorized to transact insurance in at least one other state must possess minimum aggregate capital and surplus of $50 million. Each syndicate with which a risk is to be placed must possess minimum capital and surplus of at least $5 million. The insurance exchange must maintain a deposit of at least $2.5 million in public custody in trust, in part, for the purpose of protecting all of the policyholders of the insurance exchange.

(Ariz. Rev. Stat. § 40-413(E))

Foreign

A U.S.-domiciled insurer is eligible to write nonadmitted insurance in Arizona for risks whose home state is Arizona if:

- It is eligible in its state of domicile to write the kinds of insurance that it intends to write in Arizona; and
- It maintains minimum capital and surplus requirements in the amount of $15 million or the minimum requirements of title 20, chapter 2, article 1, whichever requirements are greater.

(Ariz. Rev. Stat. § 20-413(B))

Alien

A surplus lines broker may not place insurance with an alien insurer unless:

- The insurer is listed on the NAIC's Quarterly Listing of Alien Insurers; or
- The alien insurer possesses minimum capital and surplus of at least $15 million and maintains assets of at least $2.5 million in U.S. public depositories or trust institutions.

(Ariz. Rev. Stat. § 20-413(C))

Nonadmitted Insurer Eligibility List

The Arizona Department of Insurance maintains a nonadmitted insurer eligibility list. The requirements to be added to the list are:

- A surplus lines broker must file a certification to propose the addition of the authorized insurer; and
- The certification must state the names of the public officials or other person who have supervision over the insurer in any other state and shall certify the amount of capital and surplus that the insurer possesses and the amount of the trust deposit that the insurer maintains.

(Ariz. Rev. Stat. § 20-413)

See https://difi.az.gov/insurers/licensingregistration/surplus-lines-insurer (last visited Apr. 6, 2023).

Types of Coverage Permitted or Prohibited

General Information

A surplus lines broker may only procure coverage that is on the export list or, if the coverage is not on the export list, only if the coverage cannot be procured from an admitted insurer after a "diligent effort."

(ARIZ. REV. STAT. § 20-407(A))

The director has declared certain lines of insurance to be recognized as surplus lines and maintains a list of those lines, called the "export list." A qualified surplus lines insurer may provide coverage for lines of insurance on the export list.

(ARIZ. REV. STAT. § 20-409)

See https://difi.az.gov/insurers/licensingregistration/surplus-lines-insurer (last visited Apr. 6, 2023). When accessing the site, scroll down to Administrative Order 13A-071-INS.

A surplus lines insurer may provide coverage for lines of insurance not on the export list if the coverage is not procurable after a "diligent effort" has been made to procure coverage, or the coverage has been procured to the full extent the insurers are willing to insure, and the placing of insurance with an unauthorized insurer is not for the purpose of securing advantages either as to premium rate or terms of the insurance contract. "Diligent effort" means having sought insurance for the same risk from at least three insurers authorized in Arizona to write the particular insurance coverage or type, class, or kind of insurance.

(ARIZ. REV. STAT. §§ 20-407(A)(2), 20-401(4))

Exempt Transactions

The following types of transactions are exempt from Ariz. Rev. Stat. §§ 20-403, 20-404, and 20-406 relating to actions against an unauthorized insurer:

- Ocean marine and foreign trade insurance
- Insurance on subjects located, resident, or to be performed wholly outside this state or on vehicles or aircraft owned and principally garaged outside this state
- Insurance on property or operations of railroads engaged in interstate commerce
- Insurance procured by a federally recognized Indian tribe, or by a member of a federally recognized tribe, covering subjects located on a federally recognized Indian reservation (Ariz. Rev. Stat. § 20-420(3)).

(Ariz. Rev. Stat. § 20-404)

Service of Process

Transacting surplus lines insurance in Arizona is deemed to constitute an appointment by the insurer of the Director of the Department of Insurance as the insurer's agent for service of process.

(Ariz. Rev. Stat. § 20-403(A))

Limitations on Actions Involving Judicial Proceedings

Arizona statutes do not set forth any limitations on actions involving judicial proceedings that apply to the lawful transaction of surplus lines business.

Domestic Surplus Lines Insurers

Arizona permits a domestic insurer with at least $15 million minimum capital and surplus to be designated as a domestic surplus lines insurer upon the written approval of the director. (Ariz. Rev. Stat. § 20-407.01)

Nonadmitted Insurer Filing Requirements

Arizona statutes do not set forth periodic filing requirements for nonadmitted insurers.

Surplus Lines Broker Licensing

All surplus lines coverage must be procured by a surplus lines broker licensed in Arizona (Ariz. Rev. Stat. § 20-407(A)). A person may not act as a surplus lines broker in Arizona on behalf of an insured whose home state is Arizona unless the person is licensed as a surplus lines broker (Ariz. Rev. Stat. § 20-411(A)). An individual who is a resident of Arizona and who is licensed as a property or casualty producer, or a business entity that is licensed as a property or casualty producer in Arizona and maintains an office in Arizona, may be licensed as a surplus lines broker (Ariz. Rev. Stat. § 20-411(B), (D)).

An individual who is not a resident of Arizona may be licensed as a surplus lines broker in Arizona if the individual is licensed as a surplus lines broker or producer in the individual's home state and the individual's home state issues licenses to Arizona residents on the same basis.

(ARIZ. REV. STAT. §§ 20-411.02, 20-287)

An entity may be licensed as a surplus lines broker in Arizona if it is licensed as a surplus lines producer or broker in the entity's home state and the entity's home state issues licenses to Arizona business entities on the same basis.

(Ariz. Rev. Stat. §§ 20-411.02, 20-287)

To obtain a surplus lines broker license, an individual or entity must submit an application to the Arizona Department of Insurance (Ariz. Rev. Stat. § 20-411). The license fee is currently $1,000 and the license term is four years (Ariz. Rev. Stat. §§ 20-411, 20-167(A)(10)). Each individual applicant for a surplus lines broker license who has not previously taken and passed a surplus lines broker examination must take and pass a written examination (Ariz. Rev. Stat. § 20-411(C)).

Due Care in Selecting Nonadmitted Insurer

A surplus lines broker must determine that a surplus lines insurer meets the minimum financial requirements of the statute and is not declared by the director to be in a hazardous financial condition, improperly managed, or unreliable in insurance transactions.

(ARIZ. REV. STAT. § 20-413)

Diligent Effort/Diligent Search

A surplus lines insurer may provide coverage for lines of insurance not on the export list if the coverage is not procurable after a "diligent effort" has been made to procure coverage or the coverage has been procured to the full extent the insurers are willing to insure, and the placing of insurance with an unauthorized insurer is not for the purpose of securing advantages either as to premium rate or terms of the insurance contract. "Diligent effort" means having sought insurance for the same risk from at least three insurers authorized in Arizona to write the particular insurance coverage or type, class, or kind of insurance.

(ARIZ. REV. STAT. §§ 20-407(A)(2), 20-401(4))

Export List

The director has declared certain lines of insurance to be recognized as surplus lines and maintains a list of those lines, called the "export list." A qualified surplus lines insurer may provide coverage for lines of insurance on the export list.

(ARIZ. REV. STAT. § 20-409)

See https://difi.az.gov/insurers/licensingregistration/surplus-lines-insurer (last visited Apr. 6, 2023). When accessing the site, scroll down to Administrative Order 13A-071-INS.

Exempt Commercial Purchasers

Although the NRRA (15 U.S.C. § 8201) exempts a broker from any diligent search requirements when the insured is an exempt commercial purchaser, Arizona statutes do not address this topic.

Surplus Lines Broker Filing Requirements

Surplus line brokers must file with the Surplus Line Association of Arizona all transactions for which Arizona is the home state. Transactions procured between January 1 and June 30 must be filed before the following August 15. Transactions procured between July 1 and December 31 must be filed before the following February 15. Surplus lines brokers must generate statements of surplus line transactions and generate tax reports using the Association's online system; and file the statement of surplus lines transactions along with the tax report and payment to the Insurance Tax Section of the Arizona Department of Insurance, either using the OPTins electronic filing system (www.optins.org) or by mail (Insurance Tax Section, 2910 North 44th St. #210, Phoenix, AZ 85018-7269).

See Surplus Line Association of Arizona, https://www.sla-az.org/filing (last visited Aug. 10, 2021).

Each surplus lines broker must semi-annually file with the director a statement of all surplus lines insurance business covering Arizona risks, showing (1) the gross amount of each kind of insurance transacted; (2) aggregate gross premiums charged; (3) aggregate return premiums paid to insureds; (4) aggregate of net premiums; (5) additional information as may reasonably be required by the director. The statements, and any related taxes, are due on or before February 15 of each year for the preceding July through December, and on or before August 15 of each year for the preceding January through June.

(Ariz. Rev. Stat. §§ 20-415, 20-416)

Notices

On any surplus lines policy issued by a non-domestic surplus lines insurer, the insurer must include in the policy conspicuously stamped or in boldface type the following language:

> Pursuant to § 20-401.01, subsection B, paragraph 1, Arizona Revised Statutes, this policy is issued by an insurer that does not possess a certificate of authority from the director of the Arizona Department of Insurance. If the insurer that issued this policy becomes insolvent, insureds or claimants will not be eligible for insurance guaranty fund protection pursuant to title 20, Arizona Revised Statutes.

(Ariz. Rev. Stat. § 20-410(B)(1))

On any surplus lines policy issued by a domestic surplus lines insurer, the insurer must include in the policy conspicuously stamped or in boldface type the following language:

> If the insurer that issued this policy becomes insolvent, insureds or claimants will not be eligible for insurance guaranty fund protection pursuant to title 20, Arizona Revised Statutes.
>
> (Ariz. Rev. Stat. § 20-410(B)(2))

Taxes, Stamping Fees, and Other Government-Imposed Charges

Arizona imposes a premium tax on surplus lines insurance of 3 percent of gross premiums, including policy fees other than stamping fees, less any premiums returned to insureds. The surplus lines broker must collect the premium tax from the insured, and is barred from absorbing or rebating any part of the tax. The premium tax is payable to the Arizona Department of Insurance.

(Ariz. Rev. Stat. § 20-416)

Arizona imposes a stamping fee on surplus lines insurance of 0.2 percent of gross premiums. The stamping fee is payable to the Surplus Lines Association of Arizona, not the Arizona Department of Insurance. The surplus lines broker is not prohibited from charging the stamping fee to the insured nor is the broker prohibited from absorbing the stamping fee.

(Ariz. Rev. Stat. §§ 20-423, 20-167(G))

See also https://www.sla-az.org/ (last visited Dec. 2, 2020).

Producer, Policy, Inspection, and Other Fees

The insurance producer may pay a fee or share a commission with a surplus lines broker who procures the surplus coverage on behalf of the insurance producer.

(Ariz. Rev. Stat. § 20-407(C))

A surplus lines broker may charge and receive a fee in addition to the premium for services provided in the transaction of surplus lines insurance if before effecting any coverage both of the following conditions are met:

1. The service fees and the specific services for which the fees are charged are disclosed to the insured or the insured's representative and are agreed to in writing by the insured or the insured's representative.
2. The taxes prescribed in § 20-416 are paid on any fees charged to the insured.

(ARIZ. REV. STAT. § 20-410(C))

Industrial Insured Exemption

Arizona exempts industrial insureds from certain requirements. Arizona's definition of industrial insured mirrors the NRRA's definition of exempt commercial purchasers.

(ARIZ. REV. STAT. § 20-401.07(C)(1))

An industrial insured may procure insurance from an admitted carrier (subject to chapter 2, article 4.1 of title 20) and such coverage is not subject to the otherwise applicable rate and form filing requirements. The insured must certify to its broker that it meets the definition of industrial insured.

(Ariz. Rev. Stat. § 20-407(B))

Any policy issued to an industrial insured must contain a conspicuously stamped or written notice in boldface type that states:

> Pursuant to Arizona Revised Statutes § 20-400.10, this policy and the rates charged for it have not been filed with or approved by the director of the Arizona department of insurance. Certain provisions of Arizona law, specified in Arizona Revised Statutes § 20-400.10, do not apply to this policy. If the insurer that issued this policy becomes insolvent, insureds or claimants will not be eligible for insurance guaranty fund protection pursuant to Arizona Revised Statutes title 20.

(ARIZ. REV. STAT. § 20-400.10(E))

Semi-annually, industrial insureds must pay a premium tax of 3 percent of gross premiums to the Director of the Department of Insurance. The premium tax is due on or before February 15 each year for the preceding July through December, and on or before August 15 each year for the preceding January through June.

(Ariz. Rev. Stat. § 20-401.07(A))

Independent or Direct Procurement Law

No provision of this title shall be deemed to require any license or other authority, or impose any penalty or requirement except as provided by § 20-421, of or upon any person for negotiation or procurement of insurance by him upon his own insurable interests, with or from an insurer not authorized to transact insurance in this state.

(Ariz. Rev. Stat. § 20-107(B))

Any person who is the insured under a surplus lines policy to, upon the director's request, shall produce documents related to the policy.

(Ariz. Rev. Stat. § 20-421)

The Department of Insurance assesses a premium tax and imposes a semi-annual filing requirement on industrial insureds.

See https://difi.az.gov/surplus-lines-broker-industrial-insured-taxes (last visited Apr. 6, 2023).

ARKANSAS

Arkansas Insurance Department
1200 West Third Street
Little Rock, AR 72201-1904
(800) 282-9134
https://insurance.arkansas.gov
(501) 371-2600

Arkansas does not have a stamping office.

Nonadmitted Insurer Eligibility

General Information

Surplus lines insurance for an insured whose home state is Arkansas may only be solicited, negotiated, contracted for, effectuated, or otherwise transacted in the state through a licensed surplus lines broker. Each nonadmitted insurer providing surplus lines insurance must be an eligible surplus lines insurer. A surplus lines broker must take reasonable steps to ascertain that the insurer is in sound financial condition as may be required by regulations adopted by the commissioner.

(ARK. CODE § 23-65-305)

Eligible surplus lines insurers transacting business in Arkansas are not otherwise authorized to transact insurance in the state.

(ARK. CODE § 23-65-303)

Surplus lines insurance may be placed by a surplus lines broker if the nonadmitted insurer:

1. Is authorized to write the type of insurance in its domiciliary jurisdiction; and
2. Has capital and surplus or its equivalent under the laws of its domiciliary jurisdiction that equals the greater of:

a. The minimum capital and surplus requirements under the laws of this state; or
b. $15 million.

The preceding requirements may be satisfied by a nonadmitted insurer possessing less than the minimum capital and surplus if the insurance commissioner makes an affirmative finding of acceptability.

The commissioner shall consider the following factors to determine a finding of acceptability for the requirements of subsection (b) of this section:

a. Quality of management
b. Capital and surplus of a parent company
c. Company underwriting profit and investment income trends
d. Market availability
e. Company record and reputation within the industry

The commissioner may not make a finding of acceptability if the nonadmitted insurer's capital and surplus is less than $4.5 million.

(ARK. CODE § 23-65-305(b)(3))

However, the preceding section does not apply to a qualified exempt commercial purchaser (see Exempt Commercial Purchasers section for this state).

Foreign

A foreign nonadmitted insurer that satisfies Nonadmitted and Reinsurance Reform Act eligibility requirements (15 U.S.C. §§ 8201 *et seq.*) may be placed on Arkansas' eligible surplus lines insurer list. Specifically, the foreign insurer must be authorized to write in its domiciliary jurisdiction and have capital and surplus, or its equivalent under the laws of its domiciliary jurisdiction which equals the greater of the minimum capital and surplus requirement under the law of its home state, or $15 million, whichever is greater.

(ARK. CODE § 23-65-310)

See https://insurance.arkansas.gov/pages/industry-regulation/finance/surplus-lines-insurers/ for additional information.

The approved list may not contain:

a. A foreign insurer that is not licensed in at least one state of the United States for the kind of insurance involved;
b. A foreign stock insurer having capital and surplus amounting to less than $3 million;
c. A type of foreign insurer, other than stock insurers, having surplus of less than $3 million.

(ARK. CODE § 23-65-310(b)(2)(a–c))

Note that these three requirements appear irrelevant given the requirements of Arkansas Code § 23-65-305(b), which parallel NRRA requirements, and Arkansas Code § 23-65-305(b)(3) which requires a minimum of $4.5 million in the event of a commissioner's waiver.

Alien

An alien surplus lines insurer writing risks in Arkansas is deemed eligible if it is listed in the Quarterly Listing of Alien Insurers maintained by the International Insurers Department (IID) of the National Association of Insurance Commissioners (NAIC).

(ARK. CODE § 23-65-310(b)(2)(F)(ii))

An alien insurer not on the NAIC IID list may be approved for the Arkansas eligible surplus lines insurer list if the insurer meets the following requirements:

a. The insurer has an established and effective trust fund within the United States administered by a recognized financial institution and held for the benefit of its policyholders; and
b. The trust fund is in the amount of not less than $1 million.

A surplus lines broker may place casualty insurance with an alien insurer or a pool of alien insurers having combined capital and surplus of $5 million or more, so long as the insured signs an affidavit accepting the insurance.

(ARK. CODE § 23-65-310(b)(2)(D)(ii)(a))

The affidavit must include a statement that the insurance is not available to him or her elsewhere.

(ARK. CODE § 23-65-310(b)(2)(D)(ii)(b))

The alien insurer must also:

a. Annually report the location and balance of the trust fund to the commissioner as the commissioner prescribes; and
b. Report to the commissioner any change in the location of the trust fund.

(ARK. CODE § 23-65-310)

Nonadmitted Insurer Eligibility List

The Arkansas commissioner maintains a list of approved foreign and alien surplus lines insurers in addition to those alien insurers maintaining status on the current Quarterly Listing of Alien Insurers maintained by the International Insurers Department of the National Association of Insurance Commissioners.

(ARK. CODE § 23-65-310(b)(1) (2015))

Arkansas relies on the National Association of Insurance Commissioners (NAIC) State Based Systems (SBS) internet service to host its eligible foreign surplus lines insurer list.

See https://sbs.naic.org/solar-web/pages/public/stateServices.jsf?dswid=4074&state=AR (last visited July 15, 2020). When accessing the site, click on Lookup – One Search.

Per the Arkansas Insurance Department's web page, the following documents must be submitted by foreign insurers to be placed on Arkansas surplus lines insurer list:

1. Notice of Intent Letter. This is simply a letter stating the intention to write in Arkansas under the NRRA. It should be addressed to the commissioner and sent to the attention of Finance Division, 1200 West Third Street, Little Rock, AR 72201-1904. It should include the documentation outlined in following 2 through 4.
2. Certificate of compliance from the surplus line insurer's state of domicile.
3. Copy of most recent financial statement filed with its state of domicile.

4. Completed Uniform Consent to Service of Process Form (UCAA Form 12). Surplus lines insurers do not have to appoint a resident agent, but should provide the full name and address where a service of process is to be forwarded on Exhibit B of the form. Admitted companies holding a certificate of authority in the state must appoint a resident agent.
5. Foreign surplus lines insurers no longer have to file any financial statement filings, renewal fees, or state-specific filings with Arkansas since the Nonadmitted and Reinsurance Reform Act of 2010 (NRRA).
6. For questions, see Finance Division contact information at https://insurance.arkansas.gov/industry-regulation/finance/.

See https://insurance.arkansas.gov/pages/industry-regulation/finance/surplus-lines-insurers/ (last visited July 15, 2020).

The insurance commissioner may remove an approved surplus lines insurer if the commissioner has reason to believe that the insurer:

1. Is in unsound financial condition;
2. Is no longer eligible under § 23-65-310;
3. Has willfully violated the laws of this state;
4. Does not make reasonably prompt payment of just losses and claims in this state or elsewhere; or
5. Has failed to file its annual statement when due.

(Ark. Code § 23-65-319(a))

Types of Coverage Permitted or Prohibited

General Information

With limited exceptions, Arkansas law does not specify the types of risks eligible for surplus lines placement in the state. Automobile liability insurance must be written by an admitted insurer to comply with AR Code § 27-22-104. Title insurance must be written by an authorized carrier (AR Code § 23-103-402(16)).

Workers compensation and employer liability insurance also appear to be excepted from surplus lines eligibility.

(ARK. CODE § 23-65-302(4))

Exempt Transactions

Arkansas Code § 23-65, relating to surplus lines insurance, does not apply to reinsurance transactions or to the following transactions:

1. Wet marine and foreign trade insurance;
2. Insurance on subjects that are:
   a. Located, resident, or to be performed outside this state; or
   b. On vehicles or aircraft principally garaged outside this state;
3. Insurance on property or operation of railroads engaged in interstate commerce; and
4. Insurance of aircraft:
   a. Owned or operated by manufacturers of aircraft;
   b. Operated in scheduled interstate flight;
   c. Cargo; or
   d. Against liability, other than workers' compensation and employer's liability, arising out of the ownership, maintenance, or use of the aircraft.

(ARK. CODE § 23-65-302)

Service of Process

When Arkansas is the home state of the insured, an unauthorized insurer may be sued upon any cause of action arising in this state under any contract issued by it as a surplus lines contract, or certificate thereof issued by the surplus lines broker, under the procedure provided in § 23-65-203.

If Arkansas is the home state of the insured, an unauthorized insurer issuing the policy or accepting the risk shall be deemed to have authorized service of process against it as provided in this section and to have appointed the insurance commissioner as its agent for service of process issuing upon any cause of action arising in this state under any policy.

The surplus lines insurance policy must contain a provision stating the substance of this section and designating the person to whom the commissioner shall mail process.

(ARK. CODE § 23-65-318)

Limitations on Actions Involving Judicial Proceedings

Before an unauthorized insurer shall file or cause to be filed any pleading in any action or proceeding instituted against it, it must procure a certificate of authority or deposit with the court cash or securities or file a bond in an amount to be fixed by the court sufficient to secure the payment of any final judgment. The court may in its discretion make an order dispensing with the deposit or bond when the insurer makes a showing satisfactory to the court that it maintains sufficient funds or securities in trust or otherwise available to satisfy any final judgment. Nothing in the statute is to be construed to prevent an unauthorized insurer from filing a motion to quash or to set aside the service of any process on the ground that either the insurer has not done any of the acts enumerated in § 23-65-202 or that the person on whom service was made pursuant to § 23-65-203(a) was not doing any of the acts therein enumerated.

(ARK. CODE § 23-65-205)

Domestic Surplus Lines Insurers

Arkansas permits a domestic insurer with at least $20 million minimum capital and surplus to be designated as a domestic surplus lines insurer upon the written approval of the commissioner.

(ARK. CODE § 23-65-320)

Nonadmitted Insurer Filing Requirements

Alien insurers listed with the NAIC's International Insurer Department are not required to submit filings with the superintendent.

(ARK. CODE § 23-65-310 and ARK. CODE § 23-65-305(b)(2)(b))

Foreign surplus lines insurers no longer have to file any financial statement filings, renewal fees, or state-specific filings with our state since the Nonadmitted and Reinsurance Reform Act of 2010 (NRRA).

See https://insurance.arkansas.gov/pages/industry-regulation/finance/surplus-lines-insurers/ (last visited Aug. 26, 2020).

Surplus Lines Broker Licensing

If an insured's home state is Arkansas, placement of surplus lines insurance requires a broker with current surplus lines broker's license issued by the insurance commissioner. A person seeking a resident surplus lines broker license in Arkansas must have at least three years' experiencc as resident or nonresident insurance producer of property, casualty, surety, and marine insurance and must be deemed by the commissioner to be competent and trustworthy. An applicant for an Arkansas nonresident license must hold a current surplus lines broker license in his or her jurisdiction. The wording of the statute indicates that an alien surplus lines broker may seek a nonresident license.

The license year shall be from the date of issuance of the license to January 1 next after its issue.

Before issuance of the license, a resident applicant shall file with the commissioner securities acceptable to the commissioner in favor of the state of Arkansas in the penal sum of fifty thousand dollars ($50,000), aggregate liability, with unaffiliated entities approved by the commissioner. See bond form at https://insurance.arkansas.gov/pages/industry-regulation/licensing/forms-instructions/ (last visited Sept. 2, 2020). When accessing the site, scroll down to Broker/Producer Bond Form.

The deposit of securities must remain in force and unimpaired while the license is in effect. The deposit is to secure the

broker's fiduciary duties and payment of taxes. Upon expiration of the license, the deposit will be returned upon 60 days' notice.
(ARK. CODE § 23-65-308)
The applicant must file the following:

1. Application on forms furnished by the commissioner, which may include the NAIC's National Insurance Producer Registration web program; and
2. The license fee of $1,035.

See https://nipr.com/licensing-center/state-requirements/arkansas-resident-licensing-individual (last visited Sept. 2, 2020).

An applicant must pass a written examination as to his or her competence to act as a surplus lines broker. The deposit and exam are not required of nonresident surplus lines brokers.

The insurance commissioner shall revoke a surplus lines broker's license:

1. If the broker fails to file his or her quarterly statement or fails to remit the tax as required by law;
2. If the broker fails to maintain an office, keep records, or allow the commissioner to examine his or her records as required by law; or
3. For any cause for which an agent's license may be revoked.

(ARK. CODE § 23-65-317(a))

Due Care in Selecting Nonadmitted Insurer

A surplus lines broker shall place surplus lines insurance only with insurers that have been approved by the insurance commissioner.
(ARK. CODE § 23-65-310)

Diligent Effort/Diligent Search

Arkansas, with some exceptions, requires a diligent effort to place a risk in the admitted market prior to placement in surplus lines. Surplus lines insurance may be procured from unauthorized insurers when, after diligent effort has been made, the full amount of insurance required cannot be procured from authorized insurers who are actually marketing that kind or class of insurance in this state, and the amount of insurance placed in an unauthorized insurer is only the balance over the amount procurable from authorized insurers. The soliciting agent or broker shall maintain written documentation of compliance with the diligent effort requirements.

(ARK. CODE § 23-65-305(a))

Export List

Arkansas does not maintain a list of coverages that may be exported to the surplus lines market without first making a diligent search of licensed insurers.

Exempt Commercial Purchasers

A diligent effort to first place a risk in the admitted market is not required for transactions on behalf of exempt commercial purchasers. The surplus lines broker procuring or placing the surplus lines insurance must disclose to the exempt commercial purchaser that the insurance may or may not be available from insurers authorized to do business in this state, which may provide greater protection with more regulatory oversight. And, the exempt commercial purchaser must subsequently request in writing the surplus lines broker to procure or place the insurance from an eligible surplus lines insurer.

(ARK. CODE § 23-65-305(d))

Surplus Lines Broker Filing Requirements

At the time of the procuring of surplus lines insurance in this state, when this state is considered the home state of the insured, the surplus lines broker shall file a report with the insurance commissioner within 60 days following the end of the calendar quarter stating the facts referenced in §§ 23-65-313 and 23-65-314 and any additional information the commissioner shall require. Reports filed under this section are not subject to public inspection unless the commissioner determines that the public interest or the welfare of the filing broker requires otherwise.

(Ark. Code § 23-65-306)

The reports are due on or before March 1, June 1, August 31, and November 30 of each year. Beginning January 1, 2020, AID will no longer accept new filings and payments by mail and all filings must be done using OPTins (www.optins.org).

See Bulletin 15-2019, Affidavit of Surplus Line Broker and other forms and instructions at https://insurance.arkansas.gov/pages/industry-regulation/accounting/surplus-lines-brokers-filing/ (last visited Oct. 14, 2020).

Notices

An insurance contract procured on behalf of an insured whose home state is this state and delivered as surplus lines coverage under this subchapter shall be initiated by or bear the name of the surplus lines broker who procured it and shall contain a conspicuous statement substantially similar to the following:

> This contract is registered and delivered as a surplus line coverage under the Surplus Lines Insurance Law, and it may in some respects be different from contracts issued by insurers in the admitted markets, and, accordingly, it may, depending upon the circumstances, be more or less favorable to an insured than a contract from an admitted carrier might be. The protection of the Arkansas Property and Casualty Guaranty Act does not apply to this contract. A tax of four percent (4%) is required to be collected from the insured on all surplus lines premiums.

(Ark. Code § 23-65-307)

Taxes, Stamping Fees, and Other Government-Imposed Charges

No later than 60 days following the end of the month in which surplus lines insurance was procured, the surplus lines broker shall remit to the Arkansas treasurer of state, through the insurance commissioner, a tax of 4 percent on the direct premiums written, less return premiums and exclusive of sums collected to cover state or federal taxes. The correct amounts must be reflected on the surplus lines affidavit.

(ARK. CODE § 23-65-315)

See https://insurance.arkansas.gov/pages/industry-regulation/accounting/surplus-lines-brokers-filing/ (last visited Nov. 11, 2020) for information and access to forms.

Producer, Policy, Inspection, and Other Fees

A licensed property or casualty agent or broker may charge a fee to the insured in addition to the proper premium, provided that:

1. Each such fee is separately disclosed on the invoice or billing statement mailed or delivered to the insured; and
2. The aggregate sum of the fees and all producers' commissions or other compensation due and owing for that policy or contract does not exceed 20 percent of the total gross premium charged the insured by the insurer for that policy or contract.

(ARK. CODE § 23-66-310(c))

Arkansas Insurance Department Bulletins No. 14-2015 and 14-2015A make important clarifications to the application of Arkansas Code § 23-66-310(c) to underwriting expenses for surplus lines brokers and others.

See https://insurance.arkansas.gov/pages/industry-regulation/legal/bulletins/ (last visited Dec. 9, 2020).

Industrial Insured Exemption

Arkansas statutes and regulations do not contain an industrial insured exemption with regard to surplus lines insurance.

Independent or Direct Procurement Law

Independently procured insurance is insurance that is directly procured, caused to be procured, continued, or renewed insurance in an unauthorized insurer, including surplus lines insurance when procured without use of a surplus lines broker. The insured shall file a written report with the insurance commissioner within 30 days of placement. The report shall show the name and address of each named insured, the name and address of the insurer, the subject of the insurance, a general description of the coverage, the amount of premium currently charged, and such additional pertinent information as is reasonably requested by the commissioner. Independently procured insurance is subject to a premium tax of 2 percent.

Insurance placed with an unauthorized insurer and procured through negotiations or an application, in whole or in part, occurring or made within Arkansas or for which premiums are remitted directly or indirectly from within the state is insurance procured, continued, or renewed in the state.

In the event of a multistate risk, the independent procurement tax is to be allocated for the percentage of Arkansas risks. Life or accident and health insurance are not subject to the Arkansas independent procured statute. If the insurance also covers subjects of insurance resident, located, or to be performed outside this state, a proper pro rata portion of the entire premium payable for the insurance shall be allocated as to the subjects of insurance resident, located, or to be performed in this state, for the purposes of this section.

(Ark. Code § 23-65-103)

CALIFORNIA

California Department of Insurance
300 Capitol Mall, Suite 1600
Sacramento, CA 95814
(800) 927-4357
www.insurance.ca.gov
licdocuments@insurance.ca.gov

California has a stamping office.

The Surplus Line Association of California
12667 Alcosta Boulevard
Bishop Ranch 15, Suite 450
San Ramon, CA 94583

Nonadmitted Insurer Eligibility

General Information

Surplus line insurers must meet eligibility standards to underwrite risks presented by specially licensed surplus line brokers. These insurers need not be licensed by California. Use of a surplus line insurer solely to obtain a lower rate than is available on the admitted market is prohibited.

(Cal. Ins. Code § 1763(c))

A California domestic insurer may have common directors with a nonadmitted insurer, but subject to very specific restrictions (Cal. Ins. Code § 1761(b)(1)). Similarly, a California domestic insurer may provide specified administrative services for an affiliated nonadmitted insurer.

(Cal. Ins. Code § 1761(b)(2))

Foreign

Foreign insurers must be licensed in their state of domicile for the lines of business they plan to write as surplus line risks in California, and either (1) maintain a minimum of $45 million of policyholder surplus, or (2) maintain a lesser amount specifically approved in writing by the commissioner.

(15 U.S.C. § 8204(1) and CAL. INS. CODE § 1765.1(a))

Alien

Alien insurers must be published on the NAIC International Insurer Department's most recent Quarterly Listing of Alien Insurers to be eligible.

(15 U.S.C. § 8204 (2) and CAL. INS. CODE § 1765.1(b))

Nonadmitted Insurer Eligibility List

California maintains a List of Approved Surplus Line Insurers (LASLI), a voluntary list of nonadmitted insurers that the California Department of Insurance has approved for use by surplus line brokers. Because the LASLI is voluntary, there are nonadmitted insurers not on the LASLI that are nonetheless eligible for use by surplus line brokers due to federal law (the NRRA). If a nonadmitted insurer is not on the LASLI, the broker must determine at the time of placement that the insurer meets the specific federal eligibility criteria.

See http://slacal.org/resources/insurer-member-lookup (last visited July 15, 2020) for the LASLI list.

The department also maintains additional information about surplus line insurers and nonadmitted insurer eligibility on its website.

Types of Coverage Permitted or Prohibited

Prohibited

The following types of coverage are not permitted to be written with a surplus line insurer:

- State-mandated private-passenger automobile coverage
- Workers' compensation

Exempt Transactions

The following types of insurance are exempt from California's surplus line laws:

1. Reinsurance
2. Insurance against perils of navigation, transit, or transportation upon hulls, freights or disbursements, or other shipowner interests; upon goods, wares, merchandise, and all other personal property and interests therein, in the course of exportation from or importation into any country, or transportation coastwise, including transportation by land or water from point of origin to final destination and including war risks; and marine builder's risks, drydocks, and marine railways, including insurance of ship repairer's liability, and protection and indemnity insurance, but excluding insurance covering bridges or tunnels
3. Aircraft or spacecraft insurance
4. Insurance on property or operations of railroads engaged in interstate commerce

However, types 2 through 4 must be placed only by a special lines' surplus line broker. Licensing information for a special lines' surplus line broker license can be found at http://www.insurance.ca.gov/0200-industry/0050-renew-license/0200-requirements/special-lines-surplus.cfm (last visited July 29, 2020).

(CAL. INS. CODE § 1760.5)

Service of Process

The commissioner is the agent for service of process for surplus line insurers.

(CAL. INS. CODE § 1610)

Limitations on Actions Involving Judicial Proceedings

Before any unauthorized person or insurer files or causes to be filed any pleading in any court action or proceeding or in any administrative proceeding before the commissioner instituted against the person or insurer by service made in accordance with the provisions of section 1612, the person or insurer shall either (1) procure a certificate of authority to transact insurance in California; or (2) give a bond in the action, suit, or proceeding in an amount to be fixed by the court sufficient to secure the payment of any final judgment that may be rendered in the action, suit, or proceeding.

(CAL. INS. CODE § 1616)

Domestic Surplus Lines Insurers

California statutes have no provision allowing domestic surplus lines insurers.

Nonadmitted Insurer Filing Requirements

A nonadmitted insurer must file the following documents with the commissioner, unless available from the NAIC or another public source:

a. Financial documents showing the insurer's condition as of a date not more than 12 months prior to submission:
    i. For a foreign insurer, an annual statement and an audited financial report.
    ii. For an alien insurer, a certified copy of the trust agreement, most recent quarterly statement, or list of the assets in the trust.
b. A certified copy of the insurer's license issued by its domiciliary jurisdiction, plus a certification of good standing, certificate of compliance, or other equivalent certificate, from either that jurisdiction or, if the jurisdiction does not issue those certificates, from a state where it is licensed.

c. Information on the insurer's agent in California for service of process, including the agent's full name and address. The agent's address must include a street address where the agent can be reached during normal business hours.
d. The complete street address, mailing address, and telephone number of the insurer's principal place of business.
e. A certified or verified explanation, report, or other statement from the insurance regulatory office or official of the insurer's domiciliary jurisdiction concerning the insurer's record regarding market conduct and consumer complaints, or, if that information cannot be obtained from that jurisdiction, then any other information that the licensee can procure to demonstrate a good reputation for payment of claims and treatment of policyholders.
f. A verified statement regarding whether the insurer or an affiliated entity is currently known to be the subject of an order or proceeding regarding conservation, liquidation, or other receivership; or regarding revocation or suspension of a license to transact insurance in any jurisdiction; or otherwise seeking to stop the insurer from transacting insurance in any jurisdiction. The statement shall identify the proceeding by date, jurisdiction, and relief or sanction sought, and shall attach a copy of the relevant order.
g. A certified copy of the most recent report of examination or an explanation if the report is not available.
h. A list of all California surplus line brokers authorized by the insurer to issue policies on its behalf, and any additions to or deletions from that list.

(Cal. Ins. Code § 1765.2(c))

Initial application and annual renewal requirements for a non-admitted insurer to be placed on the List of Approved Surplus Line Insurers (LASLI) can be found at http://slacal.org/resources/lasli-insurer-filing-requirements (last visited Aug. 26, 2020).

Surplus Lines Broker Licensing

The initial and renewal fees are as follows:

a. For an individual surplus line broker who only transacts on behalf of a surplus line broker business entity: $646 for a two-year term
b. For an individual surplus line broker that has a $50,000 bond on file: $1,296 for a two-year term
c. For a surplus line broker business entity license: $1,296 for a two-year term

Both nonresident individuals and nonresident business entities applying for a surplus line license must hold an active surplus line license in another state.

Both individuals and business entities applying for a surplus line broker license must be currently licensed and in good standing as a California property and casualty broker-agent. For a business entity to obtain/maintain a license, there needs to be at least one designated license responsible person (DLRP) who is actively surplus line licensed in California.

There are no pre-licensing or continuing education requirements for the surplus line license. However, there are education requirements for the underlying property and casualty broker-agent license. Similarly, there is no separate exam for the surplus line license, but an individual has to pass both the property broker-agent and casualty broker-agent examinations to receive the surplus line license.

A $50,000 bond is generally required. If an individual surplus line broker will only be transacting business on behalf of a licensed surplus line broker business entity, no bond is required.

(CAL. INS. CODE § 1765)

Due Care in Selecting Nonadmitted Insurer

Surplus line brokers must ensure that they place policies only with nonadmitted insurers that have met the requirements set forth in section 1765.2; provided, however, if a nonadmitted insurer has been placed on the List of Approved Surplus Line

Insurers (LASLI), then it shall be presumed that the insurer is an approved surplus line insurer and meets the requirements of section 1765.2.

(CAL. INS. CODE § 1765.2)

Diligent Effort/Diligent Search

Surplus line brokers may place insurance with eligible surplus line insurers only if, after diligent effort to place the coverage in the authorized market, a particular coverage, or part thereof, is not available from licensed insurers or a residual market mechanism. Coverage placed in the surplus line market can only be excess over the amount of insurance that can be procured from authorized insurers.

A diligent effort is presumed to have been made if a standardized form is filed establishing that three admitted insurers that actually write the particular type of insurance in California have declined the risk, or that fewer than three admitted insurers actually write the particular type of insurance. The form promulgated by the Surplus Line Association of California must be used.

(CAL. INS. CODE § 1763)

Export List

The insurance department maintains an "export list," which is available at https://www.slacal.com/brokers/export-list (last visited Sept. 30, 2020). The department holds a hearing at least once per year to allow applicants to ask to add or delete from the export list.

Exempt Commercial Purchasers

California has adopted the NRRA (15 U.S.C. § 8201) definition of exempt commercial purchasers. Coverage for these insureds may be exported to the surplus line market without making a diligent effort to place the coverage with authorized insurers provided (1) the surplus line broker has disclosed to the exempt commercial purchaser that coverage may or may not be available from an authorized insurer that may provide greater protection with more regulatory oversight, and (2) such exempt commercial purchaser has subsequently requested such broker, in writing, to procure such policy from an unauthorized insurer.

(CAL. INS. CODE § 1763(h))

Surplus Lines Broker Filing Requirements

Within 60 days of placing any insurance for a California home state insured with a surplus line insurer, the surplus line broker must file (1) a copy of the declaration page, certificate, cover note, or binder; (2) a Confidential Report of Placements (Form SL-1); and (3) a Diligent Search Report (Form SL-2).

(CAL. INS. CODE § 1763)

On or before March 1, surplus line brokers must file an annual sworn statement of all business transacted under their surplus line licenses during the last preceding calendar year. The statement must contain an account of the business done by the surplus line broker placing business for a home state insured for the prior year, and must include (1) the total amount of gross premium; (2) the total gross premium for single state risks where 100 percent of the premium is attributable to risks in California; and (3) for multistate risks, the percentage of gross premium allocated to California and each other state.

(CAL. INS. CODE § 1774)

Notices

Every insurance policy written on a surplus line basis must include a stand-alone separate note (Form D-2) in not less than sixteen-point boldface type in capital letters, the following:

NOTICE:

1. THE INSURANCE POLICY THAT YOU [HAVE PURCHASED] [ARE APPLYING TO PURCHASE] IS BEING ISSUED BY AN INSURER THAT IS NOT LICENSED BY THE STATE OF CALIFORNIA. THESE

COMPANIES ARE CALLED "NONADMITTED" OR "SURPLUS LINE" INSURERS.

2. THE INSURER IS NOT SUBJECT TO THE FINANCIAL SOLVENCY REGULATION AND ENFORCEMENT THAT APPLY TO CALIFORNIA LICENSED INSURERS.

3. THE INSURER DOES NOT PARTICIPATE IN ANY OF THE INSURANCE GUARANTEE FUNDS CREATED BY CALIFORNIA LAW. THEREFORE, THESE FUNDS WILL NOT PAY YOUR CLAIMS OR PROTECT YOUR ASSETS IF THE INSURER BECOMES INSOLVENT AND IS UNABLE TO MAKE PAYMENTS AS PROMISED.

4. THE INSURER SHOULD BE LICENSED EITHER AS A FOREIGN INSURER IN ANOTHER STATE IN THE UNITED STATES OR AS A NON-UNITED STATES (ALIEN) INSURER. YOU SHOULD ASK QUESTIONS OF YOUR INSURANCE AGENT, BROKER, OR "SURPLUS LINE" BROKER OR CONTACT THE CALIFORNIA DEPARTMENT OF INSURANCE AT THE FOLLOWING TOLL-FREE TELEPHONE NUMBER __________. ASK WHETHER OR NOT THE INSURER IS LICENSED AS A FOREIGN OR NON-UNITED STATES (ALIEN) INSURER AND FOR ADDITIONAL INFORMATION ABOUT THE INSURER. YOU MAY ALSO CONTACT THE NAIC'S INTERNET WEB SITE AT WWW.NAIC.ORG.

5. FOREIGN INSURERS SHOULD BE LICENSED BY A STATE IN THE UNITED STATES AND YOU MAY CONTACT THAT STATE'S DEPARTMENT OF INSURANCE TO OBTAIN MORE INFORMATION ABOUT THAT INSURER.

6. FOR NON-UNITED STATES (ALIEN) INSURERS, THE INSURER SHOULD BE LICENSED BY A COUNTRY OUTSIDE OF THE UNITED STATES AND SHOULD BE ON THE NAIC'S INTERNATIONAL INSURERS DEPARTMENT (IID) LISTING OF APPROVED NONADMITTED NON-UNITED STATES INSURERS. ASK YOUR AGENT, BROKER, OR "SURPLUS LINE" BROKER TO OBTAIN MORE INFORMATION ABOUT THAT INSURER.

7. CALIFORNIA MAINTAINS A LIST OF APPROVED SURPLUS LINE INSURERS. ASK YOUR AGENT OR BROKER IF THE INSURER IS ON THAT LIST, OR VIEW THAT LIST AT THE INTERNET WEB SITE OF THE CALIFORNIA DEPARTMENT OF INSURANCE: WWW.INSURANCE.CA.GOV.

8. IF YOU, AS THE APPLICANT, REQUIRED THAT THE INSURANCE POLICY YOU HAVE PURCHASED BE BOUND IMMEDIATELY, EITHER BECAUSE EXISTING COVERAGE WAS GOING TO LAPSE WITHIN TWO BUSINESS DAYS OR BECAUSE YOU WERE REQUIRED TO HAVE COVERAGE WITHIN TWO BUSINESS DAYS, AND YOU DID NOT RECEIVE THIS DISCLOSURE FORM AND A REQUEST FOR YOUR SIGNATURE UNTIL AFTER COVERAGE BECAME EFFECTIVE, YOU HAVE THE RIGHT TO CANCEL THIS POLICY WITHIN FIVE DAYS OF RECEIVING THIS DISCLOSURE. IF YOU CANCEL COVERAGE, THE PREMIUM WILL BE PRORATED AND ANY BROKER'S FEE CHARGED FOR THIS INSURANCE WILL BE RETURNED TO YOU.

(CAL. INS. CODE § 1764.1(b))

A similar disclosure (Form D-1) must be signed by the prospective insured at the time the surplus line broker accepts an application for any surplus line insurance policy, other than a renewal of that policy.

(CAL. INS. CODE § 1764.1(a))

Taxes, Stamping Fees and Other Government-Imposed Charges

The surplus line tax is 3 percent. Tax returns are generally filed annually; however, if the annual tax during the preceding year was $20,000 or more, then the surplus line broker must make monthly installment payments for the current year.

(CAL. INS. CODE §§ 1775.1, 1775.5)

There is also a 0.25 percent stamping fee, payable monthly.

(Surplus Line Association of California Bulletin #1373, June 10, 2019)

Producer, Policy, Inspection, and Other Fees

A surplus line broker may charge a fee to provide services that constitute or arise out of an insurance transaction, provided that the surplus line broker discloses the fees to the prospective insured, who must agree to these fees prior to the placement of the coverage. Broker fees and other charges levied solely by and for the benefit of the surplus line broker and not remitted to the surplus line insurer are generally not considered taxable premium and thus not subject to surplus line premium taxes.

(CAL. CODE REGS. tit. 10 § 2189; Surplus Line Association of California Bulletin #628 (Feb. 9, 1994))

Industrial Insured Exemption

A surplus line broker must provide an industrial insured with the policyholder notice required by § 1764.1(b) only once (at confirmation of coverage) rather than twice (at application and again at confirmation). An industrial insured is defined as employing at least 25 employees on average during the past 12 months, and either (a) having at least $25,000 aggregate annual premiums for insurance, excluding workers compensation and health insurance, or (b) procuring insurance by the use of the services of a full-time employee acting as an insurance manager or a continuously retained insurance consultant.

(CAL. INS. CODE § 1764.1(c))

Independent or Direct Procurement Law

Direct procurement is permitted. A 3 percent premium tax applies.

(CAL. INS. CODE § 1760; CAL. REV. & TAX. CODE § 13210)

COLORADO

Colorado Division of Insurance
1560 Broadway, Suite 850
Denver, CO 80202
(303) 894-7499 or (800) 930-3745
https://www.colorado.gov/pacific/dora/division-insurance
licensingandce@dora.state.co.us

Colorado does not have a stamping office.

Nonadmitted Insurer Eligibility

Foreign

No unauthorized insurer shall be or become an eligible surplus lines insurer unless declared eligible by the commissioner in accordance with the following conditions:

- For each line of insurance it proposes to write as an eligible surplus lines insurer, the insurer must be currently licensed in the state of its domicile if chartered, incorporated, organized, or constituted within the United States; and
- The insurer must maintain capital and surplus to policyholders of at least $15 million.

(Colo. Rev. Stat. § 10-5-108(B)(I); 3 Colo. Code Regs. § 702-2-4-1-10(A))

Alien

A surplus lines broker may place business with an alien insurer provided the insurer is listed on the Quarterly Listing of Alien Insurers maintained by the International Insurers Department of the National Association of Insurance Commissioners.

(3 Colo. Code Regs. § 702-2-4-1-10(B))

An alien insurer that is part of a Lloyd's plan or other similar unincorporated group of individual insurers, or a combination of both unincorporated and incorporated insurers must maintain a trust fund, in the United States, in an amount of not less than $100 million, which trust fund must be available for the benefit of U.S. surplus lines policyholders of any member of the group.

(COLO. REV. STAT. § 10-5-108(c)(II))

Nonadmitted Insurer Eligibility List

Colorado maintains a list of active surplus lines insurers, which is available online.

See https://www.colorado.gov/pacific/dora/surplus-lines-premium-taxes (last visited July 15, 2020).

Types of Coverage Permitted or Prohibited

Permitted

Disability, property, and casualty insurance may be exported to the surplus lines market.

(COLO. REV. STAT. § 10-5-101.1(1))

Exempt Transactions

Reinsurance transactions are exempt from the surplus lines procedures.

(COLO. REV. STAT. § 10-5-101.5(1))

The following types of insurance are also exempt from the surplus lines procedures, except that brokers placing these types of business must keep a full and true record of each such coverage in detail as required of surplus lines insurance:

a. Insurance on vessels or crafts or their hulls or cargoes or on marine builders' risks or marine protection and indemnity or other risks, including strikes and war risks commonly insured under ocean or wet marine forms of policy;

b. Insurance on subjects located, resident, or to be performed wholly outside of this state or on vehicles or aircraft owned and principally garaged outside this state;
c. Insurance on the operations of railroads engaged in transportation in interstate commerce and their property used in such operations;
d. Insurance on aircraft owned or operated by manufacturers of aircraft or on aircraft operated in commercial scheduled interstate flight or the cargo of such aircraft or against liability, other than workers' compensation and employers' liability, arising out of the ownership, maintenance, or use of such aircraft; and
e. Insurance on satellites or other devices intended for launch beyond the earth's atmosphere.

The records for these types of business must be preserved for not less than three years after the effective date of the insurance, kept in the broker's office and open to the commissioner's examination and on forms designated and furnished by the commissioner, and contain a report of all such coverages so placed in a designated calendar year.

(Colo. Rev. Stat. § 10-5-101.5)

Service of Process

The commissioner is the agent for service of process for surplus lines insurers.

(Colo. Rev. Stat. § 10-5-114(3))

Limitations on Actions Involving Judicial Proceedings

Before any unauthorized foreign or alien insurer files or causes to be filed any pleading in any action, suit, or proceeding instituted against it, the unauthorized insurer must either (1) deposit cash or securities with the clerk of the court in which such action, suit, or proceeding is pending, or (2) file with the clerk a bond with good and sufficient sureties, to be approved by the court, in an amount to be fixed by the court sufficient to secure the payment of any final judgment that may be rendered in such action, or (3) procure a certificate of authority to transact the business of insurance in this state, unless one or more of the following is applicable:

a. The insurer makes a showing satisfactory to the court and the commissioner that there are, in this state or in another state, cash, securities, bond, or other assets sufficient and available to secure the payment of any final judgment which may be rendered in the action, suit, or proceeding or that the insurance was placed lawfully in the jurisdiction in which the transaction took place and which was not an unlawful placement under the laws of this state;
b. At the time the insurer files any pleading in any action, suit, or proceeding instituted against it, the insurer is listed on the eligible nonadmitted insurers list;
c. With respect to a contract of reinsurance, the reinsurer has complied with the rules necessary to permit the ceding insurer to take credit on its financial statement for the reinsurance.

(Colo. Rev. Stat. § 10-3-1004)

Domestic Surplus Lines Insurers

Colorado statutes have no provision allowing domestic surplus lines insurers.

Nonadmitted Insurer Filing Requirements

A foreign or alien nonadmitted insurer that wants to be included on the Division of Insurance's list of eligible surplus lines insurers must, on or before March 1 of every year, submit the following to the Division of Insurance:

- Fee Form F and requisite fees (fees will vary by the direct premiums written in the previous year)
- A current copy of Certificate of Authority/Compliance from the insurer's state of domicile

(Colo. Rev. Stat. § 10-5-108(1)(a))

Surplus Lines Broker Licensing

Any person who holds either a Colorado insurance producer license, a resident surplus lines license, or the equivalent issued by another state or territory that offers Colorado surplus lines producers' nonresident licenses on a reciprocal basis and is deemed by the commissioner to be competent and trustworthy may be licensed as a surplus lines producer.

(Colo. Rev. Stat. § 10-2-408(6))

Notwithstanding any other provision of article 2 of title 10 of the Colorado Revised Statutes, a person licensed as a surplus lines producer in the surplus lines producer's home state shall receive a nonresident surplus lines producer.

(Colo. Rev. Stat. § 10-2-502(5))

The initial fee and renewal fee is $144 for residents and $294 for nonresidents.

(3 Colo. Code Regs. § 702-1-2-10-12)

For a business entity to obtain/maintain a license, there needs to be one designated responsible producer listed on the application/renewal who is actively surplus lines licensed in Colorado.

See https://home.pearsonvue.com/co/insurance (last visited Sept. 2, 2020). When accessing the site, scroll down to the link titled Agency Personnel Registration Instructions.

There are no pre-licensing or continuing education requirements for surplus lines licensees. However, there are education requirements for an underlying resident Property and Casualty Producer license. Also, for a resident individual applying for a surplus lines license, there is a written examination requirement. *See* https://home.pearsonvue.com/co/insurance (last visited Sept. 2, 2020) for more information about the written examination.

Due Care in Selecting Nonadmitted Insurer

A broker shall not place any coverage with a nonadmitted insurer unless, at the time of placement, the nonadmitted insurer meets all applicable eligibility requirements contained in the NRRA (15 U.S.C. § 8201) or is an insurance exchange, Lloyds plan, or group of incorporated insurers under common administration that has been approved by the commissioner and is included on the list of eligible nonadmitted insurers prepared by the commissioner at least annually.

(Colo. Rev. Stat. § 10-5-108(1))

The list of eligible nonadmitted insurers is available at https://www.colorado.gov/pacific/dora/surplus-lines-premium-taxes (last visited Sept. 16, 2020).

Diligent Effort/Diligent Search

Surplus lines brokers may place insurance with eligible surplus lines insurers only if, after diligent effort to place the coverage in the authorized market, the full amount of insurance required is not procurable from among admitted insurers authorized to transact and actually transacting that kind of insurance in Colorado.

Placement with a surplus lines insurer must not be for the purpose of securing a lower premium rate than that which would be accepted by an admitted insurer unless the premium rate quoted by the admitted insurer is more than 10 percent higher than that quoted by the surplus lines insurer for comparable benefits and provisions.

(Colo. Rev. Stat. § 10-5-103(b); 3 Colo. Code Regs. § 702-2-4-1-5)

An affidavit documenting the diligent effort must be completed by the surplus lines broker, demonstrating that the coverage required was not procurable after a comprehensive search was made from a minimum of three admitted insurers authorized to and currently transacting that line of business in this state. If there are fewer than three admitted insurers in Colorado authorized and currently transacting the line of business needed, such diligent effort must be met by searching the available insurers (3 Colo. Code Regs. § 702-2-4-1-6(A)). The affidavit must be filed with the commissioner within 30 days after the insurance is procured (Colo. Rev. Stat. § 10-5-103(c)). An affidavit from a retail broker may be submitted in lieu of the affidavit from the surplus lines broker (Colo. Rev. Stat. § 10-5-103.5). The determination of placement and evidence of diligent search efforts must be made each policy period prior to placement of coverage with an eligible nonadmitted insurer (3 Colo. Code Regs. § 702-2-4-1-6(C)).

Export List

Colorado does not maintain a list of coverages that may be exported to the surplus lines market without first making a diligent search of licensed insurers.

Exempt Commercial Purchasers

Although the NRRA (15 U.S.C. § 8201) exempts a broker from any diligent search requirements when the insured is an exempt commercial purchaser, Colorado statutes do not address this topic.

Surplus Lines Broker Filing Requirements

No later than the 15th of each month for the prior month, surplus lines brokers are required to submit a report to the Division of Insurance showing each policy written, including those accepted from licensed producers. Such report must include (1) the name of the insured, (2) line of business, (3) name of nonadmitted insurer, (4) surplus lines premium, (5) policy fees charged, and (6) surplus lines taxes due. Monthly filings are required, even for zero business.

The broker should only include a surplus lines policy on their Colorado monthly report, if:

1. The insured's home state is Colorado; or
2. The insured's home state is not Colorado, but the insurance policy covers risks or exposures located in Colorado, and:
   a. One-hundred percent of the insured risk is located outside the insured's home state, and
   b. The greatest percentage of the taxable premium for that policy is payable to Colorado.

(3 COLO. CODE REGS. § 702-2-4-1-7(B); Division of Insurance Bulletin B-2.10 (June 15, 2015))

Tax returns are filed annually on or before March 1.

(COLO. REV. STAT. §§ 10-5-111, -111.5; 3 COLO. CODE REGS. § 702-2-4-1-7(D))

Notices

Every insurance contract procured and delivered as a surplus lines coverage must be initialed by or bear the name of the surplus lines broker who procured it and must have stamped upon it the following:

> This contract is delivered as a surplus lines coverage under the "Nonadmitted Insurance Act." The insurer issuing this contract is not licensed in Colorado but is an eligible nonadmitted insurer. There is no protection under the provisions of the "Colorado Insurance Guaranty Association Act."

(COLO. REV. STAT. § 10-5-104)

If a contract procured or placed by a Colorado surplus lines broker is on a claims-made or other nonoccurrence policy form, the broker or the nonadmitted insurer must stamp on the face of the policy the following disclosure, which must be in a predominate type:

> This policy is a claims-made policy which provides liability coverage only if a claim is made during the policy period or any applicable extended reporting period.

This disclosure is not required for transactions with exempt commercial policyholders.

(COLO. REV. STAT. § 10-5-119; 3 COLO. CODE REGS. § 702-2-4-1-4(B))

If an automobile policy does not provide the basic complying policy coverages (legal liability coverage for bodily injury or death arising out of the use of the motor vehicle to a limit, exclusive of interest and costs, of $25,000 to any one person in any one accident and $50,000 to all persons in any one accident and for property damage arising out of the use of the motor vehicle to a limit, exclusive of interest and costs, of $15,000 in any one accident) the following disclosure must appear on the policy:

> This policy does not meet the statutory requirements of this State's financial responsibility laws. It does not provide liability coverage for bodily injury and property damage.

(3 COLO. CODE REGS. § 702-2-4-1-4(C))

The exemption for insurance on subjects located, resident, or to be performed wholly outside of this state or on vehicles or aircraft owned and principally garaged outside Colorado shall apply to policies of property and casualty insurance issued or delivered in this state by an unauthorized insurer affording coverage only on property located temporarily or permanently, or operations conducted temporarily or permanently outside the boundaries of the United States of America, its territories or possessions when the policy is placed by Colorado-licensed property and casualty producers or brokers, who shall remain responsible for verifying that the insuring company is licensed or authorized by the appropriate regulatory bodies to transact the business of insurance in that jurisdiction, and contains the following disclaimer:

> This policy is issued by an insurance company that is not regulated by the Colorado Division of Insurance. The insurance company may not provide claims service and may not be subject to service of process in Colorado. If the insurance company becomes insolvent, insureds or claimants will not be eligible for protection under Colorado insurance law.

(3 Colo. Code Regs. § 702-2-4-1-4(D))

These required disclosures must be affixed to the declaration page of the contract given to the insured. A copy, bearing the disclosures, must also be maintained by the broker; in the case of the issuance of a binder prior to the formal policy, such disclosure must also appear on the binder.

(3 Colo. Code Regs. § 702-2-4-1-4(E))

Taxes, Stamping Fees, and Other Government-Imposed Charges

The surplus lines tax is 3 percent of net premiums. Tax returns are filed annually on or before March 1. Each broker and every person that enters into an independent procurement for nonadmitted insurance must file their annual statement of, and remit the premium taxes for, all nonadmitted insurance transacted during the preceding calendar year.

(Colo. Rev. Stat. §§ 10-5-111, -111.5; 3 Colo. Code Regs. § 702-2-4-1-7(D))

Producer, Policy, Inspection, and Other Fees

Insurance producers may charge fees for specific services which are beyond the scope of services pertaining to acquiring and/or maintaining specific insurance policies, including, but not limited to, risk management services, financial planning, investment counseling, qualified retirement plan design or administration, estate planning, third party employee benefit plans, or any other service for which the insurance producer does not receive a commission from an insurance company. Such fees may be charged only under the following circumstances:

1. When a person signs a disclosure statement in advance of the performance of the specific services, which states that the person is under no obligation to purchase any insurance product through the insurance producer in exchange for receiving the specific services. This requirement may be met by including the disclosure language in any disclosure statement required by federal or state securities law.
2. In those cases where it is clear from the outset that no insurance product sale related to the specific services rendered will occur through the insurance producer.

The insurance producer must maintain records, and must retain a copy of the disclosure statement just described for not less than three years after completion of services. A copy must be provided to the commissioner upon request.

Insurance wholesale intermediaries must advise the retail insurance producer, in writing, that "the cost of the insurance coverage provided herein includes a fee to a wholesale intermediary in addition to the premium charges."

(3 Colo. Code Regs. § 702-1-2-9-6)

However, agreements between the insurer and insurance producers must include a commission schedule that lists the insurance producer's compensation. Insurance producers are prohibited from charging separate fees in addition to their commissions for the solicitation and procurement of insurance products or for servicing existing insurance policies. These services may include, but are not limited to, inspections; quoting premiums; issuing or signing policies; examining and mailing policies, applications, and daily reports; compiling figures for accounts current and mailing billing notices; correspondence and other bookkeeping and clerical work; issuing certificates of insurance and endorsements; issuing proof of insurance cards and notices (SR-22s); making copies of insurance documents; and taking loss information.

Insurance producers are also prohibited from charging fees for purchasing new computer equipment, extending business hours, adding new sales facilities, or other overhead expenses associated with the solicitation or procurement of insurance products or the servicing of existing insurance policies. Further, insurance producers may not condition the placement of insurance upon the provision of other services for which fees may be charged.

These restrictions do not apply to an insurance wholesale intermediary, who is a person or organization that deals directly with a licensed retail producer and not with a consumer.

(3 COLO. CODE REGS. § 702-1-2-9-5)

Industrial Insured Exemption

Transactions involving an industrial insured are exempt from the surplus lines procedures, except payment of premium tax pursuant to Colorado Revised Statutes § 10-3-909. An industrial insured is an insured:

a. Who procures the insurance of any risk other than life and annuity contracts by use of the services of a full-time employee acting as an insurance manager or buyer or the services of a regularly and continuously retained qualified insurance consultant who does not receive a commission or compensation for placing the risk; and
b. Whose aggregate annual premiums for insurance on all risks total at least $100,000; and
c. That has at least 100 full-time employees.

(COLO. REV. STAT. § 10-3-910)

Independent or Direct Procurement Law

Direct procurement is permitted. Each surplus line broker and every person that enters into an independent procurement for nonadmitted insurance must file with the commissioner a verified statement of all insurance transacted by the broker or other person during the preceding reporting period, which statement must show: gross amount of each kind of insurance transacted, aggregate gross premiums charged, aggregate of returned premiums paid to insureds, aggregate of net premiums, and additional information as required by the commissioner. A 3 percent premium tax applies.

(Colo. Rev. Stat. §§ 10-5-110, -111, -111.5)

The insured under an insurance contract procured from an unauthorized insurer, obtained through methods other than through a surplus lines broker or independent procurement, is required to pay a tax of 2.25 percent on such insurance.

(Colo. Rev. Stat. § 10-3-909)

CONNECTICUT

Connecticut Insurance Department
153 Market Street, 7th Floor
Hartford, CT 06103
(860) 297-3800
www.ct.gov/cid
(800) 203-3447

Connecticut does not have a stamping office.

Nonadmitted Insurer Eligibility

General Information

Surplus lines insurers are not licensed, but must meet eligibility standards in order to underwrite risks presented by surplus lines producers.

(CONN. AGENCIES REGS. § 38a-740-4)

Foreign

No unauthorized insurer shall be or become an eligible surplus lines insurer unless declared eligible by the commissioner in accordance with the following conditions:

1. For each line of insurance it proposes to write as an eligible surplus lines insurer, the insurer shall:
   a. Be currently licensed in the state of its domicile if chartered, incorporated, organized, or constituted within the United States;
   b. Show that it writes the lines of business that it proposes to write in Connecticut in sufficient volume as to demonstrate expertise in insuring such product lines.

(CONN. AGENCIES REGS. § 38a-740-4(a))

Each insurer must have capital and surplus to policyholders of at least $15 million.

(CONN. AGENCIES REGS. § 38a-740-4(b))

Alien

Each insurer must be currently licensed in its U.S. domiciliary jurisdiction if as an alien insurer, it does business through a U.S. branch; or be currently licensed in its domiciliary jurisdiction outside the United States if an alien insurer.

(CONN. AGENCIES REGS. § 38a-740-4(a))

A surplus lines broker may place business with an alien insurer provided the insurer is listed on the Quarterly Listing of Alien Insurers maintained by the International Insurers Department of the National Association of Insurance Commissioners.

(CONN. AGENCIES REGS. § 38a-740-4; Insurance Department Bulletin SL-2)

Each alien group of Lloyd's plan must have aggregate surplus of $10 billion. Each insurer that is a member of the group shall individually maintain capital and surplus of not less than $25 million.

(CONN. AGENCIES REGS. § 38a-740-4(f))

Nonadmitted Insurer Eligibility List

Connecticut maintains a list of active surplus lines insurers that can be accessed at https://portal.ct.gov/CID/Licensing/Surplus-Lines-Broker-FAQs--Individual-and-Business-Entities (last visited Apr. 6, 2023). Scroll to "FAQ #15 - Where Is the White List (listing of surplus lines insurers) located?"

Types of Coverage Permitted or Prohibited

Prohibited

The following is permitted to be written with an excess and surplus line insurer:

- Any insurance coverage which can be placed through a residual market mechanism—home, auto, and workers compensation.

(CONN. GEN. STAT. § 38a-794)

Exempt Transactions

The premium tax and reporting requirements do not apply to any policy issued to the state of Connecticut or any agency of the state, or to any policy issued to any Connecticut town, or agency of such town or special taxing district when such town, agency, or department thereof or special taxing district appears in the policy as the named insured and as such is responsible for the payment of premiums shown on such policy.

(CONN. GEN. STAT. § 38a-743(f))

Service of Process

The commissioner is the agent for service of process for surplus lines insurers.

(CONN. GEN. STAT. § 38a-25)

Limitations on Actions Involving Judicial Proceedings

Before any unauthorized person or insurer files or causes to be filed any pleading in any court action or proceeding or in any administrative proceeding before the commissioner instituted against the person or insurer by service made in accordance with the provisions of section 38a-25, section 38a-26, or section 38a-273, the person or insurer shall either: (1) deposit with the clerk of the court in which the action or proceeding is pending, or with the commissioner in administrative proceedings before the commissioner, cash or securities or a bond with good and sufficient sureties to be approved by the court or the commissioner, in an amount to be fixed by the court or the commissioner sufficient to secure the payment of any final judgment that may be rendered in the action or proceeding, provided the court or the commissioner in administrative proceedings may in its or his discretion make an order dispensing with the deposit or bond where the insurer shows to the satisfaction of the court or the commissioner that it maintains in this state funds or securities, in trust or otherwise, sufficient and available to satisfy any final judgment that may be entered in the action or proceeding; or (2) procure proper authorization to do an insurance business in this state.

(CONN. GEN. STAT. § 38a-27(a))

Domestic Surplus Lines Insurers

Connecticut permits a domestic insurer with at least $15 million minimum capital and surplus to be designated as a domestic surplus lines insurer upon the written approval of the commissioner.

(CONN. GEN. STAT. § 38a-271a)

Nonadmitted Insurer Filing Requirements

U.S.-based surplus lines insurers are required to file financial statements with the insurance commissioner on a quarterly basis.

(CONN. AGENCIES REGS. § 38a-740-6(b)(3))

These reports must include a breakdown of the company's Connecticut business showing premiums and losses by line.

See Department Bulletin FS-4SL-15, https://portal.ct.gov/CID/Financial-Division/Financial-Regulation-Division (last visited Aug. 26, 2020). When accessing the site, scroll down to Surplus Lines Insurers: Financial Reporting Requirements for ALL ELIGIBLE SURPLUS LINES INSURERS.

Surplus Lines Broker Licensing

The initial and reinstatement fees are each $675. The renewal fee is $625.

Surplus lines licenses renew October 1st of even-numbered years. Renewals must be done electronically via the National

Producer License Registry (NIPR) up to 90 days prior to the expiration date.

There are no continuing education requirements for surplus lines licensees.

Both nonresident individuals and nonresident business entities applying for a surplus lines license must hold an active surplus lines license in another state.

Both individuals and business entities applying for a surplus lines broker license must be currently licensed and in good standing as a Connecticut property and casualty producer. For a business entity to obtain/maintain a license, there needs to be at least one designated license responsible person (DLRP) who is actively surplus lines licensed in Connecticut.

A bond is not required.

A pre-licensing course is not required.

See http://www.ct.gov/cid/cwp/view.asp?q=301744%20 (last visited Sept. 2, 2020) and CONN. GEN. STAT. § 38a-794.

Due Care in Selecting Nonadmitted Insurer

The broker must place business only with eligible surplus lines insurers.

(CONN. AGENCIES REGS. § 38a-740-2)

See http://www.catalog.state.ct.us/cid/portalApps/FindCompany.aspx (last visited Sept. 16, 2020) for the list of eligible surplus lines insurers.

Diligent Effort/Diligent Search

In order to export a risk to the surplus lines market, the surplus lines producer must first conduct a diligent search and attempt to procure the coverage from authorized insurers.

(CONN. GEN. STAT. § 38a-741(b)(1))

The diligent search requirement does not apply to flood insurance.

(CONN. GEN. STAT. § 38a-741(b)(2))

The diligent search requirement is fulfilled by obtaining declinations from three insurers licensed in Connecticut to transact the class of insurance being procured.

The insured is required to sign the diligent search statement filed by the surplus lines broker with the department.

(CONN. GEN. STAT. § 38a-741(b)(1)).

See Department Bulletin SL-04, https://portal.ct.gov/CID/Bulletins/Surplus-Lines-SL-Bulletins (last visited Sept. 23, 2020).

Export List

The insurance commissioner maintains a list of coverages that are eligible for export due to that fact that they are generally unavailable from licensed insurers.

(CONN. GEN. STAT. § 38a-741(a))

See https://portal.ct.gov/CID/Financial-Division/Exportable-List (last visited Sept. 30, 2020) for the export list.

Exempt Commercial Purchasers

Connecticut has adopted the NRRA (15 U.S.C. § 8201) definition of exempt commercial purchasers. Coverage for these insureds may be exported to the surplus lines market without making a diligent effort to place the coverage with authorized insurers provided (1) the surplus lines broker has disclosed to the exempt commercial purchaser that coverage may or may not be available from an authorized insurer that may provide greater protection with more regulatory oversight, and (2) such exempt commercial purchaser has subsequently requested such broker, in writing, to procure such policy from an unauthorized insurer.

(CONN. GEN. STAT. § 38a-741(b)(2))

Surplus Lines Broker Filing Requirements

Surplus line brokers are required to submit quarterly written statements to the insurance department by the insured and by the licensee, attesting that they were unable to procure the necessary coverage in the authorized market. National Flood Insurance

Program policies and insurance procured for an exempt commercial purchaser are exempt from this requirement.

(CONN. GEN. STAT. § 38a-741(b)(1))

Surplus lines producers must make quarterly reports including signed copies of their diligent search statements and the taxes associated with each placement.

(CONN. GEN. STAT. § 38a-743(c)(3) and Department Bulletin SL-4, https://portal.ct.gov/CID/Bulletins/Surplus-Lines-SL-Bulletins (last visited Oct. 14, 2020))

Notices

Every insurance policy written on a surplus line basis must have a statement stamped on its cover in not less than 12-point boldface type in capital letters, the following:

> NOTICE
>
> THIS IS A SURPLUS LINES POLICY AND IS NOT PROTECTED BY THE CONNECTICUT INSURANCE GUARANTY ASSOCIATION OR SUBJECT TO REVIEW BY THE CONNECTICUT INSURANCE DEPARTMENT. IT IS IMPORTANT THAT YOU READ AND UNDERSTAND THIS POLICY.

(CONN. GEN. STAT. § 38a-745)

Taxes, Stamping Fees, and Other Government-Imposed Charges

The surplus lines tax is 4 percent of gross premiums. Premium tax does not apply to any policy issued to the state of Connecticut or any agency of the state or to any policy issued to any town, or agency of such town or special taxing district when such town, agency, or department thereof or special taxing district appears in the policy as the named insured and as such is responsible for the payment of premiums shown on such policy. Taxes must be filed on a quarterly basis to the insurance commissioner. Where Connecticut is the home state, tax is due on the entire U.S. premium.

(CONN. GEN. STAT. § 38a-743)

Producer, Policy, Inspection, and Other Fees

A duly licensed producer and surplus lines broker involved in the same transaction may each charge a flat fee per policy for new or renewal business placed in the surplus lines market, provided that the sum of the fee charged by such producer and the fee charged by such surplus lines broker shall not exceed $250 in the aggregate. In the alternative, such producer and surplus lines broker may charge a fee of up to 5 percent of the applicable premium, not to exceed $500 in the aggregate.

(CONN. AGENCIES REGS. § 38a-770-7)

In addition to the scheduled fees a producer or surplus lines broker may charge as reimbursement, any moneys expended by him for any (1) inspection report fees, (2) motor vehicle department reports, (3) policy reports, (4) credit card service fees, (5) regulatory fees from other jurisdictions, such as licensing fees, necessary for the placement of Connecticut risks with out-of-state exposure, (6) costs for overnight mail, or (7) telegrams or telephone calls necessary for the placement of the risk under consideration.

(CONN. AGENCIES REGS. § 38a-707-1)

Industrial Insured Exemption

Connecticut permits an insured that meets the definition of an "industrial insured" to acquire insurance coverage directly from an insurer not authorized to do an insurance business in the state. Industrial insured is defined as "an insured (a) which procures the insurance of any risk by the use of the services of a full-time employee acting as an insurance manager or buyer, or the services of a regularly and continuously retained qualified insurance consultant, and (b) whose aggregate annual premiums for insurance, excluding life, accident and health insurance, total at least fifty thousand dollars."

(CONN. GEN. STAT. § 38a-271(b)(6))

The insured must pay premium tax to the commissioner of revenue services at the independently procured tax rate of 4 percent within 45 days of the end of the quarter during which the transaction took place.

(CONN. GEN. STAT. § 38a-277(g)(3))

Independent or Direct Procurement Law

Connecticut law permits an insured to acquire insurance coverage directly from an unauthorized insurer pursuant to the unsolicited application of the insured or his or her agent.

(CONN. GEN. STAT. § 38a-271(b)(4))

The insured must pay premium tax to the commissioner of revenue services at the independently procured tax rate of 4 percent within 45 days of the end of the quarter during which the transaction took place.

(CONN. GEN. STAT. § 38a-277(g)(3))

DELAWARE

Department of Insurance
1351 West North Street
Suite 101
Dover, DE 19904
(302) 674-7300
http://insurance.delaware.gov/

Alternate Address:
1007 Orange Street
Suite 1010
Wilmington, DE 19801
(302) 577-5280

Delaware does not have a stamping office.

Nonadmitted Insurer Eligibility

General Information

Surplus lines insurers are not licensed, but must meet eligibility standards in order to underwrite risks presented by surplus lines producers. Alien insurers listed on the NAIC International Insurers Department's Quarterly Listing of Alien Insurers are considered eligible.

(DEL. CODE tit. 18, § 1931)

Nonadmitted Insurer Eligibility List

Delaware maintains a list of eligible domestic surplus lines insurers and relies on the Quarterly Listing of Alien Insurers maintained by the International Insurers Department of the National Association of Insurance Commissioners.

See http://insurance.delaware.gov/information/surpluslines/ (last visited July 15, 2020). Scroll to Eligible Non-admitted Surplus Lines Companies, under General Information.

Types of Coverage Permitted or Prohibited

General Information

Life and health insurance are specifically not eligible for export (DEL. CODE tit. 18, § 1905). In addition, nonadmitted insurance, which includes surplus lines insurance, is defined as property and casualty insurance.

(DEL. CODE tit. 18, § 1904(15))

Exempt Transactions

The provisions of surplus lines law do not apply to reinsurance or to the risks enumerated provided that they are placed by Delaware licensed producers or surplus lines brokers. The following risks are considered exempt and may be written by unauthorized insurers without regard to the surplus lines requirements:

- Wet marine and transportation insurance
- Insurance on subjects located, resident, or to be performed wholly outside Delaware or on vehicles or aircraft owned and principally garaged outside Delaware
- Insurance on operations of railroads engaged in transportation in interstate commerce and their property used in such operations
- Insurance of aircraft owned or operated by manufacturers of aircraft or of aircraft operated in commercial interstate flight or cargo of such aircraft or against liability, other than workers' compensation and employer's liability, arising out of the ownership, maintenance, or use of such aircraft
- Transactions for which a certificate of authority to do business is not required of an insurer under the insurance laws of Delaware

(DEL. CODE tit. 18, § 1905)

Service of Process

The commissioner is deemed the agent for service of process on a surplus lines insurer.

(DEL. CODE tit. 18, § 1934)

Limitations on Actions Involving Judicial Proceedings

Before an unauthorized insurer files or causes to be filed any pleading in any action or proceeding instituted against it under §§ 2104 and 2105 of this title, such insurer shall (1) procure a certificate of authority to transact insurance in this state; or (2) deposit with the clerk of the court in which such action or proceeding is pending cash or securities, or file with such clerk a bond with good and sufficient sureties, to be approved by the court, in an amount to be fixed by the court sufficient to secure the payment of any final judgment that may be rendered in such action. The court may in its discretion make an order dispensing with such deposit or bond where the insurer makes a showing satisfactory to the court that it maintains in a state of the United States funds or securities, in trust or otherwise, sufficient and available to satisfy any final judgment that may be entered in such action or proceeding, and that the insurer will pay any final judgment entered therein without requiring suit to be brought on such judgment in the state where such funds or securities are located.

(DEL. CODE tit. 18, § 2107)

Domestic Surplus Lines Insurers

Delaware permits a domestic insurer with at least $15 million minimum capital and surplus to be designated as a domestic surplus lines insurer upon the written approval of the commissioner.

(DEL. CODE tit. 18, § 1932).

Nonadmitted Insurer Filing Requirements

Surplus lines insurers are required to file a financial statement with the insurance commissioner on an annual basis and pay a filing fee.

(DEL. CODE tit. 18, § 1935)

Surplus Lines Broker Licensing

In order to obtain surplus lines authority, a producer must first obtain a property and casualty producer license.

(DEL. CODE tit. 18, § 1920)

A business entity acting as an insurance producer is required to obtain an insurance producer license. The business entity must designate a Delaware licensed insurance producer to be responsible for the business entity's compliance with Delaware insurance laws, rules, and regulations.

(DEL. CODE tit. 18, § 1706(f))

Due Care in Selecting Nonadmitted Insurer

A broker shall not knowingly place surplus lines insurance with an insurer that is unsound financially or that does not meet the eligibility requirements. Before placing insurance with a nonadmitted insurer, all surplus lines brokers shall make a thorough inquiry into the financial condition and operating history of such insurer. During the course of placing business with a nonadmitted insurer, either foreign or alien, each surplus lines broker shall be under a continuous duty to apprise himself or herself that such insurer maintains a condition of solvency and general financial health, and that the company processes claims and pays losses expeditiously. Whenever any reasonable doubt arises as to the capacity, competence, stability, or good faith of a nonadmitted insurer with which a surplus lines broker places insurance, the broker is under a further duty to inform the insurance commissioner of the basis of such doubt. Any broker in a position of doubt shall immediately cease and desist placing further business with such insurer.

(DEL. CODE tit. 18, § 1913)

Diligent Effort/Diligent Search

In order to export a risk to the surplus lines market, the surplus lines producer must first conduct a diligent search and attempt to procure the coverage from authorized insurers (DEL. CODE tit. 18, § 1912). The diligent search requirement is fulfilled by obtaining declinations from three insurers licensed in Delaware to transact the class of insurance being procured and reporting using form SL-1923, which is available at https://insurance.delaware.gov/information/surpluslines/ (last visited Sept. 23, 2020).

Export List

Delaware does not maintain a list of coverages that may be exported to the surplus lines market without first making a diligent search of licensed insurers.

Exempt Commercial Purchasers

Delaware has adopted the NRRA (15 U.S.C. § 8201) definition of exempt commercial purchasers. Coverage for these insureds may be exported to the surplus lines market without making a diligent effort to place the coverage with authorized insurers provided (1) the surplus lines broker has disclosed to the exempt commercial purchaser that coverage may or may not be available from an authorized insurer that may provide greater protection with more regulatory oversight, and (2) such exempt commercial purchaser has subsequently requested such broker, in writing, to procure such policy from an unauthorized insurer.

(DEL. CODE tit. 18, § 1914)

Surplus Lines Broker Filing Requirements

Surplus lines producers must report each policy placed to the department within 30 days. Surplus lines producers are required to make annual transactional filings with the insurance commissioner by March 1 each year.

(DEL. CODE tit. 18, § 1924)

Notices

Every surplus lines producer is obligated to notify each insured in writing that:

a. The insurer with which the broker places the insurance is not licensed by this state and is not subject to its supervision; and
b. In the event of the insolvency of the surplus lines insurer, losses will not be paid by the state insurance guaranty fund.

The department has promulgated Form SL-1917 to fulfill the notification requirement. The form must be signed by the producer and the insured. The use of this form is mandatory.

Every surplus lines policy must have stamped or printed upon it, initialed by and bearing the name of the individual surplus lines producer who procured it, the following disclosure statement:

> This insurance contract is issued pursuant to the Delaware Insurance Laws by an insurer neither licensed by nor under the jurisdiction of the Delaware Insurance Department. This insurer does not participate in insurance guaranty funds created by state law. In the event of the insolvency of the surplus lines insurer, losses will not be paid by the state insurance guaranty fund.

(Del. Code tit. 18, § 1917)

Taxes, Stamping Fees, and Other Government-Imposed Charges

Surplus lines premiums are subject to a tax of 3 percent of gross premiums. Taxes must be filed on a quarterly basis to the insurance commissioner. Where Delaware is the home state, tax is due on the entire U.S. premium.

(Del. Code tit. 18, § 1925)

Producer, Policy, Inspection, and Other Fees

Any assessment, or any membership, policy, survey, inspection, service, or similar fee or other charge in consideration for an insurance contract is deemed part of the taxable premium.

(DEL. CODE tit. 18, § 1904(8))

Industrial Insured Exemption

Delaware statutes and regulations do not contain an industrial insured exemption with regard to surplus lines insurance.

Independent or Direct Procurement Law

Delaware law permits an insured to acquire insurance coverage directly from an unauthorized insurer without the involvement of a surplus lines licensee. The insured must report the transaction to the insurance commissioner on or before March 1 each year and is subject to the same tax requirements as a surplus lines producer.

(DEL. CODE tit. 18, § 1926)

DISTRICT OF COLUMBIA

Government of the District of Columbia
Department of Insurance, Securities and Banking
1050 First Street, NE, #801
Washington, DC 20002
(202) 727-8000
http://disb.dc.gov
disb@dc.gov

District of Columbia does not have a stamping office.

Nonadmitted Insurer Eligibility

General Information

An unauthorized insurer must have standards of solvency and management that meet the requirements necessary for the protection of the policyholders.

(D.C. Code § 31-2502.40(b))

Surplus lines insurers are not required to have a license or register with the department, nor are they required to file annual statements. There is no list of approved surplus lines insurers.

See https://disb.dc.gov/page/surplus-line-information (last visited July 15, 2020).

Nonadmitted Insurer Eligibility List

The Department of Insurance, Securities and Banking does not maintain a nonadmitted insurer eligibility list.

See https://disb.dc.gov/page/surplus-line-information (last visited July 15, 2020).

Types of Coverage Permitted or Prohibited

General Information

There are no restrictions regarding which lines of business may be exported to the surplus lines market in the District of Columbia.

Exempt Transactions

Each agent or broker engaged by the District of Columbia government to procure insurance on its behalf shall be exempt from the requirement, as set forth in § 31-2502.40(a), to pay the 2 per centum of the amount of the gross premiums upon all kinds of policies procured by the agent or broker on behalf of the District of Columbia government. The transaction must still be included on the monthly affidavit, but an accompanying statement must identify the portions relating to policies procured on behalf of the District of Columbia government.

(D.C. CODE § 31-2502.40(c))

The provisions requiring a surplus lines license, premium tax, and reporting do not apply to the business of ocean marine insurance, nor to insurance covering the property of railroad companies and other common carriers engaged in interstate commerce.

(D.C. CODE § 31-2502.38)

Service of Process

District of Columbia statutes do not address service of process specific to surplus lines insurers.

Limitations on Actions Involving Judicial Proceedings

District of Columbia statutes do not set forth any limitations on actions involving judicial proceedings that apply to the lawful transaction of surplus lines business.

Domestic Surplus Lines Insurers

District of Columbia statutes have no provision allowing domestic surplus lines insurers.

Nonadmitted Insurer Filing Requirements

District of Columbia statutes do not set forth filing requirements for nonadmitted insurers. This is confirmed on the department's website.

See https://disb.dc.gov/page/surplus-line-information (last visited Aug. 26, 2020).

Surplus Lines Broker Licensing

An applicant may obtain a producer's license with surplus lines authority by going to nipr.com at https://nipr.com/licensing-center/state-requirements (last visited Sept. 2, 2020). All applicants for surplus lines authority must have or obtain simultaneously casualty authority. Also, nonresident applicants must have surplus lines in their resident state at time of application.

See https://disb.dc.gov/page/surplus-line-information (last visited Sept. 2, 2020).

Applicable to both resident and nonresident surplus lines producers, no person will be issued a surplus lines license unless they hold or are simultaneously issued a license in the property or casualty lines of insurance.

(D.C. Mun. Regs. tit. 26-A, § 100(100.10))

Due Care in Selecting Nonadmitted Insurer

Surplus lines brokers/agents can get their surplus lines licenses revoked for a number of reasons that include procuring "policies from unauthorized companies whose standards of solvency and management do not meet the requirements necessary for the protection of the policyholders."

(D.C. Code Ann. § 31-2502.40(b))

Diligent Effort/Diligent Search

Surplus lines producers must make diligent efforts to procure policies to cover the kind or kinds of business required from companies duly authorized to transact business in the District of Columbia before placing those policies with nonadmitted insurers.

(D.C. Code Ann. § 31-2502.40(a))

Export List

Washington D.C. does not maintain a list of coverages that may be exported to the surplus lines market without first making a diligent search of licensed insurers.

Exempt Commercial Purchasers

Although the NRRA (15 U.S.C. § 8201) exempts a broker from any diligent search requirements when the insured is an exempt commercial purchaser, the District of Columbia statutes do not address this topic.

Surplus Lines Broker Filing Requirements

Surplus lines brokers and agents must file with the department, on or before the 10th day of each month, an affidavit covering the previous calendar month's transaction, including:

1. The description and location of the insured property or risk, and the name of the assured;
2. The amount insured in the policy or contract;
3. The gross premiums charged thereon;
4. The name of the company whose policy or contract is issued, and the kind or kinds of business effected; and
5. That said agent or broker after diligent effort was unable to procure the policies or contracts required to protect the property or risk described in the affidavit from companies duly authorized to transact business in the District.

(D.C. Code Ann. § 31-2502.40(a)(1–5))

Notices

The District of Columbia statutes and regulations do not address disclosure or notice requirements for placement of surplus lines coverage.

Taxes, Stamping Fees, and Other Government-Imposed Charges

Each D.C. licensed surplus lines agent or broker must pay, on February 1st and August 1st of each year, "a sum equal to 2 per centum of the amount of the gross premiums upon all kinds of policies procured by him during the immediately preceding 6 months' period ending December 31st and June 30th, respectively, and, in default of such payment, the Commissioner, through the Corporation Counsel, may bring suit to recover the same."

(D.C. Code Ann. § 31-2502.40(a))

Surplus lines agents or brokers are exempt from the 2 percent tax on gross premiums for policies procured by the agent or broker on behalf of the District of Columbia government.

(D.C. Code Ann. § 31-2502.40(c))

Producer, Policy, Inspection, and Other Fees

A surplus lines agent may only charge fees that are incidental and necessary to placing the risk. Any fee charged must be itemized separately. Taxable premium includes the premium specified in the policy and any and all other revenue earned or fee charged that is incidental to placing the risk.

See https://disb.dc.gov/page/surplus-line-information (last visited Dec. 9, 2020).

Industrial Insured Exemption

District of Columbia statutes and regulations do not contain an industrial insured exemption with regard to surplus lines insurance.

Independent or Direct Procurement Law

District of Columbia statutes and regulations do not contain provisions addressing independently procured insurance.

FLORIDA

Office of Insurance Regulation
200 East Gaines Street, RM 101A
Tallahassee, FL 32399-0305
(850) 413-5914
http://www.floir.com/

Florida has a stamping office.

Florida Surplus Lines Service Office
1441 Maclay Commerce Drive, Suite 200
Tallahassee, FL 32312
(800) 562-4496
www.fslso.com

Nonadmitted Insurer Eligibility

General Information

Surplus lines insurers are not licensed, but must meet eligibility standards in order to underwrite risks presented by surplus lines brokers (FLA. STAT. § 626.918). Alien insurers listed on the NAIC International Insurers Department's Quarterly Listing of Alien Insurers are considered eligible.

If a risk is eligible for export, but coverage cannot be obtained from eligible surplus lines insurers, the surplus lines broker may place the risk with an unauthorized insurer. The surplus lines broker must file a signed statement setting forth the facts of the placement. Unauthorized insurers desiring to accept risks in this manner must first post $50,000 security with the department for each individual risk, contract, or certificate. The surplus lines broker must also file with the department a certified copy of the insurer's financial statement as of the close of the last calendar year, which must show net assets of at least that amount required for licensure of a domestic insurer. The policy, binder, or cover note must contain the following disclosure signed by the insured and the broker:

> The insured is aware that certain insurers participating in this risk have not been approved to transact business in Florida nor have they been declared eligible as surplus lines insurers by the Office of Insurance Regulation of Florida. The placing of such insurance by a duly licensed surplus lines agent in Florida shall not be construed as approval of such insurer by the Office of Insurance Regulation of Florida. Consequently, the insured is aware that the insured has severely limited the assistance available under the insurance laws of Florida. The insured is further aware that he or she may be charged a reasonable per policy fee, as provided in § 626.916(4), Florida Statutes, for each policy certified for export.

All other provisions of the surplus lines law apply to the placement (FLA. STAT. § 626.918(5)).

Nonadmitted Insurer Eligibility List

The department maintains a list of surplus lines insurers that includes alien insurers that appear on the Quarterly Listing of Alien Insurers maintained by the International Insurers Department of the National Association of Insurance Commissioners. *See* https://floir.com/resources-and-reports/surplus-lines-search (last visited Apr. 6, 2023).

Types of Coverage Permitted or Prohibited

General Information

There are no restrictions regarding which lines of business may be exported to the surplus lines market in Florida.

Exempt Transactions

Florida statutes do not set forth any transactions exempt from surplus lines laws.

Service of Process

The chief financial officer is deemed the agent for service of process on a surplus lines insurer.

(FLA. STAT. § 626.937)

Limitations on Actions Involving Judicial Proceedings

Before an unauthorized insurer or person representing or aiding such insurer files or causes to be filed any pleading in any action or proceeding instituted against it under § 626.906, § 626.907, or § 626.909, or a suit instituted by the office or the department enforcing agency action against unauthorized insurers under § 120.69, an unauthorized insurer or person representing or aiding such insurer shall (a) procure a certificate of authority to transact insurance in this state, or (b) deposit with the clerk of the court in which such action or proceeding is pending cash or securities or file with such clerk a bond with good and sufficient sureties, to be approved by the court, in an amount to be fixed by the court sufficient to secure the payment of any final judgment which may be rendered in such action. The court may in its discretion make an order dispensing with such deposit or bond where the insurer makes a showing satisfactory to the court that it maintains in a state of the United States funds or securities, in trust or otherwise, sufficient and available to satisfy any final judgment which may be entered in such action or proceeding, and that the insurer or person representing or aiding such insurer will pay any final judgment entered therein without requiring suit to be brought on such judgment in the state where such funds or securities are located, and that if, nevertheless, such suit is brought on such final judgment the insurer or person representing or aiding such insurer shall waive all defenses thereto.

(FLA. STAT. ANN. § 626.908)

Domestic Surplus Lines Insurers

Florida statutes have no provision allowing domestic surplus lines insurers.

Nonadmitted Insurer Filing Requirements

All U.S. domestic surplus lines insurers are required to file quarterly transactional information with the Florida Surplus Lines Stamping Office no later than 90 days after the quarter ends.

(Fla. Stat. § 626.931(3))

Alien insurers are required to file annual transaction reports by June 30.

(Fla. Stat. § 626.931(4))

See https://www.fslso.com/File/FilingRequirements (last visited Aug. 2, 2021) for foreign and alien insurer filing criteria, due dates, and other information.

Surplus Lines Broker Licensing

In order to obtain surplus lines authority, a broker must first obtain a general lines property and casualty broker license (Fla. Stat. § 626.927(1)). A nonresident applicant must hold an active P&C license and surplus lines license in another state (Fla. Stat. § 626.9272). Agencies must be separately licensed (Fla. Stat. § 626.112(7)(a)). The agency must have a designated agent-in-charge that has an individual license.

After receiving a surplus lines agent license, the agent must become a member of the Florida Surplus Lines Service Office. To become a member, complete a New Agent Membership form by visiting https://slip.fslso.com and selecting Register.

See https://www.fslso.com/licensing-registration/agent-licensing-requirements (last visited Apr. 6, 2023).

Due Care in Selecting Nonadmitted Insurer

A surplus lines agent may not place any coverage with any unauthorized insurer that is not then an eligible surplus lines insurer. There are certain exceptions described in § 626.918(5).

(Fla. Stat. § 626.918)

Diligent Effort/Diligent Search

In order to export a risk to the surplus lines market, the surplus lines broker must first conduct a diligent search and attempt to procure the coverage from authorized insurers.

(Fla. Stat. § 626.916(1)(a))

The diligent search requirement is fulfilled by obtaining declinations from three insurers licensed in Florida to transact the class of insurance being procured. For residential dwellings with a placement cost of $700,000 or more, declination from only one insurer licensed in Florida and currently writing this type of business is required.

(Fla. Stat. § 626.914)

A diligent search affidavit must be filed with the Florida Surplus Lines Service office by the 45th day following the end of each calendar quarter.

(Fla. Stat. § 626.931(1), (2))

Export List

Florida does not have an export list; however, the state has deregulated certain types of commercial and professional lines for the admitted market. The deregulation statute also provides that the deregulated lines of business are exportable to the surplus lines market without a diligent search, provided the required disclosure is made. In order to take advantage of this export rule, the surplus lines broker must have the insured sign the following disclosure:

> You are agreeing to place coverage in the surplus lines market. Superior coverage may be available in the admitted market and at a lesser cost. Persons insured by surplus lines carriers are not protected under the Florida Insurance Guaranty Act with respect to any right of recovery for the obligation of an insolvent unlicensed insurer.

(FLA. STAT. § 626.916(3)(b))

The law providing deregulation for admitted insurers and free export for surplus lines insurers applies to coverage under the following lines of business:

- Excess or umbrella policies
- Surety and fidelity business
- Boiler, machinery, leakage and fire extinguishing equipment
- Errors and omissions
- Directors and officers liability, employment practices, fiduciary liability, and management liability
- Intellectual property and patent infringement liability
- Advertising injury and internet liability insurance
- Property risks rated under a highly protected risks rating plan
- General liability
- Nonresidential property (except for collateral protection insurance)
- Nonresidential multiperil
- Excess property
- Burglary and theft
- Medical malpractice for a facility that is not a hospital, nursing home, or assisted-living facility
- Medical malpractice for a health care practitioner that is not a licensed dentist, physician, osteopathic physician, chiropractic physician, podiatric physician, pharmacist, or pharmacy technician

(FLA. STAT. § 627.062(3)(d)(1))

Exempt Commercial Purchasers

Although the NRRA (15 U.S.C. § 8201) exempts a broker from any diligent search requirements when the insured is an exempt commercial purchaser, Florida statutes do not address this topic.

Surplus Lines Broker Filing Requirements

Each surplus lines agent that has transacted business during a calendar quarter shall on or before the 45th day following the calendar quarter file with the Florida Surplus Lines Service Office an affidavit, on forms as prescribed and furnished by the Florida Surplus Lines Service Office, stating that all surplus lines insurance transacted by him or her during such calendar quarter has been submitted to the Florida Surplus Lines Service Office as required.

(Fla. Stat. § 626.931(1))

All premium bearing policy transactions placed with a surplus lines insurer, taxable or nontaxable, must be electronically submitted to the FSLSO via SLIP or in the prescribed electronic format for XML Batch file submissions within 30 days from the effective date of the premium bearing transaction.

See https://www.fslso.com/File/FilingRequirements (last visited Aug. 2, 2021).

Notices

The surplus lines broker must write or print on the outside of the policy and on any certificate, cover note, or other confirmation of the insurance his or her name, address, and identification number and the name and address of the producing broker through whom the business originated, and must have stamped or written upon the first page of the policy or the certificate, cover note, or confirmation of insurance the following notice:

> THIS INSURANCE IS ISSUED PURSUANT TO THE FLORIDA SURPLUS LINES LAW. PERSONS INSURED

BY SURPLUS LINES CARRIERS DO NOT HAVE THE PROTECTION OF THE FLORIDA INSURANCE GUARANTY ACT TO THE EXTENT OF ANY RIGHT OF RECOVERY FOR THE OBLIGATION OF AN INSOLVENT UNLICENSED INSURER.

Surplus lines policies must have stamped or printed on the face of the policy in at least 14-point, boldface type, the following disclosure:

SURPLUS LINES INSURERS' POLICY RATES AND FORMS ARE NOT APPROVED BY ANY FLORIDA REGULATORY AGENCY.

(FLA. STAT. § 626.924)

Taxes, Stamping Fees, and Other Government-Imposed Charges

Surplus lines premiums are subject to a tax of 4.94 percent of gross premiums. The surplus lines broker must collect the tax from the insured and file it along with the quarterly transaction reports to the Florida Surplus Lines Stamping Office. Where Florida is the home state, tax is due on the entire premium.

The tax does not apply as to insurance of vessels, cargo, or aircraft written under § 626.917, or as to insurance of risks of the state government or its agencies, or of any county or municipality or of any agency thereof.

(FLA. STAT. § 626.932)

Producer, Policy, Inspection, and Other Fees

The surplus lines agent and retail agency may charge a reasonable per-policy fee. Any per-policy fee must be itemized separately to the customer before purchase and enumerated in the policy.

(FLA. STAT. § 626.916(4))

Fees are included in the definition of taxable premium.

(FLA. STAT. § 626.932(6))

Industrial Insured Exemption

Florida statutes and regulations do not contain an industrial insured exemption with regard to surplus lines insurance.

Independent or Direct Procurement Law

Florida law permits insureds to purchase insurance directly from unauthorized insurers without the use of a licensed surplus lines broker. The placement must take place entirely outside the state. The insured must report the transaction to the Florida Surplus Lines Stamping Office within 30 days after the date the insurance was so procured, continued, or renewed. The insured must also pay a premium tax of 5 percent and a 0.3 percent service fee on or before the 45th day following the calendar quarter in which the placement was made.

The statute does not authorize independent procurement of workers' compensation insurance, life insurance, or health insurance.

(FLA. STAT. § 626.938)

GEORGIA

Georgia Office of Insurance and Safety Fire Commissioner
Two Martin Luther King, Jr. Drive
West Tower, Suite 704
Atlanta, GA 30334
(404) 656-2070
https://www.oci.ga.gov/PublicInformation/ContactUs.aspx

Georgia does not have a stamping office.

Nonadmitted Insurer Eligibility

Foreign

A U.S.-domiciled insurer is eligible to write nonadmitted insurance in Georgia for risks whose home state is Georgia if:

- It is eligible in its state of domicile to write the kinds of insurance that it intends to write in Georgia; and
- It maintains minimum capital and surplus (or equivalent) requirements of at least $15 million. These requirements may be reduced, but not below $4.5 million, for an insurer as a result of an affirmative finding of acceptability by the commissioner based upon such factors as quality of management, capital, and surplus of any parent company, company underwriting profit and investment income trends, market availability, and company record and reputation within the industry.

(GA. CODE § 33-5-25(b)(1)(A))

Alien

A surplus line broker may not place insurance with an alien insurer unless the insurer is listed on the Quarterly Listing of Alien Insurers published by the International Insurers Department of the National Association of Insurance Commissioners.

(GA. CODE § 33-5-25(b)(1)(C))

Nonadmitted Insurer Eligibility List

The Georgia Office of Insurance and Safety Fire Commissioner does not maintain a nonadmitted insurer eligibility list.

Types of Coverage Permitted or Prohibited

General Information

Surplus line coverage may be procured from nonadmitted insurers if:

- The insurance is procured through a licensed surplus line broker;
- The insured or his agent made an effort to procure the desired coverage from authorized insurers but was unsuccessful; and
- The insurance is not procured for personal passenger motor vehicle coverage or residential dwelling property coverage unless such insurance cannot be obtained from an authorized insurer.

(GA. CODE § 33-5-21(a))

Exempt Transactions

The following types of transactions are exempt from all Georgia surplus line laws:

- Reinsurance
- Insurance on property or operations of railroads engaged in interstate commerce

- Insurance of aircraft owned or operated by manufacturers of aircraft or operated in scheduled interstate flight, or cargo of the aircraft, or against liability, other than workers' compensation and employer's liability, arising out of the ownership, maintenance, or use of the aircraft

(Ga. Code § 33-5-35)

Service of Process

An unauthorized insurer issuing a policy in Georgia is deemed to have consented to service of process upon the commissioner.
(Ga. Code §§ 33-5-34(b), 33-5-52)

Limitations on Actions Involving Judicial Proceedings

Before any unauthorized insurer may defend an action, it must deposit cash or securities with the clerk of the court, or file a bond, in an amount to be determined by the court to be sufficient to secure the payment of any final judgment. In the alternative, the insurer may procure a certificate of authority to transact insurance in Georgia.
(Ga. Code § 33-5-57(a))

Domestic Surplus Lines Insurers

Georgia permits a domestic insurer with at least $15 million minimum capital and surplus to be designated as a domestic surplus lines insurer upon the written approval of the commissioner.
(Ga. Code § 33 5 20.2)

Nonadmitted Insurer Filing Requirements

Surplus line insurers are not required to file annual financial statements with the commissioner, but must provide their brokers with financial statements.
(Ga. Code § 33-5-25(a))

Surplus Lines Broker Licensing

An individual who holds a current Georgia property and casualty broker license may be licensed as a surplus line broker by applying to the commissioner, paying the license fee (currently $615), passing an examination, and filing a $50,000 bond with the commissioner.

(GA. CODE §§ 33-5-22, 33-23-37(b); GA. COMP. R. & REGS. 120-2-3-.20)

An individual who holds a current surplus line broker license in a state other than Georgia, and who holds a current nonresident agent license for property and casualty insurance in Georgia, may receive a nonresident surplus line broker license in Georgia by submitting an application to the commissioner and paying the fee (currently $615).

(GA. CODE § 33-23-16(d); GA. COMP. R. & REGS. 120-2-3-.34(4))

Georgia does not license business entities, whether resident or nonresident, as surplus line brokers.

(GA. CODE §§ 33-23-37(b), 33-23-16(d))

See also commissioner website, https://oci.georgia.gov/agents-agency-licensing/adjusters-counselors-surplus-lines-brokers (last visited Aug. 2, 2021).

Due Care in Selecting Nonadmitted Insurer

Before placing surplus line insurance, brokers must ensure the surplus line insurer meets the financial requirements to transact surplus line insurance.

(GA. CODE § 33-5-25(a))

Diligent Effort/Diligent Search

Surplus line coverage may be procured from nonadmitted insurers if the insured or his agent makes an effort to procure the desired coverage from authorized insurers but was unsuccessful. Surplus line coverage may not be procured for personal

passenger motor vehicle coverage or residential dwelling property coverage unless such insurance cannot be obtained from an authorized insurer.
(GA. CODE § 33-5-21(a))

Export List

Georgia does not maintain a list of coverages that may be exported to the surplus line market without first making a diligent search of licensed insurers.

Exempt Commercial Purchasers

Georgia has adopted the NRRA (15 U.S.C. § 8201) definition of exempt commercial purchasers. Coverage for these insureds may be exported to the surplus line market without making a diligent effort to place the coverage with authorized insurers, provided (1) the surplus line broker has disclosed to the exempt commercial purchaser that coverage may or may not be available from an authorized insurer that may provide greater protection with more regulatory oversight, and (2) such exempt commercial purchaser has subsequently requested such broker, in writing, to procure such policy from an unauthorized insurer.
(GA. CODE § 33-5-20.1(1))

Surplus Lines Broker Filing Requirements

Each surplus line broker must submit quarterly affidavits to the commissioner on or before April 15, July 15, October 15, and January 15, stating that the insurance was not procurable through authorized insurers and was not placed to obtain better terms or premium. The affidavit must also provide the following information for all surplus line transactions placed by the broker: certificate or cover note number; the name of the insured; the amount of the premium and tax paid; and any other information required by the commissioner.
(GA. CODE §§ 33-5-29, 33-5-21)

Notices

Every surplus line policy must bear the name of the surplus line broker who procured it and must have the following language printed or stamped on it: "This contract is registered and delivered as a surplus line coverage under the Surplus Line Insurance Law, O.C.G.A. Chapter 33-5."

(GA. CODE § 33-5-26(a))

If the annual premium of a surplus line policy is $5,000 or less, the standard disclosure form or brochure explaining surplus line insurance must be attached to or made a part of the policy or certificate.

(GA. CODE § 33-5-26(b); GA. COMP. R. & REGS. 120-2-89-.03)

Taxes, Stamping Fees, and Other Government-Imposed Charges

Georgia imposes a premium tax on surplus line insurance of 4 percent of gross premiums, including policy and inspection fees.

(GA. CODE § 33-5-31(a); Ga. Bulletin No. 11-EX-3 (2011))

The surplus line broker shall remit the premium tax to the commissioner at the time the broker files his or her quarterly affidavits.

(GA. CODE § 33-5-31(a); *see also* § 16, *infra*)

All quarterly and annual tax returns must be filed electronically.

(Ga. Bulletin No. 13-EX-3 (2013))

Producer, Policy, Inspection, and Other Fees

Any assessment or any membership, policy, survey, inspection, service, or similar fee or charge in consideration for an insurance contract is deemed part of the premium and subject to the surplus line tax.

(GA. CODE § 33-24-1(2))

Any fees charged must be authorized by the insurer.

(GA. CODE § 33-60-5(6)(B)(i))

Industrial Insured Exemption

Georgia statutes and regulations do not contain an industrial insured exemption with regard to surplus line insurance.

Independent or Direct Procurement Law

An insured who independently procures insurance must, within 30 days, file a report with the commissioner. The report must state the name and address of the insured, the name and address of the insurer, the subject of the insurance, a general description of the coverage, the amount of the premium, and any other information required by the commissioner. The insured must also submit the premium tax to the commissioner at the time it files the report.

(GA. CODE § 33-5-33)

HAWAII

State of Hawaii Insurance Divisions
Department of Commerce & Consumer Affairs
P.O. Box 3614
Honolulu, HI 96811-3614
(808) 586-2790
http://cca.hawaii.gov

Alternate Address:
335 Merchant Street, 2nd Floor
Honolulu, HI 96813
(808) 586-2799

Hawaii does not have a stamping office.

Nonadmitted Insurer Eligibility

General Information

For all insurers, there is no imposition of a fee or a request of financial premium or other information from foreign and/or alien surplus lines insurers for surplus lines eligibility purposes. Under Hawaii surplus lines law, the surplus lines broker may only place surplus lines insurance with insurers authorized to write that type of insurance in the insurer's domiciliary state. The surplus lines broker is responsible for determining if the surplus lines insurer meets the eligibility requirements.

(HAW. REV. STAT. ANN. § 431:8-302(b)(c))

Foreign

For unauthorized insurers domiciled in a U.S. jurisdiction, a broker is permitted to place unauthorized insurance with such insurers provided they are authorized to write such business in their state of domicile and maintain minimum capital and surplus of $15 million.

(Haw. Rev. Stat. Ann. § 431:8-302(c)(1))

The commissioner is authorized to enter into a cooperative agreement or interstate agreement or compact to establish additional and alternative nationwide uniform eligibility requirements that shall be applicable to unauthorized insurers domiciled in another state.

(Haw. Rev. Stat. Ann. § 431:8-302(d))

Alien

For unauthorized insurers domiciled outside the United States, a broker may place business with such insurers provided the insurer is listed on the Quarterly Listing of Alien Insurers maintained by the International Insurers Department of the National Association of Insurance Commissioners.

(Haw. Rev. Stat. Ann. § 431:8-302(2))

If an alien insurer is not on the Quarterly Listing of Alien Insurers, the surplus lines broker shall maintain in the broker's office evidence of the financial responsibility of the insurer; and provide evidence to the commissioner that the insurer maintains a $5.4 million trust fund in the United States.

(Haw. Rev. Stat. Ann. § 431:8-302(2)(A)(B))

Nonadmitted Insurer Eligibility List

Hawaii does not maintain a nonadmitted insurer eligibility list.

Types of Coverage Permitted or Prohibited

General Information

Insurance may be procured from an unauthorized insurer; provided that:

1. The insurance is procured through a surplus lines broker licensed in the insured's home state;

2. The full amount or kind of insurance cannot be obtained from insurers who are authorized to do business in this state; provided that a diligent search is made among the insurers who are authorized to transact and are actually writing the particular kind and class of insurance in this state each time the insurance is placed or renewed;
3. The surplus lines insurance procured is in addition to or in excess of the amount and coverage which can be procured from the authorized insurers; and
4. The insurance is not procured at a rate lower than the lowest rate that is generally acceptable to authorized insurers transacting that kind of business and providing insurance affording substantially the same protection.

Exempt Transactions

Exemptions from the surplus lines law include reinsurance or the following insurance when placed by a licensed producer of this state:

1. Ocean marine insurance;
2. Insurance on subjects located, resident, or to be performed wholly outside this state, or on vehicles or aircraft owned and principally garaged outside this state; or
3. Insurance of aircraft or cargo of such aircraft, or against liability, other than workers' compensation and employer's liability, arising out of the ownership, maintenance, or use of such aircraft.

(Haw. Rev. Stat. Ann. § 431:8-300)

Service of Process

An unauthorized insurer's act of transacting business in this state constitutes the insurer's appointment of the commissioner or the commissioner's successor in office to be the true and lawful attorney upon whom process may be served. Any act of transacting an insurance business in this state by any unauthorized insurer shall be acknowledgment of its agreement that such service of process is of the same legal force and validity as personal service of process in this state upon the insurer.

(HAW. REV. STAT. ANN. § 431:8-207(A))

Surplus lines policies issued by the surplus lines broker shall contain a provision stating the substance of that section and designating the person to whom the commissioner shall mail process. Insurers assuming surplus lines insurance are deemed to have subjected itself to this article.

(HAW. REV. STAT. ANN. § 431:8-319)

Limitations on Actions Involving Judicial Proceedings

a. Before any unauthorized insurer files or causes to be filed any pleading in any court action, suit, or proceeding, or any notice, order, pleading, or process in an administrative proceeding before the commissioner, instituted against such person or insurer by service made as provided in section 431:8-207, such insurer shall either:
    i. Deposit with the clerk of the court in which such action, suit, or proceeding is pending, or with the commissioner in administrative proceedings, cash or securities, or file a bond with good and sufficient sureties to be approved by the court or commissioner, in an amount fixed by the court or commissioner sufficient to secure the payment of any final judgment which may be rendered in such action or administrative proceeding, or
    ii. Procure a certificate of authority to transact insurance in this state.
b. The commissioner, in any administrative proceeding in which service is made as provided in section 431:8-207, may in the commissioner's discretion order such postponement as may be necessary to afford the defendant

reasonable opportunity to comply with the provisions of subsection (a) and to defend such action.

c. Nothing in subsection (a) shall be construed to prevent an unauthorized insurer from filing a motion to quash a writ or to set aside service made in the manner provided in section 431:8-207 on the ground that the unauthorized insurer has not transacted any insurance business in this state.

(Haw. Rev. Stat. Ann. § 431:8-208)

Domestic Surplus Lines Insurers

Hawaii statutes have no provision allowing domestic surplus lines insurers.

Nonadmitted Insurer Filing Requirements

Hawaii statutes do not set forth periodic filing requirements for nonadmitted insurers.

Surplus Lines Broker Licensing

A person applying for a surplus lines broker license shall apply to the commissioner on the uniform application and declare under penalty of denial, suspension, or revocation of the license that the statements made in the application are true, accurate, and complete to the best of the applicant's knowledge and belief. Before approving the application, the commissioner shall find that the applicant (1) is at least 18 years of age; (2) has not committed any act that is a ground for a licensure sanction; (3) has paid the applicable fees; (4) has passed, within the two years immediately preceding the date of the application or issuance of the license, whichever is later, the applicable examination; and (5) has submitted a full set of fingerprints, including a scanned file from a hard copy fingerprint, for the commissioner to obtain and receive national and state criminal history records checks from the Federal Bureau of Investigation and the Hawaii criminal justice data center.

(HAW. REV. STAT. ANN. § 431:8-310)

Business entities shall be eligible to be surplus lines brokers, upon meeting the following conditions: (1) the business entity licensee shall list individuals within the business entity who have satisfied all requirements of this part to become surplus lines brokers; (2) only those individuals listed on the business entity's license shall transact surplus lines business; and (3) a natural person licensed as a surplus lines broker shall be identified as the business entity's designated representative.

(HAW. REV. STAT. ANN. § 431:8-310)

Due Care in Selecting Nonadmitted Insurer

No surplus lines broker shall, either knowingly or without reasonable investigation of the financial condition and general reputation of the insurer, place insurance with a financially unsound insurer or with an insurer engaging in an unfair practice. The broker must also first determine that insurer meets all of the eligibility requirements.

(HAW. REV. STAT. ANN. § 431:8-302)

Diligent Effort/Diligent Search

Insurance may be procured from an unauthorized insurer when:

1. The full amount or kind of insurance cannot be obtained from insurers who are authorized to do business in this state after a diligent search is made among the insurers who are authorized to transact and are actually writing the particular kind and class of insurance in this state each time the insurance is placed or renewed;
2. The surplus lines insurance procured is in addition to or in excess of the amount and coverage that can be procured from the authorized insurers; and

3. The insurance is not procured at a rate lower than the lowest rate that is generally acceptable to authorized insurers transacting that kind of business and providing insurance affording substantially the same protection.

(HAW. REV. STAT. ANN. § 431:8-301)

Export List

Hawaii does not maintain a list of coverages that may be exported to the surplus lines market without first making a diligent search of licensed insurers.

Exempt Commercial Purchasers

Hawaii has adopted the NRRA (15 U.S.C. § 8201) definition of exempt commercial purchasers. Coverage for these insureds may be exported to the surplus lines market without making a diligent effort to place the coverage with authorized insurers provided (1) the surplus lines broker has disclosed to the exempt commercial purchaser that coverage may or may not be available from an authorized insurer that may provide greater protection with more regulatory oversight, and (2) such exempt commercial purchaser has subsequently requested such broker, in writing, to procure such policy from an unauthorized insurer.

(HAW. REV. STAT. ANN. §§ 431:8-301(b), 431:8-102)

Surplus Lines Broker Filing Requirements

Each Hawaii surplus lines broker who transacted business where Hawaii is the home state of the risk during a calendar quarter must file within 45 days after the end of that quarter a report using OPTins (www.optins.org).

(HAW. REV. STAT. ANN. § 431:8-315 and *see* Insurance Division's website, https://cca.hawaii.gov/ins/surplus-lines-tax/ (last visited Oct. 14, 2020))

Notices

No contract of insurance placed by a surplus lines broker under this part and no premium charged therefor shall be due and payable until the surplus lines broker, when business is originated by a surplus lines broker, or the producer, when business is referred to a surplus lines broker from a licensed producer, has notified the insured in writing that:

1. The insurer with which the surplus lines broker placed the insurance is not licensed by this state and is not subject to its supervision; and
2. In the event of the insolvency of the surplus lines insurer, losses will not be paid by any of the state's insurance guaranty funds.

A copy of the notice shall be maintained by the broker with the records of the contract and available for examination.

Nothing in this section shall nullify any agreement by any insurer to provide insurance.

(HAW. REV. STAT. ANN. § 431:8-307)

Every insurance contract procured and delivered as a surplus lines coverage pursuant to this part, including any evidence of insurance other than a policy, shall:

1. Bear the name and address of the surplus lines broker who procured it, and
2. Have stamped or written conspicuously upon the first page of the contract the following:

   This insurance contract is issued by an insurer which is not licensed by the State of Hawaii and is not subject to its regulation or examination. If the insurer is found insolvent, claims under this contract are not covered by any guaranty fund of the State of Hawaii.

(HAW. REV. STAT. ANN. § 431:8-306)

Taxes, Stamping Fees, and Other Government-Imposed Charges

After June 30, 2011, within 45 days after the end of each calendar quarter, each surplus lines broker shall pay to the director of finance, through the commissioner, a premium tax on surplus lines insurance transacted by the broker during the calendar quarter for insurance for which this state is the home state of the insured. The tax rate shall be in the amount of 4.68 percent of gross premiums, less return premiums, on surplus lines insurance for which the home state is this state.

(HAW. REV. STAT. ANN. § 431:8-315(a))

Producer, Policy, Inspection, and Other Fees

A licensed surplus lines broker may accept and place surplus lines business from any producer licensed in this state for the class of insurance involved, and may compensate the producer therefor.

(HAW. REV. STAT. ANN. § 431:8-311)

Any charges for policy, survey, inspection, service, or similar fees or other charges added by the broker shall not be considered part of taxable premiums.

(HAW. REV. STAT. ANN. § 431:8-315(a))

Industrial Insured Exemption

Hawaii statutes and regulations do not contain an industrial insured exemption with regard to surplus lines insurance.

Independent or Direct Procurement Law

An insured who independently procures insurance shall file within 45 days after the end of the calendar quarter in which the insurance was procured, continued, or renewed, a written report with the commissioner. The report shall be on forms prescribed by the commissioner, showing (1) the name and address of the insured or insureds; (2) the name and address of the insurer; (3) the subject of the insurance; (4) a general description of the coverage; (5) the itemized amount of premiums, taxes, and fees currently charged for each state; (6) the policy number, effective date of the policy, and home state of the insured; and (7) other additional, pertinent information requested by the commissioner. At the time of filing the report, if Hawaii is the home state of the insured, the insured shall pay the tax and fees of this state and all other states to the director of finance, through the commissioner. If Hawaii is not the home state of the insured, the insured shall pay the tax and fees of this state to the home state of the insured.

(Haw. Rev. Stat. Ann. § 431:8-205)

In determining the calendar quarter of procurement, continuation, or renewal, utilize the later of the date bound, or when coverage begins.

See Hawaii Commissioner Memorandum 2013-1E, https://cca.hawaii.gov/ins/commissioners_memo/commissioners-memorandum-2013/ (last visited Jan. 13, 2021).

IDAHO

Idaho Department of Insurance
700 West State Street
3rd Floor
Boise, ID 83720-0043
(208) 334-4250
www.doi.idaho.gov/
agent@doi.idaho.gov

Alternate Address:
P.O. Box 83720
Boise, ID 83720-0043

Idaho has a stamping office.

Surplus Line Association of Idaho, Inc.
595 South 14th Street
Boise, ID 83702-6836
(208) 336-2901
www.idahosurplusline.org

Nonadmitted Insurer Eligibility

Foreign

The surplus line broker may only place insurance with a foreign insurer if it is authorized to write the type of insurance in its domiciliary jurisdiction and has capital and surplus under the laws of its domiciliary jurisdiction greater than the minimum capital and surplus requirements of this state, or $15 million.

(Idaho Code Ann. § 41-1214(6))

Alien

The surplus line broker may only place insurance with alien insurers if it is listed on the Quarterly Listing of Alien Insurers maintained by the International Insurers Department of the National Association of Insurance Commissioners.

(IDAHO CODE ANN. § 41-1214(6))

Nonadmitted Insurer Eligibility List

The director may issue a "white list" of surplus line insurers from time to time. The current white list is available on the Association's website.

See https://www.idahosurplusline.org/surplus-lines-insurers (last visited Apr. 6, 2023).

Types of Coverage Permitted or Prohibited

Prohibited

Workers' compensation is mandated to be placed with authorized insurance carriers.

(IDAHO CODE ANN. § 72-301(2))

Exempt Transactions

Surplus line regulations do not apply to:

- Reinsurance;
- Ocean marine;
- Foreign trade;
- Insurance on property located, resident, or to be performed wholly outside Idaho, or on vehicles or aircraft owned and principally garaged outside of Idaho;
- Interstate railroad operations; and
- Aircraft insurance owned or operated by manufacturers of aircraft, or aircraft operated in commercial interstate flight or against liability, other than worker's

compensation and employer's liability, arising out of the ownership, maintenance, or use of the aircraft.

(IDAHO CODE ANN. § 41-1212)

Service of Process

Transaction of insurance constitutes an appointment by an unauthorized insurer of the director to be its true and lawful attorney, upon whom may be served all lawful process in any action, suit, or proceeding instituted by or on behalf of an insured.

(IDAHO CODE ANN. § 41-1206)

Limitations on Actions Involving Judicial Proceedings

Before any unauthorized foreign or alien insurer shall file or cause to be filed any pleading in any action, suit, or proceeding instituted against it, such unauthorized insurer shall post a bond or procure a certificate of authority. However, this shall not be construed to prevent an unauthorized foreign or alien insurer from filing a motion, in accordance with the applicable rules of civil procedure, to quash a writ or to set aside service thereof on the ground that such unauthorized insurer did not transact insurance in Idaho.

(IDAHO CODE ANN. § 41-1208)

Domestic Surplus Lines Insurers

Idaho statutes have no provision allowing domestic surplus lines insurers.

Nonadmitted Insurer Filing Requirements

A foreign surplus line insurer must:

a. File with the director of insurance a letter of intent indicating:

    i. That the company wishes to be placed on the List of Eligible Surplus Line Insurers in the state of Idaho;
    ii. The reason why the company is not seeking admission as an authorized insurer;
    iii. That the company will abide by the surplus line laws of Idaho;
    iv. That the company will accept only business placed through licensed surplus line brokers who are to collect and remit the applicable premium taxes and stamping fees; and
    v. The lines of insurance the company plans to write in this state.

b. File a copy of its annual statement in the form recommended by the National Association of Insurance Commissioners. The statement must have an original certification by the public insurance supervisory official of the insurer's state of domicile or be sworn to by at least two of the company's executive officers. This filing must include a statement of actuarial opinion, a copy of the management discussion and analysis, and a copy of the company's most recent audited financial statement, including the accountant's letter of qualification and the accountant's report on internal controls.
c. File a certificate of compliance certified by the insurance supervisory official of the state of domicile.
d. File a completed designation of legal agent form certified by the proper corporate official.
e. Pay fees: $500.

See https://doi.idaho.gov/industry/tpa-pbms-other-entities/surplus-lines/ (last visited Apr. 6, 2023).

Surplus Lines Broker Licensing

A resident individual must be licensed as a property or casualty agent with at least two years of experience in the lines of insurance he or she is seeking to be licensed as a surplus line broker. Idaho does not issue surplus line licenses to a business entity.

(Idaho Code Ann. § 41-1223)

A nonresident individual may be licensed as a surplus line broker if the individual holds a surplus line license in their home state and has a property and casualty license and the applicant's home state grants nonresident licenses to Idaho residents on the same basis.

(IDAHO CODE ANN. § 41-1009(e))

Idaho does not require a surety bond for a surplus line license.

See https://doi.idaho.gov/industry/licensing-services/license-types/surplus-lines/ (last visited Apr. 6, 2023).

Due Care in Selecting Nonadmitted Insurer

A broker must not knowingly place surplus line insurance with an insurer that is financially unsound.

(IDAHO CODE ANN. § 14-1217)

Diligent Effort/Diligent Search

A surplus line broker is required to perform a diligent search of authorized insurers before procuring insurance through a surplus line insurer. The broker must keep a record of each surplus line transaction including documentation of his or her diligent effort to secure coverage with at least three admitted carriers in Idaho before writing coverage through a surplus line carrier. The diligent search requirement is waived if the risk is approved for export.

(IDAHO CODE §§ 41-1214(2), 41-1227)

Export List

Idaho maintains an export list which is available at https://www.idahosurplusline.org/export-list (last visited Apr. 6, 2023).

Exempt Commercial Purchasers

Idaho has adopted the NRRA (15 U.S.C. §8201) definition of exempt commercial purchasers. Coverage for these insureds may be exported to the surplus line market without making a diligent effort to place the coverage with authorized insurers provided (1) the surplus line broker has disclosed to the exempt commercial purchaser that coverage may or may not be available from an authorized insurer that may provide greater protection with more regulatory oversight, and (2) such exempt commercial purchaser has subsequently requested such broker, in writing, to procure such policy from an unauthorized insurer.

(Idaho Code Ann. § 41-1214)

Surplus Lines Broker Filing Requirements

The surplus line broker must file an affidavit with the Surplus Line Association within 30 days of receiving the policy using the InsCipher filing system (https://inscipher.com).

The annual report and premium tax payment must be transmitted electronically by the licensed Broker to the Idaho Insurance Department through TriTech Software, which can be found at https://nonsub.tritechsoft.com/#/ (last visited Apr. 6, 2023).

Tax payment is made in full annually on or before March 1st. A $25.00 per day penalty is assessed by the Department of Insurance commencing April 1st for late payments and reporting—including reports of "zero" transactions.

See https://www.idahosurplusline.org/faq (last visited Apr. 6, 2023).

Notices

Every insurance policy written with a surplus line carrier shall bear the name of the placing broker and shall have a notice stamped in red ink with at least ten-point bold print or in black ink with at least 12-point bold print that reads:

> This surplus line contract is issued pursuant to the Idaho insurance laws by an insurer not licensed by the Idaho Department of Insurance. There is no coverage provided for surplus line insurance by either the Idaho Insurance Guaranty Association or by the Idaho Life and Health Insurance Guaranty Association.

(Idaho Code Ann. § 41-1220)

Taxes, Stamping Fees, and Other Government-Imposed Charges

A tax of 1.5 percent is imposed on all premium written with an unauthorized insurer. The taxes are required to be remitted to the director on or before March 1st of each year on all policies transacted from the previous year.

For property and casualty insurance on multi-state risks other than worker's compensation tax is computed on the entire premium if Idaho is the home state.

(IDAHO CODE ANN. § 41-1229)

Producer, Policy, Inspection, and Other Fees

The surplus line broker must collect taxes and fees on premium paid from the insured. Fees are considered part of the premium and subject to the tax.

(IDAPA 18.06.06-015 (01))

Industrial Insured Exemption

Idaho statutes and regulations do not contain an industrial insured exemption with regard to surplus lines insurance.

Independent or Direct Procurement Law

Every insured who purchases insurance directly with a surplus line insurer must file a written report on forms designated by the director with the Surplus Line Association within 30 days from the date the policy was received by the insured. The report must include the name and address of the insured; the name and address of the insurer; the subject of insurance; a description of coverage; and the premium amount.

A tax of 1.5 percent of the premium is required to be payable within 30 days after the insured receives the policy and at the same time the report is submitted to the Association.

(IDAHO CODE ANN. § 41-1233)

ILLINOIS

Illinois Department of Insurance
320 W. Washington Street
Springfield, IL 62767-0001
(217) 782-4515
https://idoi.illinois.gov/

Alternate Address:
122 S. Michigan Avenue
19th Floor
Chicago, IL 60603
(312) 814-2420

Illinois has a stamping office.

Surplus Line Association of Illinois
222 S. Riverside Plaza, Suite 2220
Chicago, IL 60606
(312) 263-1993
www.slai.org

Nonadmitted Insurer Eligibility

General Information

A surplus line licensee may, if necessary, use an insurer that does not meet the foreign and alien insurer requirements only if prior written warning is given to the insured in a format substantially similar to the example in 50 Illinois Administrative Code 2701, Illustration A.

(Ill. Admin. Code tit. 50, § 2701.30)

Foreign

To be eligible, a surplus line insurer domiciled in the United States must

- Be permitted in its domiciliary jurisdiction to write the type of insurance involved;
- Have $15 million in policyholders surplus; and
- Have standards of solvency and management adequate for the protection of policyholders.

(215 Ill. Comp. Stat. 5/445(1.5)(b))

Alien

To be eligible, a surplus line insurer domiciled outside the United States must either meet the same standards as an insurer domiciled in the United States or must be on the Quarterly Listing of Alien Insurers maintained by the International Insurers Department of the National Association of Insurance Commissioners.
(215 Ill. Comp. Stat. 5/445(1.5)(c))

Nonadmitted Insurer Eligibility List

Illinois does not maintain a nonadmitted insurer eligibility list. The surplus line licensee is responsible for determining that the insurer meets the eligibility requirements before procuring the insurance.
(Ill. Admin. Code tit. 50, § 2701.30)

Types of Coverage Permitted or Prohibited

Permitted

In order to procure coverage from a surplus line insurer, the coverage must be of the types specified in Classes 2 and 3 of Section 4 of the Illinois Insurance Code.
(215 Ill. Comp. Stat. 5/445(1))
Classes 2 and 3 include all classes except life insurance.
(215 Ill. Comp. Stat. 5/4)

Prohibited

A producer cannot procure surplus line insurance for primary workers' compensation; for primary personal lines risks when there is residual market coverage available for the coverage and limits requested by the insured; or for a primary policy designed to satisfy proof of financial responsibility and insurance requirements in any Illinois law where the law requires that the proof of insurance is issued by an authorized insurer or residual market mechanism. Excess or umbrella coverage for these risks can be procured from a surplus line insurer.

(215 ILL. COMP. STAT. 5/445(1.5)(d))

Exempt Transactions

Reinsurance is not considered surplus line insurance.

(215 ILL. COMP. STAT. 5/121-2.01 and 121-2.02)

The Illinois surplus line law does not apply to insurance of property and operations of railroads or aircraft engaged in interstate or foreign commerce, insurance of vessels, crafts or hulls, cargoes, marine builder's risks, marine protection and indemnity, or other risks including strikes and war risks insured under ocean or wet marine forms of policies.

(215 ILL. COMP. STAT. 5/445(11))

Service of Process

Surplus line policies must contain a provision designating the director as attorney of the insurer for service of process. This requirement does not apply to domestic surplus line insurers.

(215 ILL. COMP. STAT. 5/445(10))

Limitations on Actions Involving Judicial Proceedings

Before any unauthorized insurer files any pleading in any court action, they must post a bond or obtain a certificate of authority. Nothing in the statute prevents an unauthorized insurer from filing a motion to quash process or to set aside service on the ground that the unauthorized insurer has not transacted business in the state.

(215 Ill. Comp. Stat. 5/121-10)

Domestic Surplus Lines Insurers

Illinois permits a domestic insurer with at least $15 million minimum capital and surplus to be designated as a domestic surplus line insurer upon the written approval of the director.

(215 Ill. Comp. Stat. 5/445a)

Nonadmitted Insurer Filing Requirements

While there is no requirement in the statutes, surplus line insurers are requested to submit annual financial statements, including statutory Page 14 for Illinois, to the Surplus Line Association of Illinois.

See www.slai.org/faq/insurer_02.html (last visited Aug. 26, 2020).

Surplus Lines Broker Licensing

Only individuals are licensed for surplus line in Illinois. In order to obtain a surplus line producer license, a producer must first obtain a producer license. The annual license fee is $400. Surplus line producers must keep a separate account of business transacted under their license for seven years.

(215 Ill. Comp. Stat. 5/445(2))

Illinois handles producer and surplus line producer licensing through the NIPR system.

See https://nipr.com/licensing-center/state-requirements/illinois-resident-licensing-individual or https://nipr.com/licensing-center/state-requirements/illinois-non-resident-licensing-individual (last visited Sept. 2, 2020).

Due Care in Selecting Nonadmitted Insurer

A producer is expected to determine that an insurer meets the statutory financial requirements in § 445(1.5). They are expected to review financial information published by the unauthorized insurer, the financial information and quarterly listing of alien insurers published by the International Insurers Department of the National Association of Insurance Commissioners, and information published by Best's Insurance Reports or other independent market reporting agencies. In determining whether the standards of solvency and management of an unauthorized insurer at the time of procurement meet requirements necessary for the protection of policyholders, the surplus line producer shall consider the financial condition of the insurer, the ready acceptance of the insurer in responsible commercial markets, the general reputation of the insurer, and the insurer's past and current performance of its obligations.

(Ill. Admin. Code tit. 50, § 2701.30)

Diligent Effort/Diligent Search

Before insurance is placed with a surplus line insurer, the producer or surplus line producer must make a diligent effort to procure the insurance from authorized insurers.

(215 Ill. Comp. Stat. 5/445(1))

Diligent effort by the surplus line producer shall be deemed to have been exercised if the surplus line producer or the referring insurance producer submits a risk to three or more authorized insurers that are engaged in writing in Illinois the type of coverage sought, or if there are no insurers actually engaged in writing that coverage, the risk shall be submitted to insurers that, in the surplus line producer's or the insurance producer's professional judgment, are the most likely to accept the risk.

(Ill. Admin. Code tit. 50, § 2701.50)

There is no required form upon which declinations must be recorded. The surplus line producer must maintain a record stating the name of the authorized insurers and the individuals contacted at each insurer who declined the risk. If the diligent effort was done by the retail producer, the surplus line producer must maintain a written record signed by the retail producer that the retail producer made the diligent effort, and the retail producer must maintain a record that states the name of the authorized insurers and the individuals contacted at each insurer who declined the risk

(ILL. ADM. CODE tit. 50, § 2701.60)

Effective January 1, 2022, commercial wholesale transactions with a retail producer who is not affiliated with the wholesaler are exempt from the diligent search requirement. Also effective January 1, 2022, master policies and program business are only subject to a single annual diligent effort for the master policy or for the program.

(215 ILL. COMP. STAT. 5/445(1.5)(f), (g), & (h))

Export List

Illinois does not maintain a list of coverages that may be exported to the surplus line market without first making a diligent search of licensed insurers.

Exempt Commercial Purchasers

Illinois has adopted the NRRA (15 U.S.C. § 8201) definition of exempt commercial purchasers. Coverage for these insureds may be exported to the surplus line market without making a diligent effort to place the coverage with authorized insurers provided (1) the surplus line broker has disclosed to the exempt commercial purchaser that coverage may or may not be available from an authorized insurer that may provide greater protection with more regulatory oversight, and (2) such exempt commercial purchaser has subsequently requested such broker, in writing, to procure such policy from an unauthorized insurer.

(215 ILL. COMP. STAT. 5/445(1.5)(e))

Surplus Lines Broker Filing Requirements

Surplus line producers submit each policy and premium bearing endorsement to the Surplus Line Association of Illinois (215 ILCS 5/445(5)). A stamping fee of 0.004 percent is billed monthly by the Association. It is unlawful to deliver the policy to the insured unless it has been submitted to the Surplus Line Association of Illinois (215 ILCS 5/445(6)). Surplus line tax returns are due twice per year on February 1 and August 1. Fire marshal tax returns are due annually on February 1. Taxes and stamping fees may be charged to and collected from the insured (215 ILCS 5/445(3)). Surplus line records must be kept for seven years and are open to examination by the director and by the Surplus Line Association of Illinois

(215 Ill. Comp. Stat. 5/445(7)).

Notices

Policies from domestic surplus line insurers must have stamped or imprinted on the first page in not less than 12-point, boldface type the following legend:

> Notice to Policyholder: This contract is issued by a domestic surplus line insurer, as defined in Section 445a of the Illinois Insurance Code, pursuant to Section 445, and as such is not covered by the Illinois Insurance Guaranty Fund.

All other surplus line policies must have stamped or imprinted on the first page in not less than 12-point, boldface type the following legend:

> Notice to Policyholder: This contract is issued, pursuant to Section 445 of the Illinois Insurance Code, by a company not authorized and licensed to transact business in Illinois and as such is not covered by the Illinois Insurance Guaranty Fund.

(215 Ill. Comp. Stat. 5/445(10.5))

Taxes, Stamping Fees, and Other Government-Imposed Charges

Surplus line premiums are subject to a tax of 3.5 percent of gross premiums. Fire marshal tax is 1 percent of the fire premium. Surplus line tax forms must be filed, and the taxes paid, twice per year by February 1 and August 1. Fire marshal tax forms must be filed, and the taxes paid, annually by February 1.

(215 Ill. Comp. Stat. 5/445(3))

For applicability of fire marshal tax to various lines of property coverage, see fire marshal tax schedule on Surplus Line Association of Illinois website at https://www.slai.org/info/procnew_ch06.asp#S03 (last visited Nov. 18, 2020).

Producer, Policy, Inspection, and Other Fees

The Department of Insurance has not historically considered broker fees and policy fees to be part of the premium subject to surplus line tax, fire marshal tax, or stamping fee. Effective January 1, 2022, the law was changed to specify that fees are not taxable.

(215 Ill. Comp. Stat. 5/445(1), Definition of "Premium")

If a producer charges a fee, he or she must comply with the following:

- Producer must provide written disclosure to insured prior to policy delivery and keep copy of disclosure for seven years.
- If the fee exceeds 10 percent of the premium, the disclosure must be signed by the insured.
- If policy is cancelled within 90 days, the producer must refund a pro rata portion of the fee. The producer cannot charge a fee for cancellation of a policy.
- If the policy file contains documentation that the producer performed a service for the fee and the disclosure stated that the fees were fully earned, then the fees are fully earned and not subject to refund.

(215 Ill. Comp. Stat. 5/500-80(e))

Industrial Insured Exemption

To qualify as an industrial insured, an insured must employ or retain a qualified risk manager and must be an exempt commercial purchaser, as these terms are identically defined in the NRRA and Illinois statutes. An industrial insured is permitted to independently procure insurance from an unauthorized insurer.

(215 ILL. COMP. STAT. 5/121-2.08(a))

Independent or Direct Procurement Law

Industrial insureds can independently procure insurance from an unauthorized insurer. Independently procured insurance contracts must be filed with the Surplus Line Association of Illinois within 90 days of the effective date. Within 30 days of filing, the 0.5 percent independent procurement tax and 1 percent fire marshal tax (applicable to some property coverages) and filing fee of 0.004 percent must be paid. Safety-Net Hospitals are not subject to the reporting requirement or taxes.

(215 ILL. COMP. STAT. 5/121-2.08)

INDIANA

Indiana Department of Insurance
311 W. Washington Street
Indianapolis, IN 46204-2787
(317) 232-2395
https://www.in.gov/idoi/

Indiana does not have a stamping office.

Nonadmitted Insurer Eligibility

Foreign

Indiana does not have specific statutory eligibility requirements for surplus lines insurers domiciled in the United States; however, surplus lines producers must annually file financial statements for surplus lines insurers they use.

(Ind. Code § 27-1-15.8-4(c))

According to the Indiana department website, if the company files its annual statement electronically with the NAIC, producers need not submit a hard copy; however, the producer should submit a letter indicating which surplus lines companies it currently places or is anticipating placing business with during the year.

See https://www.in.gov/idoi/2489.htm (last visited July 15, 2020).

Alien

Indiana does not have specific statutory eligibility requirements for surplus lines insurers domiciled outside of the United States. Under the NRRA (15 U.S.C. §§ 8201, *et seq.*), states cannot prohibit surplus lines producers from using alien insurers on the

Quarterly Listing of Alien Insurers maintained by the International Insurers Department of the National Association of Insurance Commissioners, and the Indiana department website (see https://www.in.gov/idoi/companyentity-financial-compliance/search-for-a-company-or-entity/lists-by-type-or-category/, last visited Apr. 14, 2023) points to that listing for eligibility.

Nonadmitted Insurer Eligibility List

Indiana has a list of eligible surplus lines insurers that are domiciled in the United States. The Department of Insurance website publishes a link to the list, hosted by Sircon.

See https://www.in.gov/idoi/companyentity-financial-compliance/search-for-a-company-or-entity/lists-by-type-or-category/#14 (last visited Apr. 14, 2023).

Types of Coverage Permitted or Prohibited

Permitted

Licensed surplus lines producers can procure from unauthorized insurers the kinds of insurance defined in Class 2 and Class 3 of Indiana Code § 27-1-5-1 when, after diligent effort, they determine that the coverage cannot be obtained from authorized insurers.

(IND. CODE § 27-1-15.8-3(a))

Exempt Transactions

Reinsurance is not considered surplus lines insurance.

(IND. CODE § 27-4-5-2(1) and (2))

Likewise, policies issued outside of Indiana involving insurance on vessels, craft or hulls, cargoes, marine builder's risk, marine protection and indemnity or other risk, including strikes and war risks commonly insured under ocean or wet marine forms of policy, are not considered surplus lines insurance.

(IND. CODE § 27-4-5-2(6))

Service of Process

An insurer that issues a policy or contract to insure a risk under Indiana's surplus lines statutes is considered to have appointed the commissioner as the insurer's attorney upon whom process may be served in Indiana in any suit, action, or proceeding based upon or arising out of the policy or contract.

(Ind. Code § 27-1-15.8-4(a))

Any act of transacting an insurance business by any unauthorized insurer constitutes an appointment of the secretary of state as attorney of such insurer upon whom may be served all lawful process in any action, suit, or proceeding.

(Ind. Code § 27-4-5-4)

Limitations on Actions Involving Judicial Proceedings

Before any unauthorized insurer files any pleading in any court action, they must post a bond or obtain a certificate of authority. However, this shall not be construed to prevent an unauthorized insurer from filing a motion to quash a writ or to set aside service thereof made in the manner provided in section 4 of this chapter on the ground that such unauthorized insurer has not done any of the acts enumerated in section 2 of chapter 27-4-5.

(Ind. Code § 27-4-5-5(a) and (c))

Domestic Surplus Lines Insurers

Indiana statutes have no provision allowing domestic surplus lines insurers.

Nonadmitted Insurer Filing Requirements

There is no statutory requirement that surplus lines insurers make filings, but when surplus lines insurers file their annual statement electronically with the NAIC, the department website states that this relieves the surplus lines producer from the requirement in Indiana Code § 27-1-15.8-4(c) to file the annual statement. However, the surplus lines producer should still submit a letter indicating which surplus lines companies it currently places or is anticipating placing business with during the year.

See https://www.in.gov/idoi/2489.htm (last visited Aug. 26, 2020).

Surplus Lines Broker Licensing

Before applying for a resident surplus lines license, a producer must be licensed in Indiana as an insurance producer qualified as to the line or lines of insurance to be written and must take an exam.

(IND. CODE §§ 27-1-15.6-5, 27-1-15.8-2, and 27-1-15.8-3(b))

Nonresidents must be licensed for surplus lines authority in their home state.

Resident business entities must hold the Resident Producer Organization license with the Property & Casualty line of authority before applying for the surplus lines license. They must also identify at least one licensed surplus lines producer. Nonresident business entities must identify at least one licensed surplus lines producer.

(IND. CODE § 27-1-15.6-8)

License applications are done at www.sircon.com, www.nipr.com, or through the uniform NAIC paper application.

Due Care in Selecting Nonadmitted Insurer

Other than determining that an insurer meets the eligibility requirements, Indiana statutes do not set forth any requirements with regard to the exercise of due care in selecting a nonadmitted insurer.

Diligent Effort/Diligent Search

Surplus lines producers must make a diligent effort to procure insurance from authorized insurers.

(IND. CODE § 27-1-15.8-3(a))

By the 20th day of each month, surplus lines producers must file an affidavit with the department showing all contracts procured during the preceding month and stating that, after diligent effort, the licensee was unable to procure the insurance from authorized insurers and that is was not placed with surplus lines insurers in order to obtain a lower premium.

(IND. CODE § 27-1-15.8-4(b))

Export List

Indiana does not maintain a list of coverages that may be exported to the surplus lines market without first making a diligent search of licensed insurers.

Exempt Commercial Purchasers

Although the NRRA (15 U.S.C. § 8201) exempts a broker from any diligent search requirements when the insured is an exempt commercial purchaser, Indiana statutes do not address this topic.

Surplus Lines Broker Filing Requirements

Surplus lines producers must file an affidavit with the department by the 20th day of each month showing all contracts procured during the preceding month and stating that, after diligent effort, the licensee was unable to procure the insurance from authorized insurers and that they were not placed with surplus lines insurers in order to obtain a lower premium.

(IND. CODE § 27-1-15.8-4(b))

Surplus lines producers are required to utilize the NAIC OPTins (http://www.optins.org/) filing system (Department Bulletin 239).

The required forms are located within the NAIC OPTins filing system. Surplus Lines Monthly affidavit filings are no longer required if no business is placed.

See https://www.optins.org/state_participation_IN.htm (last visited Oct. 21, 2020).

Surplus lines producers must file with the department by March 31st the financial statement for the preceding year of each unauthorized insurer from whom they procured policies.

(IND. CODE § 27-1-15.8-4(c))

When surplus lines insurers file their annual statement electronically with the NAIC, the department website states that this relieves the surplus lines producer from the filing requirement. However, the surplus lines producer should still submit a letter indicating which surplus lines companies it currently places or is anticipating placing business with during the year.

See https://www.in.gov/idoi/2489.htm (last visited Oct. 21, 2020).

Notices

The Indiana statutes and regulations do not address disclosure or notice requirements for placement of surplus lines coverage.

Taxes, Stamping Fees, and Other Government-Imposed Charges

Surplus lines producers must, on or before February 1 and August 1 of each year, collect from the insured and remit to the department 2.5 percent of surplus lines premiums procured during the preceding six-month period ending December 31 and June 30, respectively. Late payments are subject to a penalty of 10 percent for the first month and 1 percent for each additional month. Semi-annual tax reports are required even if no business has been written for the past six months.

(IND. CODE § 27-1-15.8-4)

Surplus lines producers are required to utilize the NAIC OPTins (http://www.optins.org/) filing system. All required forms are located within the NAIC OPTins filing system.

(Department Bulletin 239)

Producer, Policy, Inspection, and Other Fees

Indiana defines taxable premium to include policy fees, admission fees, membership fees, and regular or special assessments and payments made on account of annuities.

(IND. CODE § 27-1-2-3(w))

Industrial Insured Exemption

To qualify as an industrial insured, an insured must procure insurance by use of the services of a full-time employee acting as an insurance manager or buyer, or the services of a regularly retained and continuously qualified insurance consultant; must have aggregate annual premiums for insurance on all risks totals at least $25,000; and must have at least 25 full-time employees. An industrial insured is exempt from the prohibition of doing business with an unauthorized insurer.

Industrial insureds must remit tax of 2.5 percent of the premium by February 1 for the preceding six months ending December 31, and August 1 for the preceding six months ending June 30. Together with the remittance they must file an affidavit describing the insurance and stating that, after diligent effort, they were unable to procure the insurance from authorized insurers.

(IND. CODE § 27-4-5-2(8))

Independent or Direct Procurement Law

Industrial insureds can independently procure insurance from an unauthorized insurer. They must remit tax of 2.5 percent of the premium by February 1 for the preceding six months end ing December 31, and August 1 for the preceding six months ending June 30. Together with the remittance they must file an affidavit describing the insurance and stating that, after diligent effort, they were unable to procure the insurance from authorized insurers.

(IND. CODE § 27-4-5-2(8))

IOWA

Division of Insurance
601 Locust Street, 4th Floor
Des Moines, IA 50309-3738
(515) 281-5705
www.iid.iowa.gov
Producer Email: producer.licensing@iid.iowa.gov
Producer Licensing: (515) 281-7761

Iowa does not have a stamping office.

Nonadmitted Insurer Eligibility

Foreign

To qualify as an eligible surplus lines insurer, a nonadmitted insurer must file an application with the commissioner and be approved.

(Iowa Code § 515I.2(7)(a))

The nonadmitted insurer submits a request in a format as directed by the commissioner, which demonstrates capital and surplus that equals the greater of the minimum Iowa capital and surplus requirements or $15 million dollars and evidence that the nonadmitted insurer is in good standing with its domiciliary regulator. The commissioner may waive the eligibility requirements of this section or set specific requirements on a case-by-case basis upon an affirmative finding of acceptability. Eligible surplus lines insurers are not required to file or seek approval of their forms and rates.

(Iowa Code § 515I.4)

A nonadmitted insurer must be authorized to write the type of insurance sought in its domiciliary jurisdiction.

(Iowa Code § 515I.3)

To qualify as an eligible surplus lines insurer, a nonadmitted insurer or domestic surplus lines insurer must make an application with the division. The application must include the name of an Iowa resident surplus lines insurance producer to accept inquiries and notices on behalf of the insurer; payment of the greater of a $100 filing fee or a retaliatory fee, and an examination fee for all new applicants; and demonstrated maintenance of the required capital and surplus. In addition, the nonadmitted insurer must have been actively in operation for at least three years without significant changes in ownership or management. This management requirement may be waived.

(IOWA ADMIN. CODE r. 191-21.5(1))

To maintain or renew eligible status, a nonadmitted insurer must by March 1 of each year following the year of approval be in compliance with the rules and statutes, pay a fee, and submit required documents and quarterly financial statements as instructed on the division's website.

(IOWA ADMIN. CODE r. 191-21.5(2) & (3))

Alien

A nonadmitted insurer domiciled outside of the United States that is listed on the Quarterly Listing of Alien Insurers maintained by the International Insurers Department of the National Association of Insurance Commissioners qualifies as an eligible surplus lines insurer.

(IOWA CODE § 515I.2(7)(b))

Nonadmitted Insurer Eligibility List

The Iowa Insurance Division maintains a nonadmitted insurer eligibility list.

See https://iid.iowa.gov/insurers (last visited July 15, 2020).

Types of Coverage Permitted or Prohibited

"Surplus lines insurance" means any property and casualty insurance in this state on properties, risks, or exposures, located or to be performed in this state that is placed through a surplus lines insurance producer with an eligible surplus lines insurer. For purposes of this chapter only, "surplus lines insurance" also includes disability insurance that is in excess of policy limits available from an admitted insurer.

(Iowa Code § 515I.1(18))

Exempt Transactions

Iowa exempts transactions in this state involving group or blanket insurance and group annuities where the master policy of such groups was lawfully issued and delivered in a state in which the company was authorized to do an insurance business. Iowa also exempts insurance on vessels, craft or hulls, cargoes, marine builder's risk, marine protection and indemnity, or other risk including strikes and war risks commonly insured under ocean or wet marine forms of policy.

(Iowa Code § 507A.4(5) & (7))

Service of Process

An eligible surplus lines insurer may be sued upon a cause of action arising in this state under a surplus lines insurance policy or contract placed by the insurer or upon evidence of insurance placed by the insurer and issued or delivered in this state by a surplus lines insurance producer. A policy or contract issued by an eligible surplus lines insurer shall contain a provision stating the substance of this section and designating the person upon whom service of process can be made on behalf of the insurer.

(Iowa Code § 515I.6)

Limitations on Actions Involving Judicial Proceedings

No action shall be maintained in any court in the state upon any policy or contract of fire insurance issued upon any property situated in the state by any company, association, partnership, individual, or individuals that have not been authorized by the commissioner of insurance to transact such insurance business, unless it shall be shown that the insurer or insured, within six months after the issuing of such policy or contract of insurance, has paid into the state treasury 2 percent of the gross premium paid or agreed to be paid for such policy or contract of insurance.

(IOWA CODE ANN. § 515.108)

Domestic Surplus Lines Insurers

Iowa permits a domestic insurer with at least $15 million minimum capital and surplus to be designated as a domestic surplus lines insurer upon the written approval of the commissioner.

(IOWA CODE ANN. § 515I.4A)

Nonadmitted Insurer Filing Requirements

Foreign surplus lines insurers are required to file a financial statement with the insurance commissioner on a quarterly basis.

(IOWA ADMIN. CODE r. 191-21(3))

Surplus Lines Broker Licensing

Surplus line licensees must be licensed. Nonresidents must certify that they are currently licensed in home state for the equivalent qualification for which the applicant is seeking an Iowa nonresident license.

Business entities may be licensed. A licensed producer must be designated to be responsible for compliance with the surplus laws and rules.

(IOWA CODE ANN. §§ 522B.5, 522B.6, 522B.7)

Excess and surplus lines applicants must have successfully completed the excess and surplus lines examination and also have successfully completed either (1) the examinations for property and casualty lines of authority; or (2) the examinations for personal lines of authority and the commercial insurance subject examination.

(IOWA ADMIN. CODE r. 10.4(8))

A license will not be issued to a nonresident producer if the producer's resident state does not issue licenses to Iowa resident producers applying for nonresident producer licenses in that state or if the producer's resident state restricts Iowa resident producers' nonresident activities in that state.

(IOWA ADMIN. CODE r. 10.5(3))

Due Care in Selecting Nonadmitted Insurer

Surplus lines insurance may be placed by a surplus lines insurance producer only with an eligible surplus lines insurer that is authorized to write the type of insurance in its domiciliary jurisdiction.

(IOWA CODE ANN. § 515I.3(1))

Diligent Effort/Diligent Search

Unless otherwise exempt from this requirement, surplus lines insurance can be placed if, after a diligent search, the full amount or type of insurance cannot be obtained from an admitted insurer.

(Iowa Code Ann. § 515I.3)

Export List

Iowa does not maintain a list of coverages that may be exported to the surplus lines market without first making a diligent search of licensed insurers.

Exempt Commercial Purchasers

Iowa has adopted the NRRA (15 U.S.C. § 8201) definition of exempt commercial purchasers. Coverage for these insureds may be exported to the surplus lines market without making

a diligent effort to place the coverage with authorized insurers provided (1) the surplus lines broker has disclosed to the exempt commercial purchaser that coverage may or may not be available from an authorized insurer that may provide greater protection with more regulatory oversight, and (2) such exempt commercial purchaser has subsequently requested such broker, in writing, to procure such policy from an unauthorized insurer.

(IOWA CODE ANN. §§ 515I.2(9), 515I.9)

Surplus Lines Broker Filing Requirements

A surplus lines insurance producer who places insurance with an eligible surplus lines insurer shall collect premium tax from the eligible surplus lines insurer by withholding 1 percent of the premiums for such tax. A surplus lines insurance producer who places insurance with an eligible surplus lines insurer shall file electronically the premium tax information with the division on or before March 1 for policies issued during the preceding calendar year. On or before March 1 of each year, every surplus lines insurance producer who has placed insurance with an eligible surplus lines insurer when the policies have been issued during the preceding calendar year shall file electronically with the division, or as otherwise directed by the division, a sworn report of all such business written during the preceding calendar year and shall submit the amount to cover the taxes due on all such business. If no business was written during the preceding calendar year, no report is required.

(IOWA ADMIN. CODE r. 191-21.3)

Notices

A surplus lines insurance producer who places coverage shall deliver to the insured, within 30 days of the date the policy is issued, a notice that states the following: "This policy is issued, pursuant to Iowa Code chapter 515I, by a nonadmitted company in Iowa and as such is not covered by the Iowa Insurance Guaranty Association." A surplus lines insurance producer may comply with this rule by placing the language in a clear and conspicuous position on the policy. They may also comply by electronic delivery of the notice, as authorized by Iowa Code chapter 505B, provided the method of delivery allows the division, the surplus lines insurance producer and the intended recipient to verify receipt.

(IOWA ADMIN. CODE r. 191-21.4(515I))

Taxes, Stamping Fees, and Other Government-Imposed Charges

A surplus lines insurance producer shall collect and pay to the state of Iowa the appropriate amount of premium tax for surplus lines insurance. The surplus lines tax is 1 percent.

(IOWA CODE ANN. §§ 432.1(3), 515I(2)(a))

If, pursuant to Iowa Code chapter 515I, coverage is placed with an eligible surplus lines insurer, but the surplus lines insurance producer fails to pay to the state of Iowa the premium tax required by Iowa Code section 515I.3(2) and rule 191-21.3(515), the eligible surplus lines insurer shall be liable for the premium tax required by Iowa Code chapter 515I and this chapter.

(IOWA ADMIN. CODE r. 191-21.2(1))

Producer, Policy, Inspection, and Other Fees

Any fees collected are considered part of the premium and subject to tax.

(IOWA ADMIN. CODE r. 191-21.2(515)(21.2)(2))

There is an exemption from tax due for a person properly licensed as an insurance producer, who, for a fee and pursuant to a written agreement, is engaged solely to offer advice, counsel, opinion, or service to an insured with respect to the benefits, advantages, or disadvantages promised under any proposed or in-force policy of insurance if the person does not, directly or indirectly, participate in the sale, solicitation, or negotiation of insurance on behalf of the insured.

(IOWA CODE ANN. § 515I.3(3))

Industrial Insured Exemption

Iowa statutes and regulations do not contain an industrial insured exemption with regard to surplus lines insurance.

Independent or Direct Procurement Law

"Independently procured insurance" means insurance obtained by a person directly from a nonadmitted insurer.

(IOWA CODE ANN. § 515I.2(11))

When Iowa is the home state of the insured, a person who directly procures, continues, or renews a surplus lines insurance policy or contract independently and without using a surplus lines insurance producer on properties, risks, or exposures located or to be performed in whole or in part in this state shall file a written report regarding the transaction with the commissioner, in a manner and method as directed by the commissioner by rule.

When this state is the home state of the insured, each person who has independently procured a surplus lines insurance policy or contract shall pay a premium tax at a rate appropriate to the amount of premium tax equal to the applicable percent, as provided in section 432.1. The tax shall be remitted via a method and schedule and in a manner as directed by the commissioner by rule.

(IOWA CODE ANN. § 515I.10)

KANSAS

Kansas Insurance Department
420 SW 9th Street
Topeka, KS 66612-1678
(785) 296-3071
www.ksinsurance.org
kid.commissioner@ks.gov
Consumer Hotline: (800) 432-2484 (KS only)

Kansas does not have a stamping office.

Nonadmitted Insurer Eligibility

The commissioner maintains a list of authorized nonadmitted insurers. To qualify, insurers must file a certified copy of their most recent annual statement with the commissioner in the form prescribed by Kansas Statute § 40-225, and amendments thereto, or, if domiciled outside the United States, must file their most recent annual statement with the National Association of Insurance Commissioners (NAIC). Capital or surplus as shown on the annual statement must equal or exceed $4.5 million. Individual unincorporated insurers not listed by the NAIC may appear on the list if they are authorized to transact an insurance business in at least one state of the United States, possess assets that are held in trust for the benefit of American policyholders in the sum of not less than $50 million, and pay the required filing fee. Insurance exchanges may appear on the list if they pay the filing fee, and if their individual members have a capital or surplus equal to or in excess of $1.5 million and the aggregate capital or surplus of all members of the exchange is at least $15 million. The nonrefundable filing fee is $200. Subsequent annual statements and filing fees must be submitted prior to May 1 of each year.

(Kan. Stat. § 40-246e)

Nonadmitted Insurer Eligibility List

The commissioner shall maintain a list of insurers not authorized to do business in this state for review by any interested person. Only those insurers who have filed a certified copy of their most recent annual statement with the commissioner in the form prescribed by Kansas Statute § 40-225, and amendments thereto, or, if domiciled outside the United States, have filed their most recent annual statement with the National Association of Insurance Commissioners may appear on the list.

See https://insurance.kansas.gov/excess-surplus-lines/ (last visited July 15, 2020).

Types of Coverage Permitted or Prohibited

Any excess lines agent may negotiate for insureds whose home state is this state, the types of contracts of fire insurance enumerated in Kansas Statute § 40-901, and amendments thereto, and the type of casualty insurance contracts enumerated in Kansas Statute § 40-1102, and amendments thereto, or reinsurance, or to place risks, or to effect insurance or reinsurance for persons or corporations other than such agent.

(KAN. STAT. § 40-246b(a))

Exempt Transactions

Kansas statutes do not set forth any transactions exempt from surplus lines laws.

Service of Process

Any act of transacting insurance by any unauthorized insurer constitutes an appointment of the commissioner as attorney of such insurer upon whom may be served all lawful process in any action, suit, or proceeding.

(KAN. STAT. § 40-2002)

Limitations on Actions Involving Judicial Proceedings

Before any unauthorized insurer files or causes to be filed any pleading in any court action, suit, or proceeding, or any notice, order, pleading, or process in an administrative proceeding before the commissioner of insurance, they must either post a bond or procure a certificate of authority. However, this shall not be construed to prevent an unauthorized insurer from filing a motion to quash a writ or to set aside service thereof on the grounds that such unauthorized insurer has not done any of the acts enumerated in Kansas Statute § 40-2702, and amendments thereto.

(KAN. STAT. § 40-2705)

Domestic Surplus Lines Insurers

Kansas statutes have no provision allowing domestic surplus lines insurers.

Nonadmitted Insurer Filing Requirements

Kansas statutes do not set forth filing requirements for nonadmitted insurers.

Surplus Lines Broker Licensing

A resident individual must be licensed as a resident fire or casualty agent, or both, for three consecutive years immediately prior to application. Only individuals may be licensed.

(KAN. STAT. § 40-246b(a))

Any nonresident individual licensed as a surplus lines agent in his or her home state may be licensed as a nonresident surplus lines agent if his or her home state awards nonresident licenses to residents of this state on the same basis. Only individuals may be licensed.

(KAN. STAT. §§ 40-246b(a), 40-4906(d))

Due Care in Selecting Nonadmitted Insurer

While the Kansas statutes do not define due care in selecting a nonadmitted insurer, if a surplus lines insurer becomes insolvent, the excess lines agent placing the insurance is relieved of any responsibility to the insured if they satisfactorily complied with all requirements pertaining to notification and consent of the insured and used due diligence in selecting the insurer. It shall be presumed that due diligence was used if such insurer was on the list of nonadmitted insurers authorized to write excess coverage compiled pursuant to Kansas Statute § 40-246e at the time coverage first became effective.

(KAN. STAT. § 40-246b(d))

Diligent Effort/Diligent Search

The agent shall on or before March 1 of each year, file with the insurance department of this state, a sworn affidavit or statement to the effect that, after diligent effort, such agent has been unable to secure the amount of insurance required to protect the property, person, or firm described in such agent's affidavit or statement from loss or damage in regularly admitted companies during the preceding year. Mere rate differential shall not be grounds for placing a particular risk in a nonadmitted carrier when an admitted carrier would accept such risk at a different rate. The licensed excess coverage agent must, prior to placing insurance with an insurer not authorized to do business in this state, obtain the written consent of the prospective named insured using the Statement of Insured form, available at https://insurance.kansas.gov/excess-surplus-lines/ (last visited Sept. 23, 2020).

(KAN. STAT. § 40-246b(b))

If business is placed with a nonadmitted company that is subsequently determined to be insolvent, the excess lines agent placing such business with such company is relieved of any responsibility to the insured as it relates to such insolvency, if the excess lines agent has satisfactorily complied with all requirements pertaining to notification of the insured, has properly obtained the written consent of the insured, and has used due diligence in selecting the insurer. It shall be presumed that due diligence was used in selecting the insurer if such insurer was on the list compiled pursuant to Kansas Statute § 40-246e, and amendments thereto, at the time coverage first became effective.

(Kan. Stat. § 40-246b(d))

Risks that may be written but are declined by admitted insurers may be placed with nonadmitted insurers in accordance with Kansas Statute § 40-246b subject to the following conditions:

a. When the coverage sought would be acceptable as a single contract to admitted insurers, artificial divisions of coverage into two or more proposed contracts shall be prohibited for the purpose of (1) rendering a portion of the coverage unacceptable to admitted companies; or (2) obtaining a rate advantage upon the entire risk.
b. With prior approval of the commissioner, a risk involving a single class of coverage may be placed with a nonadmitted insurer if a portion of the risk is unacceptable to admitted insurers and the nonadmitted insurer will not write the unacceptable portion separately.
c. A risk shall not be placed with a nonadmitted insurer if the risk includes a combination of classes of insurance that may be procured from separate admitted insurers under separate contracts.
d. A risk shall not be placed with a nonadmitted insurer if the risk includes a combination of classes of insurance that a single admitted insurer is prohibited from writing in either a single contract or in separate contracts, or both. In these cases, separate forms of contracts, each incorporating a class or a lawful combination of classes, shall be offered to and refused by admitted insurers for each class or combination of classes, before the insurance can be placed with nonadmitted insurers.

(Kan. Admin. Regs. § 40-8-2)

Export List

Kansas does not maintain a list of coverages that may be exported to the surplus lines market without first making a diligent search of licensed insurers.

Exempt Commercial Purchasers

Kansas has adopted the NRRA (15 U.S.C. § 8201) definition of exempt commercial purchasers. Coverage for these insureds may be exported to the surplus lines market without making a diligent effort to place the coverage with authorized insurers provided (1) the surplus lines broker has disclosed to the exempt commercial purchaser that coverage may or may not be available from an authorized insurer that may provide greater protection with more regulatory oversight, and (2) such exempt commercial purchaser has subsequently requested such broker, in writing, to procure such policy from an unauthorized insurer.

(KAN. STAT. § 40-246g)

Surplus Lines Broker Filing Requirements

The agent so licensed shall, on or before March 1 of each year, file with the insurance department of this state, a sworn affidavit or statement to the effect that, after diligent effort, such agent has been unable to secure the amount of insurance required to protect the property, person, or firm described in such agent's affidavit or statement from loss or damage in regularly admitted companies during the preceding year.

(KAN. STAT. § 40-246b)

On March 1 of each year, each licensed agent shall collect and pay to the commissioner a tax of 6 percent on the total gross premiums charged, less any return premiums, for surplus lines insurance transacted by the licensee pursuant to the license for insureds whose home state is Kansas. The individual responsible for filing the statement shall be the agent who signs the policy or the agent of record with the company. The commissioner of insurance shall collect double the amount of tax herein provided from any licensee or other responsible individual as herein described who shall fail, refuse, or neglect to transmit the required statement or shall fail to pay the tax imposed by this section, to the commissioner within the period specified.

(Kan. Stat. § 40-246c)

Notices

Any policy issued under the provisions of this statute shall have stamped or endorsed in a prominent manner thereon, the following:

> This policy is issued by an insurer not authorized to do business in Kansas and, as such, the form, financial condition and rates are not subject to review by the commissioner of insurance and the insured is not protected by any guaranty fund.

(Kan. Stat. § 40-246b(d))

A statement with the following information must be presented to and signed by the insured:

1. A statement that the coverage will be obtained from an insurer not authorized to do business in this state;
2. A statement that the insurer's name appears on the list of companies maintained by the commissioner pursuant to Kansas Statute 40-246e, and amendments thereto;
3. A notice that the insurer's financial condition, policy forms, rates, and trade practices are not subject to the review or jurisdiction of the commissioner;
4. A statement that the protection of the guaranty associations is not afforded to policyholders of the insurer; and
5. A statement or notice with respect to any other information deemed necessary by the commissioner pertinent to insuring with an insurer not authorized to do business in this state.

(Kan. Stat. § 40-246b(b))

The form for this "Statement of Insured" is available on the department's website at https://insurance.kansas.gov/excess-surplus-lines/ (last visited Nov. 11, 2020).

Taxes, Stamping Fees, and Other Government-Imposed Charges

On March 1 of each year, each licensed agent shall collect and pay to the commissioner a tax of 6 percent on the total gross premiums charged, less any return premiums, for surplus lines insurance transacted by the licensee pursuant to the license for insureds whose home state is Kansas.

(KAN. STAT. § 40-246c)

Producer, Policy, Inspection, and Other Fees

Fees are permitted if based upon a written agreement between the insurance agent and insured specifying the amount of the compensation.

(KAN. STAT. § 40-4911)

Taxable premium includes any cost charged in the placement of the insurance including policy or inspection fees.

See Statement & PRF Instructions, https://insurance.kansas.gov/excess-surplus-lines/ (last visited Dec. 9, 2020).

Industrial Insured Exemption

Kansas statutes and regulations do not contain an industrial insured exemption with regard to surplus lines insurance.

Independent or Direct Procurement Law

Any assured who shall knowingly insure such assured's property contrary to the provisions of this act or with a company not authorized to do business in this state, shall be personally liable for double the amount of the tax provided by law on the premiums paid for such insurance.

(KAN. STAT. § 40-246a)

Any excess line agent shall not place risks or effect insurance or reinsurance for themselves, or for the persons, company, or corporation with whom the excess line agent is employed.

(KAN. STAT. § 40-8-10)

KENTUCKY

Department of Insurance (the "Department")
P.O. Box 517
Frankfort, KY 40602-0517
(502) 564-6004
http://insurance.ky.gov/home.aspx

Kentucky does not have a stamping office.

Nonadmitted Insurer Eligibility

Surplus lines insurers are not licensed, but must meet eligibility standards in order to underwrite risks presented by surplus lines brokers. Alien insurers listed on the Quarterly Listing of Alien Insurers maintained by the International Insurers Department of the National Association of Insurance Commissioners are considered eligible.

(Ky. Rev. Stat. § 304.10-070)

Nonadmitted Insurer Eligibility List

Kentucky does not maintain a nonadmitted insurer eligibility list.

Types of Coverage Permitted or Prohibited

In Kentucky, nonadmitted insurance, which includes surplus lines insurance, is defined as property and casualty insurance.

(Ky. Rev. Stat. § 304.10-030(7))

Exempt Transactions

The provisions of surplus lines law do not apply to reinsurance or to the following enumerated risks provided that they are placed by Kentucky licensed producers or surplus lines brokers. The following risks are considered exempt and may be written by unauthorized insurers without regard to the surplus lines requirements:

- Ocean marine and foreign trade insurances
- Insurance on subjects located, resident, or to be performed wholly outside Kentucky or on vehicles or aircraft owned and principally garaged outside Kentucky
- Insurance on operations of railroads engaged in transportation in interstate commerce and their property used in such operations
- Insurance of aircraft owned or operated by manufacturers of aircraft or of aircraft operated in commercial interstate flight or cargo of aircraft or against liability, other than workers' compensation and employer's liability, arising out of the ownership, maintenance, or use of such aircraft

(Ky. Rev. Stat. § 304.10-020)

A certificate of insurance is not required to place insurance on vessels, craft or hulls, cargoes, marine builder's risk, marine protection and indemnity, or other risk, including strikes and war risks commonly insured under ocean or wet marine forms of policy. Therefore these risks may be placed by unauthorized insurers.

(Ky. Rev. Stat. § 304.11-030(1)(h))

Service of Process

Service of lawful process against unauthorized insurers shall be made upon the secretary of state.

(Ky. Rev. Stat. § 304.3-230)

Limitations on Actions Involving Judicial Proceedings

Before any unauthorized person or insurer files or causes to be filed in any pleading in any court action, suit, or proceeding or in any notice, order, pleading, or process in such administrative proceeding before the commissioner instituted against such person or insurer, by services made as provided in subsections (1) to (5), inclusive, of this section, such person or insurer shall either (1) deposit with the clerk of the court in which such action, suit, or proceeding is pending, or with the commissioner in administrative proceedings before the commissioner, cash or securities, or file with such clerk or commissioner a bond with good and sufficient sureties, to be approved by the clerk or commissioner in an amount to be fixed by the court or commissioner sufficient to secure the payment of any final judgment that may be rendered in such action or administrative proceeding; or (2) procure a certificate of authority to transact the business of insurance in this state.

(KY. REV. STAT. ANN. § 304.11-040)

Domestic Surplus Lines Insurers

Kentucky statutes have no provision allowing domestic surplus lines insurers.

Nonadmitted Insurer Filing Requirements

Kentucky statutes do not set forth periodic filing requirements for nonadmitted insurers.

Surplus Lines Broker Licensing

In order to obtain surplus lines authority, a Kentucky resident broker must first obtain a property and casualty agent license.

(KY. REV. STAT. § 304.10-120(6))

A nonresident must be licensed in their home state.
(Ky. Rev. Stat. §§ 304.10-120, 304.9-140)

A business entity acting as an insurance broker is required to obtain an insurance broker license.
(Ky. Rev. Stat. § 304.9-080)

Due Care in Selecting Nonadmitted Insurer

A broker shall place surplus lines insurance only with an insurer that he or she knows, or in the exercise of reasonable diligence could know meets the eligibility requirements.
(Ky. Rev. Stat. § 304.10-070)

Diligent Effort/Diligent Search

In order to export a risk to the surplus lines market, the surplus lines broker must first conduct a diligent search and attempt to procure the coverage from authorized insurers. The Kentucky diligent search statute requires that the full amount of insurance must not be available from insurers licensed to transact and actually writing that class of insurance in Kentucky. Only the amount of insurance in excess of the amount available from licensed insurers may be exported to the surplus lines market. Coverage may not be exported in order to secure a lower premium or better terms than those offered by admitted insurers.
(Ky. Rev. Stat. § 304.10-040)

Export List

Kentucky does not maintain a list of coverages that may be exported to the surplus lines market without first making a diligent search of licensed insurers.

Exempt Commercial Purchasers

Kentucky has adopted the NRRA (15 U.S.C. § 8201) definition of exempt commercial purchasers. Coverage for these insureds may be exported to the surplus lines market without making

a diligent effort to place the coverage with authorized insurers provided (1) the surplus lines broker has disclosed to the exempt commercial purchaser that coverage may or may not be available from an authorized insurer that may provide greater protection with more regulatory oversight, and (2) such exempt commercial purchaser has subsequently requested such broker, in writing, to procure such policy from an unauthorized insurer.

(KY. REV. STAT. § 304.10-040(2)).

Surplus Lines Broker Filing Requirements

Surplus lines brokers must submit an affidavit of eligibility for export for each policy with the Department of Insurance. The affidavit must be filed within 15 days after the invoice date or effective date, whichever occurs later. The affidavit must be filed electronically with the Department of Insurance at https://insurance.ky.gov/doieservices/UserRole.aspx (last visited Apr. 18, 2023).

(806 KY. ADMIN. REGS. 10:030)

The department shall generate quarterly reports, based on filed affidavits, available to licensed surplus lines brokers at https://insurance.ky.gov/doieservices/UserRole.aspx. Each licensed surplus lines broker must reconcile the taxes on the quarterly report with the broker's own records and notify the department of any discrepancy. Surplus lines premium tax and any applicable penalties must be paid within thirty (30) days of the end of the calendar quarter..

(806 KY. ADMIN. REGS. 10:030)

Notices

Every surplus lines policy must have stamped upon the face page, initialed by or bearing the name of the individual surplus lines broker who procured it, the following disclosure statement:

> This insurance has been placed with an insurer not licensed to transact business in the Commonwealth of Kentucky but eligible as a surplus lines insurer. The insurer is not a member of the Kentucky Insurance Guaranty Association. Should the insurer become insolvent,

the protection and benefits of the Kentucky Insurance Guaranty Association are not available.

(KY. REV. STAT. § 304.10-090)

Taxes, Stamping Fees, and Other Government-Imposed Charges

Surplus lines premiums are subject to a tax of 3 percent of gross premiums. The surplus lines premium tax is not assessed upon the premium surcharge tax, the local government premium tax, or any other state or federal tax. Taxes must be filed on a quarterly basis to the insurance commissioner within 30 days of the end of the quarter.

(KY. REV. STAT. § 304.10-180(1))

Surplus lines brokers are responsible for collecting the 1.8 percent policy surcharge, which is payable to the Kentucky Revenue Cabinet on a monthly basis.

(KY. REV. STAT. §§ 304.10-180(2), 136.392)

Surplus lines brokers are responsible for collecting local government premium taxes, which must be submitted to the relevant authorities on a quarterly basis within 30 days of the end of the quarter.

(KY. REV. STAT. §§ 304.10-180(3), 98A.080(8))

Producer, Policy, Inspection, and Other Fees

A licensed surplus lines broker may accept and place surplus lines business for a Kentucky licensed insurance agent for the kind of insurance involved, and may compensate the agent therefor.

(KY. REV. STAT. § 304.10-150)

Industrial Insured Exemption

Industrial insureds are permitted to independently procure insurance without the involvement of an agent or broker. Surplus lines coverages issued to these insureds are exempt from the diligent search requirement. Tax is required to be paid by the insured.

Kentucky law requires each class of exempt policyholder to file a self-certification form and pay a registration fee ($100) once every three years.

"Industrial insured" is defined as and insured: (1) who procures the insurance of any risk or risks other than life and annuity contracts by use of the services of a full-time employee acting as an insurance manager or buyer or the services of a regularly and continuously retained qualified insurance consultant; (2) whose aggregate annual premiums for insurance on all risks total at least $25,000; and (3) that has at least 25 full-time employees; and (4) qualified as an industrial insured as of July 1, 1999. The industrial insured exemption expired effective July 1, 1999. Only qualifying entities that filed the mandatory forms prior to July 1, 1999, and subsequently maintained current registration for that status, remain eligible for the industrial insured class. (Ky. Rev. Stat. § 304.11-020 and 806 Ky. Admin. Regs. 11:010)

Independent or Direct Procurement Law

Kentucky law permits an insured to acquire insurance coverage directly from an unauthorized insurer provided that the negotiations take place entirely outside Kentucky. The insured must pay tax on the transaction and report it to the insurance commissioner.

(Ky. Rev. Stat. § 304.11-030(1)(d))

LOUISIANA

Louisiana Commissioner of Insurance
1702 N. 3rd Street
Baton Rouge, LA 70802
(225) 342-5900
www.ldi.la.gov

Louisiana does not have a stamping office.

Nonadmitted Insurer Eligibility

Surplus lines insurance, as defined in Louisiana Revised Statutes § 22:46(17), may be procured from a surplus lines insurer, as defined in Louisiana Revised Statutes § 22:46(17.1), and shall be procured through a licensed surplus lines broker. It may be procured without regard to the availability of coverage from authorized insurers.

(La. Rev. Stat. § 22:432)

Nonadmitted Insurer Eligibility List

The commissioner of insurance shall maintain a list of approved unauthorized insurers from those eligible unauthorized insurers that apply for approval and satisfy the criteria established by the commissioner.

(La. Rev. Stat. § 22:436)

The list is available on the department's website.

See https://www.ldi.la.gov/onlineservices/WhiteList/ (last visited July 15, 2020).

Types of Coverage Permitted or Prohibited

There are no specific limitations concerning the type of coverage that may be written by a surplus lines insurer. It is noteworthy however that the exemption from rate and form requirements for surplus lines insurers (LA. REV. STAT. § 22:446) does not apply to public carrier vehicles.

(LA. REV. STAT. § 22:1456(B)(2))

The commissioner may require surplus lines insurers to file their forms and rates for health and accident insurance, other than health stop loss and limited benefit policies, when necessary to comply with federal laws or regulations.

(LA. STAT. ANN. § 22:446)

Exempt Transactions

The provisions of Louisiana Revised Statutes § 22:432 through 442, 444, and 1910 controlling the placing of insurance with unauthorized insurers do not apply to reinsurance, ocean marine and foreign trade insurance, insurance on property or operation of railroads engaged in interstate commerce, or insurance of aircraft owned or operated by manufacturers of aircraft, or of aircraft operated in scheduled interstate flight, or cargo of such aircraft, or against liability, other than workers' compensation and employer's liability, arising out of the ownership, maintenance, or use of such aircraft. However, a tax on the portion of the premiums received from ocean marine and foreign trade coverages that is properly allocable to Louisiana does apply. Surplus lines brokers must keep records of these placements in the same detail as required of surplus lines insurance for not less than five years from the effective date of the insurance.

(LA. REV. STAT. § 22:443)

Service of Process

Service of legal process against the insurer may be made in any such action by service upon the secretary of state or some other person in his office whom he may designate during his absence. An unauthorized insurer issuing such policy shall be deemed thereby to have authorized service of process against it in the manner and to the effect as provided by statute.

(LA. REV. STAT. § 22:442)

Limitations on Actions Involving Judicial Proceedings

Before any unauthorized insurer shall file or cause to be filed any pleading in any action, suit, or proceeding instituted against it, such unauthorized insurer shall either (1) file with the clerk of the court in which such action, suit, or proceeding is pending a bond with good and sufficient sureties, to be approved by the court, in an amount to be fixed by the court sufficient to secure the payment of any final judgment that may be rendered in such action; or (2) procure a certificate of authority to transact the business of insurance in this state.

(LA. REV. STAT. § 22:442)

Domestic Surplus Lines Insurers

Louisiana permits a domestic insurer with at least $15 million minimum capital and surplus to be designated as a domestic surplus lines insurer upon the written approval of the commissioner.

(LA. REV. STAT. § 22:436.1)

Nonadmitted Insurer Filing Requirements

To obtain and maintain placement on the list of approved unauthorized insurers, an unauthorized insurer shall comply with the provisions of Louisiana Revised Statutes § 22:435 applicable to foreign or alien insurers, respectively, and shall annually file with the commissioner the following, unless available to the commissioner through the NAIC or from public sources:

1. A copy of the insurer's annual statement as of the preceding December 31st, evidencing that the insurer has complied with the provisions of Louisiana Revised Statutes § 22:435.
2. Evidence that, if the insurer issues workers' compensation insurance in this state, it has established and maintained a workers' compensation claims office pursuant to Louisiana Revised Statutes § 23:1161.1 or has retained a licensed claims adjuster.

3. A copy of the producer production report in a form required by the commissioner listing all business placed with the company by licensed surplus lines brokers. The report shall be filed with the commissioner no later than April 15th of each year.
4. Evidence obtained from the insurer's domiciliary jurisdiction showing the types of insurance it may write in that jurisdiction.

(LA. STAT. ANN. § 22:436)

Surplus Lines Broker Licensing

The fee for the first-time applicant shall be $250; thereafter, the renewal fee is $350 (every two years).

Any licensed property and casualty or health and accident insurance producer maintaining an office at a designated location in this state and having at least two years' experience in the insurance business with an insurer or as an insurance producer may be licensed as a surplus lines broker as follows:

1. The applicant shall submit an application to the commissioner for the license on forms approved by the commissioner.
2. The applicant shall submit the required license fee, as authorized by Louisiana Revised Statutes § 22:821, for each license year during any part of which the license is in effect. The license shall remain in force until the biannual renewal date.
3. The applicant shall pass an examination approved by the commissioner.

(LA. STAT. ANN. § 22:1547)

Due Care in Selecting Nonadmitted Insurer

A surplus lines broker shall place surplus lines insurance only with surplus lines insurers that meet eligibility requirements, are financially sound, and authorized in their domiciliary jurisdictions to write the type of insurance placed.

(La. Rev. Stat. § 22:435)

Diligent Effort/Diligent Search

The requirement for diligent search was repealed by Act 203 of the 2013 Regular Session.

Export List

Louisiana does not maintain a list of coverages that may be exported to the surplus lines market without first making a diligent search of licensed insurers.

Exempt Commercial Purchasers

Although the NRRA (15 U.S.C. § 8201) exempts a broker from any applicable diligent search requirements when the insured is an exempt commercial purchaser, Louisiana statutes do not address this topic.

Surplus Lines Broker Filing Requirements

Surplus lines brokers placing insurance with an unauthorized insurer shall keep a full and true record of such coverage in detail. The record shall be preserved for not less than five years from the effective date of the insurance and shall be kept available in this state and open to the examination of the commissioner of insurance. The surplus lines broker shall furnish to the commissioner of insurance at his request and on forms as designated and furnished by him a report of all such coverage by calendar year.

(La. Stat. Ann. § 22:443)

Notices

Any licensed surplus lines broker that procures a personal lines policy with a surplus lines insurer shall obtain from the applicant for insurance no later than the date of binding coverage, an acknowledgment on a standardized form promulgated by the commissioner of insurance, which shall be maintained by the licensed surplus lines broker.

(LA. STAT. ANN. § 22:438)

Advisory Letter 2018-05 Personal Lines Surplus Lines Coverage Form (Form 438) is used for this purpose and is available from the department's website at https://www.ldi.la.gov/industry/taxes-and-assessments/surplus-lines-premium-tax (last visited Nov. 11, 2020).

Each surplus lines insurance policy or contract shall have the following notice:

> NOTICE
>
> This insurance policy is delivered as surplus lines coverage under the Louisiana Insurance Code.
>
> In the event of insolvency of the company issuing this contract, the policyholder or claimant is not covered by the Louisiana Insurance Guaranty Association or the Louisiana Life and Health Insurance Guaranty Association, which guarantees only specific types of policies issued by insurance companies authorized to do business in Louisiana.
>
> This surplus lines policy has been procured by the following licensed Louisiana surplus lines broker:
>
> ____
>
> ____
>
> Signature of Licensed Louisiana Surplus Lines Broker or Authorized Representative
>
> ____
>
> ____

Printed Name of Licensed Louisiana Surplus Lines Broker

The notice required pursuant to this section shall be:

1. Prominently displayed in the color red or prominently offset by a black border;
2. Printed or stamped on the policy or contract in bold and in not less than ten-point type;
3. Signed by the surplus lines broker who procured the policy or contract.

(LA. STAT. ANN. § 22:433)

Taxes, Stamping Fees, and Other Government-Imposed Charges

There shall be a tax of four and eighty-five one hundredths of 1 percent per annum on the gross premium for all surplus lines insurance for which Louisiana is the home state of the policyholder as defined in Louisiana Statutes Annotated § 22:46(8.1). On or before March 1, June 1, September 1, and December 1 of each year, each surplus lines broker shall transmit to the commissioner a surplus lines tax report and remit the tax payable.

(LA. STAT. ANN. § 22:439(A))

Producer, Policy, Inspection, and Other Fees

The premium quoted by the insurer shall be inclusive of all fees, charges, premiums, or other consideration charged for the insurance or for the procurement thereof.

No fees may be charged except for reimbursement of expenses and an agency fee. The producer may receive reimbursement from the insured for expenses incurred by the producer directly related to the insurance coverage for the insured. In addition, the producer may charge a reasonable agency fee related to the services provided by the producer. Any reimbursement or agency fee shall be itemized separately on an invoice statement. Each such charge must be prominently disclosed and itemized separately on the invoice.

The reimbursement for expense and agency fees shall not be considered premium for any purpose, nor shall they be subject to premium taxes or surplus lines premium taxes. Agency fees for criminal bail bond, homeowners insurance, or personal automobile insurance that are standard risks insurable at standard rates shall not exceed $25.

(La. Stat. Ann. § 22:855)

Industrial Insured Exemption

Louisiana statutes and regulations do not contain an industrial insured exemption with regard to surplus lines insurance.

Independent or Direct Procurement Law

Direct procurement is permitted. A 4.85 percent premium tax applies. Every person placing insurance without a licensed Louisiana producer or surplus lines broker shall transmit a report and remit the tax to the commissioner.

(La. Stat. Ann. § 22:439)

MAINE

Maine Bureau of Insurance
(all USPS deliveries including overnight express)
34 State House Station
Augusta, ME 04333-0034
(800) 300-5000
https://www.maine.gov/pfr/insurance/
Insurance.PFR@maine.gov

Alternate Address:
(Private deliveries such as FedEx and UPS):
76 Northern Avenue
Gardiner, ME 04345

Maine does not have a stamping office.

Nonadmitted Insurer Eligibility

Foreign

A U.S. insurer may be approved by the superintendent as an eligible surplus lines insurer if the insurer:

a. Is authorized to write such insurance in its domiciliary jurisdiction;
b. Has established satisfactory evidence of good repute and financial integrity; and
c. Maintains capital and surplus, or its equivalent under the laws of its state of domicile, in an amount at least equal to the greater of:
   i. The minimum capital and surplus that would be required if the insurer were licensed in this state; and
   ii. $15 million.

(ME. STAT. tit. 24-A, § 2007(3))

Alien

A non-U.S. insurer is considered eligible to write insurance on an unauthorized basis in Maine if it is listed on the Quarterly Listing of Alien Insurers maintained by the International Insurers Department of the National Association of Insurance Commissioners.

(ME. STAT. tit. 24-A, § 2007(5))

Nonadmitted Insurer Eligibility List

Maine maintains a searchable database that includes active surplus lines companies online.

See https://www.pfr.maine.gov/almsonline/almsquery/SearchCompany.aspx (last visited July 15, 2020). When accessing the database, choose Department: PROF. AND FINANCIAL REGULATION; Agency: INSURANCE; click Show Additional Search Options; Business Type: Surplus Lines Companies.

Types of Coverage Permitted or Prohibited

The following types of insurance are not permitted to be written with a surplus line insurer and must be procured from an authorized insurer:

a. Life insurance;
b. Health insurance, except disability insurance; or
c. Employee benefit excess insurance.

(ME. STAT. tit. 24-A, § 2002-A(1))

The surplus lines law may not be used to place reinsurance.

(ME. STAT. tit. 24-A, § 2002-A(2))

However, a certificate of authority is not required for a foreign reinsurer to operate as such.

(ME. STAT. tit. 24-A, § 405(4))

Exempt Transactions

Surplus lines producers may procure the following kinds of insurance from eligible surplus lines insurers without otherwise adhering to the surplus lines procedures:

a. Wet marine and transportation insurance;
b. Insurance on subjects located, resident, or to be performed wholly outside of Maine, or on vehicles or aircraft owned and principally garaged outside Maine;
c. Insurance on operations of railroads engaged in transportation in interstate commerce and their property used in such operations; or
d. Insurance on aircraft owned or operated by manufacturers of aircraft or of aircraft operated in commercial interstate flight, or cargo of such aircraft, or against liability other than workers' compensation and employer's liability arising out of the ownership, maintenance or use of such aircraft.

(ME. STAT. tit. 24-A, § 2104)

Service of Process

The superintendent is the agent for service of process for surplus lines insurers.
(ME. STAT. tit. 24-A, § 2002(A)(3))

Limitations on Actions Involving Judicial Proceedings

Before any unauthorized person or insurer files or causes to be filed any pleading in any action or proceeding instituted against it under sections 2104 and 2105, the insurer must either (1) procure a certificate of authority to transact insurance in Maine; or (2) deposit with the clerk of the court in which such action or proceeding is pending cash or securities, or file with such clerk a bond with good and sufficient sureties, to be approved by the court, in an amount to be fixed by the court sufficient to secure the payment of any final judgment that may be rendered in such action, provided however that the court may in its discretion make an order dispensing with such deposit or bond where the insurer makes a showing satisfactory to the court that it maintains in a state of the United States funds or securities, in trust or otherwise, sufficient and available to satisfy any final judgment that may be entered in such action or proceeding, and that the insurer will pay final judgment entered therein without requiring suit to be brought on such judgment in the state where such funds or securities are located.

(ME. STAT. tit. 24-A, § 2107)

Domestic Surplus Lines Insurers

Maine statutes have no provision allowing domestic surplus lines insurers.

Nonadmitted Insurer Filing Requirements

The initial filing requirements for an insurer applying for eligibility status are set forth in 31 Code of Maine Rules 160 § 4(A). If the insurer is a U.S. corporation, on or before April 15 of each year succeeding the initial filing or if the insurer is an alien corporation (organized pursuant to laws of countries other than the U.S.) within 75 days subsequent to the close of its elected fiscal year but not later than September 30 in any calendar year, such insurer must file with the superintendent a certified copy of the annual statement for the year immediately preceding and such other information as the superintendent may deem necessary.

(31 ME. CODE R. 160 § 4(B))

Surplus Lines Broker Licensing

Any person while licensed in this state as a resident producer may apply for a surplus lines license. A nonresident producer who is considered by the superintendent to be competent and trustworthy with respect to the handling of surplus lines may apply for surplus lines authority if the home state issues licenses to Maine producers on a reciprocal basis.

(24-A Me. Code R. 19 § 2012)

The application fee is $15, and the license fee is $150.

(24-A Me. Code R. 7 §§ 601(9-A), 601(32))

A bond of at least $20,000 must be maintained by a surplus lines producer.

(24-A Me. Code R. 19 § 2020)

See bond form at https://nipr.com/licensing-center/state-requirements/maine-resident-licensing-individual or https://nipr.com/licensing-center/state-requirements/maine-non-resident-licensing-individual (last visited Sept. 2, 2020). When accessing the site, scroll down to Special Instructions and click on Surplus Lines Bond Form.

Due Care in Selecting Nonadmitted Insurer

A surplus lines broker may not knowingly place surplus lines insurance with an insurer that is unsound financially or that is ineligible.

(24-A Me. Code R. 19 § 2007)

See list of eligible surplus lines insurers at https://www.pfr.maine.gov/almsonline/almsquery/SearchCompany.aspx (last visited Sept. 16, 2020). When accessing the list, choose Department: PROF. AND FINANCIAL REGULATION; Agency: INSURANCE; click Show Additional Search Options; Business Type: Surplus Lines Companies.

Diligent Effort/Diligent Search

Surplus lines brokers may place insurance with eligible surplus lines insurers only if the insurance is not available after diligent effort has been made to place the coverage with authorized insurers. Maine does not require a certain number of declinations for a diligent search. No affidavits are required.

(Me. Stat. tit. 24-A, § 2004)

Export List

Maine does not maintain a list of coverages that may be exported to the surplus lines market without first making a diligent search of licensed insurers.

Exempt Commercial Purchasers

Maine has adopted the NRRA (15 U.S.C. § 8201) definition of exempt commercial purchasers. Coverage for these insureds may be exported to the surplus lines market without making a diligent effort to place the coverage with authorized insurers provided (1) the surplus lines broker has disclosed to the exempt commercial purchaser that coverage may or may not be available from an authorized insurer that may provide greater protection with more regulatory oversight, and (2) such exempt commercial purchaser has subsequently requested such broker, in writing, to procure such policy from an unauthorized insurer.

(ME. STAT. tit. 24-A, 2002-A)

Surplus Lines Broker Filing Requirements

Surplus line brokers are required to maintain in their office a monthly report showing the amount of insurance placed for any person or organization, the location of each risk, the gross premium charged, the name of each insurer with which the insurance was placed, the date and term of each insurance contract issued during the preceding month, and any other pertinent information required by the superintendent. The report must show in the same detail each contract cancelled during the month covered by the report and the return premium on it. The monthly report must be made available to the superintendent for examination at the producer's office location at any time or by delivery to the Bureau of Insurance upon five days' notice by the superintendent.

(ME. STAT. tit. 24-A § 2016)

Notices

Every insurance contract procured and delivered as a surplus lines policy must have stamped upon it, and bearing the name of the producer with surplus lines authority who procured it, the following:

> This insurance contract is issued pursuant to the Maine Insurance Laws by an insurer neither licensed by nor under the jurisdiction of the Maine Bureau of Insurance.
>
> (ME. STAT. tit. 24-A, § 2009)

Taxes, Stamping Fees, and Other Government-Imposed Charges

The surplus lines tax is 3 percent. Tax returns are filed quarterly. For surplus lines policies, the tax must be paid by the surplus lines producer.

(ME. STAT. tit. 36, §§ 2521-A, 2531)

Producer, Policy, Inspection, and Other Fees

A surplus lines broker is permitted to collect a small nominal service charge to cover communication expenses, in addition to the premium required by the insurer and applicable state and federal taxes.

(ME. STAT. tit. 24-A, § 2174)

Industrial Insured Exemption

Maine statutes and regulations do not contain an industrial insured exemption with regard to surplus lines insurance.

Independent or Direct Procurement Law

Direct procurement is permitted. A 3 percent premium tax applies and must be paid by the insured.

(ME. STAT. tit. 36, §§ 2101(2)(F), 2531)

MARYLAND

Maryland Insurance Administration
200 St. Paul Place, Suite 2700
Baltimore, MD 21202
(410) 468-2000
http://www.mdinsurance.state.md.us

Maryland does not have a stamping office.

Nonadmitted Insurer Eligibility

Foreign

A foreign insurer must be authorized in its domiciliary jurisdiction to write the type of insurance it seeks to write, have capital and surplus that is the greater of the minimum capital and surplus required under the laws of its domiciliary jurisdiction, or $15 million. If a foreign insurer's surplus is at least $4.5 million and after consideration of quality of management, capital and surplus of any parent company, company underwriting profit and investment income trends, market availability, and company record and reputation of the foreign insurer in the industry, the Commissioner of Insurance may waive these requirements.

(MD. INS. CODE § 3-318)

Alien

A surplus lines broker may only place business with alien insurers that are listed on the Quarterly Listing of Alien Insurers, maintained by the International Insurers Department of the National Association of Insurance Commissioners.

(MD. INS. CODE § 3-303)

Nonadmitted Insurer Eligibility List

A list of eligible alien surplus lines insurers may be found through the "Company Search" function on the Maryland Insurance Administration website. See https://www.apps.insurance.maryland.gov/CompanyProducerInfo/InsCompanySearch.aspx?NAV=HOME (last visited July 15, 2020). When accessing the site, choose Status: Alien Non-Admitted Insurer.

For foreign surplus lines insurers, you can look up an insurer by company name and click on Information and Documents to see if the Company Status is Active and the Application Field is Surplus Lines.

Types of Coverage Permitted or Prohibited

Permitted

Disability insurance and short-term medical insurance may be procured from a nonadmitted insurer if it is excess of admitted coverage, or if it is not available from an admitted insurer.

(Md. Ins. Code § 3–306.2)

Prohibited

The surplus line statute does not apply to the coverages enumerated in Maryland Insurance Code § 3-302.

Exempt Transactions

Maryland statutes do not set forth any transactions exempt from surplus lines laws.

Service of Process

An unauthorized insurer shall appoint in writing the commissioner as agent for the acceptance of service of process.

(Md. Ins. Code § 3-318(e))

Limitations on Actions Involving Judicial Proceedings

Maryland statutes do not set forth any limitations on actions involving judicial proceedings that apply to the lawful transaction of surplus lines business.

Domestic Surplus Lines Insurers

Maryland statutes have no provision allowing domestic surplus lines insurers.

Nonadmitted Insurer Filing Requirements

Eligible surplus lines insurer approvals expire annually on June 30. Insurers must renew annually by filing an application with the commissioner, paying the applicable fee, and submitting any additional information or documentation that the commissioner requires.

The application for renewal of approval as a surplus lines insurer shall be signed by an officer of the insurer certifying that, to the best knowledge and belief of the officer, the insurer is in compliance with all statutes and regulations of the insurer's domiciliary jurisdiction.

(Md. Ins. Code § 3-318(c) and (d))

Surplus Lines Broker Licensing

A certificate of qualification is required. Applicants must be qualified as an insurance producer, hold an insurance producer's license for the kind of insurance being solicited or sold, and be competent and trustworthy as determined by the commissioner.

(Md. Ins. Code § 3-311)

A $10,000 bond must be posted. A pre-licensing course is not required.

See https://insurance.maryland.gov/Producer/Pages/Surplus LinesBrokers.aspx (last visited Sept. 9, 2020). When accessing the site, click on Initial and Renewal License Application.

Due Care in Selecting Nonadmitted Insurer

A surplus lines broker may not place surplus lines insurance with an insurer if the broker knows, or reasonably should know, that the insurer is in an unsafe or insolvent financial condition.

(MD. INS. CODE § 3-319(c))

Diligent Effort/Diligent Search

A diligent search shall be deemed completed if the insured or the surplus lines broker or insurance producer obtains declinations of a risk from three authorized insurers that are writing the particular kind and class of insurance in the state, and the declinations are included in the affidavit required under § 3-307 of the insurance code. In addition, an insurance producer shall obtain a declination from each insurer for which the insurance producer has been appointed that the insurance producer knows, or should know, is actually writing on a broad basis the particular kind and class of insurance sought.

(MD. INS. CODE §§ 3-306(a)(2), § 3-306.1)

Export List

The Insurance Administration maintains an "Exportable List."

(MD. CODE REGS. 31.03.06.10)

Exempt Commercial Purchasers

Maryland has adopted the NRRA (15 U.S.C. § 8201) definition of exempt commercial purchasers. Coverage for these insureds may be exported to the surplus lines market without making a diligent effort to place the coverage with authorized insurers provided (1) the surplus lines broker has disclosed to the exempt commercial purchaser that coverage may or may not be available from an authorized insurer that may provide greater protection with more regulatory oversight, and (2) such exempt commercial purchaser has subsequently requested such broker, in writing, to procure such policy from an unauthorized insurer.

(MD. INS. CODE § 3-306.1)

Surplus Lines Broker Filing Requirements

A surplus lines placement compliance affidavit must be personally executed by the surplus lines broker or the originating insurance producer at the time the surplus lines insurance is placed. The affidavit must be filed with the commissioner on or before the 45th day after the last day of the calendar quarter in which the surplus lines insurance was placed. For short-term medical insurance procured from a nonadmitted insurer under this subtitle, the affidavit shall include, for each declining authorized insurer, the reason for the declination.

(MD. INS. CODE § 3-307)

Notices

Every insurance policy written on a surplus line basis must contain a separate attachment stating the following:

> Please Read the Following Carefully Before Purchasing Insurance From a Surplus Lines Insurer.
>
> This policy is issued by a surplus lines insurer that has been approved by the Maryland Insurance Administration to issue insurance policies in the surplus lines insurance market. Surplus lines insurers are not under the jurisdiction of the Maryland Insurance Administration and do not possess a certificate of authority to transact insurance business in the State of Maryland. Because surplus lines insurers are not under the jurisdiction of the Maryland Insurance Administration, your ability to seek assistance from the State if you have a problem with your insurance company is limited.
>
> Property and Casualty Insurance Guaranty Corporation and Maryland Life and Health Insurance Guaranty Corporation provide funds that permit certain claimants or policyholders to receive payment of covered claims if their insurance company becomes insolvent (i.e., bankrupt) and is unable to pay the claims. However, these funds do not apply to surplus lines insurers, as a surplus lines insurer is not a member insurer of the Property and Casualty Insurance Guaranty Corporation or the

Maryland Life and Health Insurance Guaranty Corporation. If a surplus lines insurer becomes insolvent (i.e. bankrupt), any claim that you have against the surplus lines insurer will not be covered by the funds administered by Property and Casualty Insurance Guaranty Corporation and Maryland Life and Health Insurance Guaranty Corporation.

If you have any questions regarding this disclosure or surplus lines insurance, please contact the Maryland Insurance Administration at 410-468-2340.

(Md. Code Regs. 31.03.06.09)

Taxes, Stamping Fees, and Other Government-Imposed Charges

The surplus line tax is 3 percent. Surplus lines brokers must file tax reports by March 15th and September 15th of each year. The reports shall be open to public inspection and shall include the gross amount of each kind of insurance business transacted and the aggregate gross premiums charged, the aggregate of returned premiums and taxes paid to insureds, the aggregate of net premiums, and any additional information required by the form.

(Md. Ins. Code § 3-324 and Md. Code Regs. 31.03.06.05)

On delivery of the cover note, certificate of insurance, policy, or other initial confirmation of insurance, a surplus lines broker shall charge the insured the amount of the premium receipts tax in addition to the full amount of the gross premium charged by the insurer for the surplus lines insurance. The surplus lines broker shall return to the insured the premium receipts tax on any unearned part of the premium.

(Md. Ins. Code § 3-324(f))

The surplus lines broker may not absorb the premium receipts tax nor rebate all or part of the premium receipts tax or the surplus lines broker's commission.

(Md. Ins. Code § 3-324(g))

Producer, Policy, Inspection, and Other Fees

Surplus lines brokers may charge a reasonable policy fee not to exceed $100 on a personal lines policy and $250 on a commercial lines policy. Surplus lines brokers may recoup from the insured the actual cost of a required inspection and actual expenses incurred for payment by use of a credit card. Brokers must disclose any fees to the insured on a form approved by the commissioner.

(Md. Ins. Code § 27-216)

Fees that are charged, collected, and retained by the surplus lines broker are not subject to the premium tax but are, instead, considered income for the broker.

See MIA Bulletin 17-18 at https://insurance.maryland.gov/Pages/newscenter/ProducerBulletins.aspx (last visited Dec. 9, 2020).

Industrial Insured Exemption

Except for the premium tax requirement of § 4-209 and the reporting requirement of § 4-210, policies issued to industrial insureds are exempt from the statutes of subtitle 2 of title 4 applicable to unauthorized insurers.

"Industrial insured" is an insured that:

1. Procures the insurance of a risk by the services of a full-time employee acting as an insurance manager or buyer or a regularly and continuously retained qualified insurance consultant;
2. Has aggregate annual premiums for insurance on all risks that total at least $100,000; or
3. Has at least 25 full-time employees.

(Md. Ins. Code § 4-201(a))

Independent or Direct Procurement Law

A full-time salaried employee of a corporate insured may act as an insurance manager or buyer in placing insurance for the corporate insured with an insurer.

(MD. INS. CODE § 4-205(d))

Direct procurements are subject to a 3 percent premium tax.

(MD. INS. CODE § 4-211(b)(1))

MASSACHUSETTS

Massachusetts Division of Insurance
1000 Washington Street, Suite 810
Boston, MA 02118
(617) 521-7794
https://www.mass.gov/orgs/division-of-insurance

Massachusetts does not have a stamping office.

Nonadmitted Insurer Eligibility

Foreign

A U.S.-domiciled insurer is eligible to write nonadmitted insurance in Massachusetts for risks whose home state is Massachusetts if:

- It is eligible in its state of domicile to write the kinds of insurance that it intends to write in Massachusetts; and
- It maintains minimum capital and surplus (or equivalent) requirements of at least $15 million. These requirements may be reduced for an insurer as a result of an affirmative finding of acceptability by the commissioner—based upon such factors as quality of management, capital and surplus of any parent company, company underwriting profit and investment income trends, market availability, and company record and reputation within the industry.

(Mass. Gen. Laws ch. 175, § 168A(c))

Alien

A surplus line broker may not place insurance with an alien insurer unless:

- The insurer is listed on the Quarterly Listing of Alien Insurers maintained by the International Insurers Department of the National Association of Insurance Commissioners, or
- The alien insurer possesses minimum capital and surplus of at least $20 million and maintains assets of at least $5.4 million in U.S. public depositories or trust institutions.

(Mass. Gen. Laws, tit. XXII, ch. 175, § 168A(c))

Nonadmitted Insurer Eligibility List

The Massachusetts Division of Insurance maintains a nonadmitted insurer eligibility list for foreign surplus lines insurers. The requirements to be on the list are:

- The company must be admitted to transact business in at least one state for three or more years.
- The company must maintain at least $300,000 in net assets.
- The company must maintain a deposit of not less $400,000 with the state treasurer or some other state.

The list can be found at https://www.mass.gov/lists/massachusetts-licensed-insurance-companies#massachusetts-eligible-surplus-lines-companies- (last visited July 15, 2020).

Types of Coverage Permitted or Prohibited

Prohibited

A broker may not procure the following types of coverage on the surplus lines market: accident and health, workers' compensation, compulsory motor vehicle liability with the exception of motor vehicle policies for transportation network vehicles, and life insurance on property or interests in Massachusetts.

(Mass. Gen. Laws ch. 175, § 168(b))

Exempt Transactions

Surplus lines laws do not apply to transportation, inland navigation, and ocean and coastwise marine risks.

(MASS. GEN. LAWS ch. 175, § 160)

Service of Process

Any act of transacting insurance by any unauthorized insurer constitutes an appointment of the commissioner as attorney of such insurer upon whom may be served all lawful process in any action, suit, or proceeding.

(MASS. GEN. LAWS ch. 175B, § 2)

Limitations on Actions Involving Judicial Proceedings

Massachusetts statutes do not set forth any limitations on actions involving judicial proceedings that apply to the lawful transaction of surplus lines business.

Domestic Surplus Lines Insurers

Massachusetts statutes have no provision allowing domestic surplus lines insurers.

Nonadmitted Insurer Filing Requirements

Massachusetts statutes do not set forth periodic filing requirements for nonadmitted insurers.

Surplus Lines Broker Licensing

An individual holding a Massachusetts property and casualty broker license may be licensed as a surplus lines broker by submitting an application, paying the application fee (currently $150), and passing an examination.

(MASS. GEN. LAWS ch. 175, §§ 168(b), 162L, 14)

A corporation or partnership holding a Massachusetts property and casualty broker license may be licensed as a surplus lines broker by submitting an application and paying the application fee (currently $150 per individual named in the license).

(MASS. GEN. LAWS ch. 175, §§ 168 (h), 173, 174)

An individual licensed as a surplus lines broker in the individual's home state may be licensed as a Massachusetts surplus lines broker if the individual's home state grants nonresident surplus lines broker licenses to Massachusetts residents on the same basis.

(MASS. GEN. LAWS ch. 175, §§ 162N, 174)

Due Care in Selecting Nonadmitted Insurer

A licensed special insurance broker shall not procure surplus lines from any unauthorized company unless the insurer meets the eligibility requirements in the statute.

(MASS. GEN. LAWS ch. 175, § 168(c))

Diligent Effort/Diligent Search

If certain insurance coverages cannot be procured from authorized insurers, surplus lines coverage may be procured from non-authorized insurers. Within 20 days after procuring such insurance, the broker must file an affidavit stating that the full amount of the insurance cannot be obtained from authorized companies after a diligent effort has been made and that such insurance is only the excess over the amount procured from admitted companies.

(MASS. GEN. LAWS ch. 175, § 168(b)(iii))

Export List

Massachusetts does not maintain a list of coverages that may be exported to the surplus lines market without first making a diligent search of licensed insurers.

Exempt Commercial Purchasers

Massachusetts has adopted the NRRA (15 U.S.C. § 8201) definition of exempt commercial purchasers. Coverage for these insureds may be exported to the surplus lines market without making a diligent effort to place the coverage with authorized insurers provided (1) the surplus lines broker has disclosed to the exempt commercial purchaser that coverage may or may not be available from an authorized insurer that may provide greater protection with more regulatory oversight, and (2) such exempt commercial purchaser has subsequently requested such broker, in writing, to procure such policy from an unauthorized insurer.

(MASS. GEN. LAWS ch. 175, §§ 168(b)(iv), 224)

Surplus Lines Broker Filing Requirements

A surplus lines broker must file an annual statement with the commissioner by January 31 for the immediately preceding calendar year. The statement must show the gross premiums charged for insurance procured or placed. The premium taxes are due and payable at the time the broker files the annual statement.

(MASS. GEN. LAWS ch. 175, §§ 168(d))

Form BR-7 Affidavit by Assured must be filed with the DOI for each new or renewal surplus lines policy within 20 days from the procurement date. Certain "sophisticated commercial insurance buyers" are exempt from the Form BR-7 filing requirement. The DOI has established an electronic mailbox to which scanned copies of the BR-7 shall be emailed by all special brokers doing business in the Commonwealth.

See https://www.mass.gov/info-details/surplus-lines-faqs (last visited Oct. 21, 2020). When accessing the site, scroll down to "When must I complete and file the disclosure statement Form BR-7 Affidavit by Assured?"

Notices

Every surplus lines policy must contain the following disclosure to the policyholder:

> This policy is insured by a company which is not admitted to transact insurance in the commonwealth, is not supervised by the commissioner of insurance and, in the event of an insolvency of such company, a loss shall not be paid by the Massachusetts Insurers Insolvency Fund under chapter 175D.
>
> (MASS. GEN. LAWS ch. 175, § 168(c))

Taxes, Stamping Fees, and Other Government-Imposed Charges

Massachusetts imposes a premium tax on surplus lines insurance of 4.0 percent of gross premiums. Each surplus lines broker must remit the premium tax to the commissioner at the time of filing its annual statement. Massachusetts does not prohibit the surplus lines insurer from absorbing or rebating the tax or charging the tax to the insured.

(MASS. GEN. LAWS ch. 175, § 168(d))

Any policy or inspection fees are "add-ons" to the actual premium and not subject to the surplus lines premium tax.

(Mass. Ins. Bulletin No. B-94-06, 1994)

Producer, Policy, Inspection, and Other Fees

The consumer may be charged an inspection fee only if the inspection is performed by a qualified third party at the request of the insurer. Before the application is taken, the consumer must be notified of the inspection requirement, the estimated cost, and the fact that the consumer will be charged for the inspection. The consumer may be charged only the actual inspection fee. No additional charges for service, handling, administration, etc. may be passed on to the consumer.

Any policy or inspection fees are "add-ons" to the actual premium and not subject to the surplus lines premium tax.

See Mass. Ins. Bulletin No. B-94-06 (1994) at https://www.mass.gov/lists/doi-bulletins (last visited Dec. 9, 2020).

Industrial Insured Exemption

Massachusetts statutes and regulations do not contain an industrial insured exemption with regard to surplus lines insurance.

Independent or Direct Procurement Law

Massachusetts statutes and regulations do not contain provisions addressing independently procured insurance.

MICHIGAN

Michigan Department of Insurance & Financial Services
530 W. Allegan Street, 7th Floor
Lansing, MI 48933
(517) 284-8800
http://www.michigan.gov/difs/Alternate Address:
PO Box 30220
Lansing, MI 48909-7720

Michigan does not have a stamping office.

Nonadmitted Insurer Eligibility

General Information

With certain restrictions, reporting, and additional notice to the insured, a surplus lines licensee may procure insurance from an unauthorized insurer that is not recognized by the commissioner as eligible.

(Mich. Comp. Laws § 500.1950)

Foreign

For insurers domiciled in the United States, the NRRA (15 U.S.C. § 8201) provides that no state shall impose eligibility requirements except in conformance with sections 5A(2) and 5C(2)(a) of the Nonadmitted Insurance Model Act of the National Association of Insurance Commissioners. These sections of the model act require that the insurer be authorized to write the type of insurance in its domiciliary jurisdiction, and possess capital and surplus of the greater of the statutory limits of the state or $15 million.

Michigan's current statutory requirement is $1.5 million.

(Mich. Comp. Laws § 500.1920(4))

However, the state's published "Application for Verifying Eligibility as Surplus Lines Insurer in the State of Michigan" requires the insurer to certify that they have capital and surplus of at least $15 million, and to pay a $500 application fee.

See https://www.michigan.gov/difs/0,5269,7-303-13044_13199---,00.html and scroll down to the Surplus Lines Insurer section.

Alien

For insurers domiciled outside of the United States, the same application requires alien insurers to provide confirmation that they are on the Quarterly Listing of Alien Insurers, maintained by the International Insurers Department of the National Association of Insurance Commissioners, in conformity with Michigan Compiled Laws § 500.1920(4) and requirements in the NRRA (15 U.S.C. § 8201).

Nonadmitted Insurer Eligibility List

Michigan maintains a list of surplus lines insurers that have verified their eligibility.

(MICH. COMP. LAWS § 500.1920)

Insurers on this list are presumed to satisfy the requirement that licensees offer surplus lines insurance only from insurers that are in a stable and unimpaired financial condition.

(MICH. COMP. LAWS § 500.1920(1))

The list can be found using the Company Lookup function on the department website at https://difs.state.mi.us/locators?searchtype=InsCompany (last visited July 15, 2020). When accessing the site, choose Entity Type: Surplus Lines Entities.

Types of Coverage Permitted or Prohibited

General Information

Any coverage that the licensee is unable to procure after diligent search among authorized insurers can be procured from an unauthorized insurer.

(MICH. COMP. LAWS § 500.1910(3)(b))

Exempt Transactions

Michigan considers marine insurance and inland navigation and transportation insurance as categories, separate from surplus lines insurance, that do not require a certificate of authority.

(MICH. COMP. LAWS § 500.402b)

Service of Process

Each eligible unauthorized insurer shall appoint the commissioner as its resident agent, for purposes of service of process.

(MICH. COMP. LAWS § 500.1921(3))

Limitations on Actions Involving Judicial Proceedings

Michigan statutes do not set forth any limitations on actions involving judicial proceedings that apply to the lawful transaction of surplus lines business.

Domestic Surplus Lines Insurers

Michigan statutes have no provision allowing domestic surplus lines insurers.

Nonadmitted Insurer Filing Requirements

Michigan statutes do not set forth periodic filing requirements for nonadmitted insurers.

Surplus Lines Broker Licensing

To obtain a surplus lines license, an applicant must first hold an active property and casualty producer license, file an application at www.nipr.com, and resident applicants must successfully complete an exam. Additionally, an applicant must agree to file semi-annual reports of surplus lines business and pay the associated tax. A resident agency must hold an active property and casualty insurance producer license in order to obtain the Surplus Lines Agency license, and must have an active Michigan licensed surplus lines producer affiliated with their agency. A nonresident agency must be licensed for surplus lines in its home state, hold an active Michigan nonresident property and casualty license, and must have an active Michigan licensed surplus lines individual producer affiliated with their agency in order to get a Nonresident Surplus Lines Agency license.

(Mich. Comp. Laws § 500.1905(3))

Due Care in Selecting Nonadmitted Insurer

Other than determining that an insurer meets the eligibility requirements, Michigan statutes do not set forth any requirements with regard to the exercise of due care in selecting a nonadmitted insurer.

Diligent Effort/Diligent Search

A licensee cannot place insurance with an unauthorized insurer if coverage is available from an authorized insurer. There is a rebuttable presumption that certain coverages are available from an authorized insurers, including auto, homeowners, worker's compensation, and any coverage available from three or more authorized insurers.

(MICH. COMP. LAWS § 500.1910)

Export List

Michigan has an export list.

(MICH. COMP. LAWS § 500.1910(4))

See also the department website at https://www.michigan.gov/difs/0,5269,7-303-13648_60666_76273-381975--,00.html (last visited Sept. 30, 2020).

Exempt Commercial Purchasers

Although not codified in Michigan statutes, the state recognized the exempt commercial purchaser provisions of the federal NRRA.

See the department website at https://www.michigan.gov/difs/0,5269,7-303-13648_60666_76549-384615--,00.html (last visited Oct. 14, 2020).

Surplus Lines Broker Filing Requirements

Surplus lines producers must, on or before February 15 and August 15 of each year, report surplus lines insurance procured during the preceding six-month period ending December 31 and June 30, respectively.

(MICH. COMP. LAWS § 500.1905(3))

Surplus lines producers are required to utilize the NAIC OPTins filing system. Zero filings are required for all quarterly and semi-annual filings.

See https://www.optins.org/state_participation_MI.htm (last visited Oct. 21, 2020).

Notices

Each surplus lines policy must have printed in not less than ten-point type, the following notice:

> This insurance has been placed with an insurer that is not licensed by the state of Michigan. In case of insolvency, payment of claims may not be guaranteed.

The notice cannot be covered over or concealed in any manner.
(MICH. COMP. LAWS § 500.1922)

Taxes, Stamping Fees, and Other Government-Imposed Charges

Surplus lines producers must, on or before February 15 and August 15 of each year, report surplus lines insurance procured during the preceding six-month period ending December 31 and June 30, respectively, and at the time of filing the statement, must pay the 2 percent tax on premiums written and a 0.5 percent regulatory fee.
(MICH. COMP. LAWS § 500.1905(3))
Surplus lines producers are required to utilize the NAIC OPTins (http://www.optins.org/) filing system.

Producer, Policy, Inspection, and Other Fees

A licensee may charge a fee in addition to a commission only if the fee is not included in the premium and the fee is reasonable to cover underwriting and other expenses that are unique to surplus lines. For a personal lines insurance policy, the fee cannot exceed the greater of $100 or 10 percent of the premium. Any fee must not be excessive or discriminatory. The fee must be fully disclosed in detail to the insured, whether directly or through another licensed insurance producer, in writing before the sale. The licensee shall maintain complete documentation of all fees charged and evidence of the required disclosure. The fee must be separately itemized on the policy declarations page, the billing statement, or other documentation provided to the purchaser setting forth the cost of the policy. The fee must not be included as a part of the policy premium in the computation of premium taxes.

(Mich. Comp. Laws § 500.1915)

Industrial Insured Exemption

Michigan statutes and regulations do not contain an industrial insured exemption with regard to surplus lines insurance.

Independent or Direct Procurement Law

Insurance independently procured through negotiations occurring entirely outside of Michigan is a category, separate from surplus lines insurance, that does not require a certificate of authority.

(Mich. Comp. Laws § 500.402b(g))

An insured who procures insurance on behalf of himself or herself, or an employee who procures insurance on behalf of his or her employer must report to the commissioner within 30 days. The report shall be accompanied by a 2 percent tax on premiums written and a 0.5 percent regulatory fee on premiums written.

(Mich. Comp. Laws § 500.1951)

MINNESOTA

Minnesota Commerce Department, Insurance Division
Main Office, Golden Rule Building
85 7th Place East, Suite 280
Saint Paul, MN 55101
(651) 539-1500
https://mn.gov/commerce/insurance/

Minnesota has a stamping office.

Surplus Line Association of Minnesota
600 Clark Street
PO Box 86
Mora, MN 55051
(320) 679-4244
https://www.mnsla.com/

Nonadmitted Insurer Eligibility

Foreign

The commissioner shall not authorize a foreign insurer as an eligible surplus lines insurer unless the insurer:

1. Is domiciled within a U.S. jurisdiction and authorized to write the type of insurance in its domiciliary jurisdiction; and
2. Has capital and surplus, or its equivalent, under the laws of the domiciliary jurisdiction which equals the greater of:
   a. The minimum capital and surplus requirements under the laws of Minnesota; or
   b. $15 million.

An insurer possessing less than the minimum capital and surplus may qualify based on factors such as quality of management, capital and surplus of any parent company, company underwriting profit and investment income trends, market availability, and company record and reputation within the industry. However, the commissioner shall not make an affirmative finding of acceptability if the surplus lines insurer's capital and surplus is less than $4.5 million.

(MINN. STAT. § 60A.206)

Alien

Eligible surplus lines insurers domiciled outside the United States shall file an annual statement on the standard nonadmitted insurers information office financial reporting format as prescribed by the National Association of Insurance Commissioners, and an annual financial audit performed by an independent accounting firm. The commissioner shall not prohibit a surplus lines broker from placing nonadmitted insurance with, or procuring nonadmitted insurance from, an alien insurer that is included on the Quarterly Listing of Alien Insurers maintained by the International Insurers Department of the National Association of Insurance Commissioners.

(MINN. STAT. § 60A.206)

Nonadmitted Insurer Eligibility List

An insurer not otherwise licensed to engage in the business of insurance in Minnesota may apply for recognition as an eligible surplus lines insurer by filing an application in the form and with the information as reasonably required by the commissioner regarding the insurer's financial stability, reputation, integrity, and operating plans, accompanied by a license fee of $500. The commissioner may delegate to an association the power to process and make recommendations on applications for recognition as an eligible surplus lines insurer. Notwithstanding delegation by the commissioner, an applicant may file an application directly with the commissioner.

(MINN. STAT. § 60A.206)

The list is maintained by the department at https://www.sircon.com/ComplianceExpress/Inquiry/consumerInquiry.do?nonSscrb=Y (last visited July 15, 2020). When accessing the list select State: Minnesota; Entity Type: Company; Company Type: Surplus Lines Insurer.

Types of Coverage Permitted or Prohibited

General Information

Insurance shall not be placed by the surplus lines broker with a nonadmitted insurer when coverage is available from a licensed insurer.

(MINN. STAT. § 60A.201)

Permitted

There shall be a rebuttable presumption that the following coverages are unavailable from a licensed insurer:

a. Coverages where one portion of risk is acceptable to licensed insurers but another portion of the same risk is not acceptable. The entire coverage may be placed with eligible surplus lines insurers if it can be shown that eligible surplus lines insurers will accept the entire coverage but not the rejected portion alone; and
b. Any coverage that the broker is unable to procure after a diligent search among licensed insurers.

Prohibited

There shall be a rebuttable presumption that the following coverages are available from a licensed insurer:

a. All mandatory automobile insurance coverages required by chapter 65B;
b. Private passenger automobile physical damage coverage;
c. Homeowners and property insurance on owner-occupied dwellings whose value is less than $500,000. This figure shall be changed annually by the commissioner by the

same percentage as the Consumer Price Index for the Minneapolis-St. Paul Metropolitan Area is changed;

d. Any coverage readily available from three or more licensed insurers unless the licensed insurers quote a premium and terms not competitive with a premium and terms quoted by an eligible surplus lines insurer and;
e. Workers' compensation insurance, except workers' compensation insurance that is not available from the Workers' Compensation Reinsurance Association.

Exempt Transactions

Minnesota statutes do not set forth any transactions exempt from surplus lines laws.

Service of Process

Each eligible surplus lines insurer shall appoint the commissioner as its resident agent for purposes of service of process.

(MINN. STAT. § 60A.206, subdiv. 7)

Limitations on Actions Involving Judicial Proceedings

Minnesota statutes do not set forth any limitations on actions involving judicial proceedings that apply to the lawful transaction of surplus lines business.

Domestic Surplus Lines Insurers

Minnesota statutes have no provision allowing domestic surplus lines insurers.

Nonadmitted Insurer Filing Requirements

Eligible surplus lines insurers domiciled within the United States must file an annual statement and an annual financial audit.

Eligible surplus lines insurers domiciled outside the United States must file an annual statement on the standard nonadmitted insurers information office financial reporting format as prescribed by the NAIC and an annual financial audit performed by an independent accounting firm.

(MINN. STAT. § 60A.206(c), (d))

Surplus Lines Broker Licensing

A person licensed as an agent in Minnesota may obtain a surplus lines license by doing the following:

a. Filing an application in the form and with the information the commissioner may reasonably require to determine the ability of the applicant to act in accordance with sections 60A.195 to 60A.209;
b. Maintaining an agents license in Minnesota;
c. Registering with the association created pursuant to section 60A.2085;
d. Agreeing to file with the commissioner of revenue all returns required by chapter 297I and paying to the commissioner of revenue all amounts required under chapter 297I;
e. Agreeing to file all documents required pursuant to section 60A.2085 and to pay the stamping fee assessed pursuant to section 60A.2085, subdivision 7; and
f. Paying a fee as prescribed by section 60K.55.

(MINN. STAT. § 60A.198)

Due Care in Selecting Nonadmitted Insurer

A surplus lines broker shall place nonadmitted insurance only with insurers that are in a stable and unimpaired financial condition. An insurer recognized by the commissioner as an eligible surplus lines insurer shall be considered to meet this requirement.

(MINN. STAT. § 60A.206)

Diligent Effort/Diligent Search

MN Commerce does not require an affidavit be filed. Surplus lines licensee is to retain evidence that a diligent search with three declinations from licensed insurers was performed. There shall be a rebuttable presumption that the following coverages are unavailable from a licensed insurer:

- Coverages where one portion of risk is acceptable to licensed insurers but another portion of the same risk is not acceptable. The entire coverage may be placed with eligible surplus lines insurers if it can be shown that eligible surplus lines insurers will accept the entire coverage but not the rejected portion alone; and
- Any coverage the broker is unable to produce after a diligent search among licensed insurers.

(MINN. STAT. § 60A.201)

Export List

Minnesota does not maintain a list of coverages that may be exported to the surplus lines market without first making a diligent search of licensed insurers.

Exempt Commercial Purchasers

Minnesota has adopted the NRRA (15 U.S.C. § 8201) definition of exempt commercial purchasers. Coverage for these insureds may be exported to the surplus lines market without making

a diligent effort to place the coverage with authorized insurers provided (1) the surplus lines broker has disclosed to the exempt commercial purchaser that coverage may or may not be available from an authorized insurer that may provide greater protection with more regulatory oversight, and (2) such exempt commercial purchaser has subsequently requested such broker, in writing, to procure such policy from an unauthorized insurer.

(MINN. STAT. § 60A.201)

Surplus Lines Broker Filing Requirements

All premium bearing placements with nonadmitted insurers by Minnesota surplus lines licensees shall be electronically filed with the Surplus Lines Association of Minnesota. Each document must be stamped prior to delivery to the insured.

(MINN. STAT. § 60A.2086)

Notices

Each policy, cover note, or instrument evidencing nonadmitted insurance from an eligible surplus lines insurer that is delivered to an insured or a representative of an insured shall have printed, typed, or stamped upon its face in no less than ten-point type, the following notice:

> THIS INSURANCE IS ISSUED PURSUANT TO THE MINNESOTA SURPLUS LINES INSURANCE ACT. THE INSURER IS AN ELIGIBLE SURPLUS LINES INSURER BUT IS NOT OTHERWISE LICENSED BY THE STATE OF MINNESOTA. IN CASE OF INSOLVENCY, PAYMENT OF CLAIMS IS NOT GUARANTEED.

This notice shall not be covered or concealed in any manner.

(MINN. STAT. § 60A.207)

Policies that are obtained from any ineligible surplus lines insurer must set forth on the face of the policy in red ink not less than ten-point type the following notice:

THIS INSURANCE IS ISSUED PURSUANT TO THE MINNESOTA SURPLUS LINES INSURANCE ACT. THIS INSURANCE IS PLACED WITH AN INSURER THAT IS NOT LICENSED BY THE STATE NOR RECOGNIZED BY THE COMMISSIONER OF COMMERCE AS AN ELIGIBLE SURPLUS LINES INSURER. IN CASE OF ANY DISPUTE RELATIVE TO THE TERMS OR CONDITIONS OF THE POLICY OR THE PRACTICES OF THE INSURER, THE COMMISSIONER OF COMMERCE WILL NOT BE ABLE TO ASSIST IN THE DISPUTE. IN CASE OF INSOLVENCY, PAYMENT OF CLAIMS IS NOT GUARANTEED.

(MINN. STAT. § 60A.209)

Taxes, Stamping Fees, and Other Government-Imposed Charges

A tax is imposed on surplus lines brokers. The rate of tax is equal to three percent of the gross premiums less return premiums paid by an insured whose home state is Minnesota. All fees charged to the insured are subject to Minnesota surplus lines tax.

(MINN. STAT. § 297I.05)

Gross premium for nonadmitted insurance includes any payment made as consideration for an insurance contract for such insurance, including premium deposits, assessments, fees, and any other compensation given in consideration for a contract of insurance. Gross premiums does not include the stamping fee or the operating assessment.

(MINN. STAT. § 2971.01)

Surplus lines tax for business written by surplus lines licensees is reported and paid to Minnesota Revenue semiannually on February 15 and August 15.

(MINN. STAT. § 2971.30)

Producer, Policy, Inspection, and Other Fees

Surplus lines licensees may charge a fee to the insured so long as it is not excessive or discriminatory.

(Minn. Stat. § 60A.204)

All fees charged to the insured are subject to Minnesota surplus lines tax.

(Minn. Stat. § 297I.05)

Industrial Insured Exemption

Minnesota statutes and regulations do not contain an industrial insured exemption with regard to surplus lines insurance.

Independent or Direct Procurement Law

Minnesota law provides for direct procurement of insurance from unauthorized insurers.

(Minn. Stat. § 60A.198)

A tax is imposed on a person, firm, corporation, or purchasing group as defined in section 60E.02, or any member of a purchasing group, that procures insurance directly from a nonadmitted insurer. The rate of tax is equal to 2 percent of the gross premiums less return premiums paid by an insured whose home state is Minnesota. Form IG255 tax report and payment must be sent to Minnesota Revenue by March 1 for the preceding calendar year.

(Minn. Stat. § 297I.05)

MISSISSIPPI

Mississippi Insurance Department
P.O. Box 79
Jackson, MS 39205-0079
(601) 359-3569
www.mid.ms.gov

Mississippi has a stamping office.

Mississippi Surplus Lines Association
504 Keywood Circle, Suite B
Flowood, MS 39232
(601) 713-1111
www.msla.org

Nonadmitted Insurer Eligibility

Foreign

Each nonadmitted insurer must have capital and surplus that is the greater of (1) the same as required of a company licensed to do business in the state of Mississippi, or (2) $15 million.

An insurer may have less than the minimum capital and surplus upon an affirmative finding of acceptability by the commissioner. The finding shall be based upon such factors as quality of management, capital and surplus of any parent company, company underwriting profit and investment income trends, market availability, and company record and reputation within the industry. In no event shall the commissioner make an affirmative finding of acceptability when the nonadmitted insurer's capital and surplus is less than $4.5 million.

(Miss. Code § 83.21.17(1)(a) and (b))

See also http://www.msla.org/insurers/insurer-procedures-manual/iii-nonadmitted-insurer-eligibility-info (last visited Oct. 25, 2021).

Alien

Section 524 of the NRRA (15 U.S.C. § 8201) provides for the automatic approval of a nonadmitted insurer domiciled outside of the United States if the insurer is listed on the Quarterly Listing of Alien Insurers maintained by the International Insurers Department of the National Association of Insurance Commissioners. Therefore, insurers appearing on the Quarterly Listing of Alien Insurers are approved to write business in Mississippi.

See http://www.msla.org/insurers/insurer-procedures-manual/iii-nonadmitted-insurer-eligibility-info (last visited Oct. 25, 2021).

There are separate requirements centered on maintenance of a trust fund for a Lloyd's plan and groups or related insurers.

(MISS. CODE § 83.21.17(1)(c))

Except for Lloyd's plans and related insurers, an alien insurer must have the greater of $15 million in capital and surplus or the same as a licensed company, and shall have in force a trust fund of not less than the greater of $5.4 million or 30 percent of the U.S. surplus lines gross liabilities, excluding aviation, wet marine, and transportation insurance liabilities, not to exceed $60 million.

(MISS. CODE § 83.21.17(1)(e))

An alien insurer shall be listed with the Quarterly Listing of Alien Insurers maintained by the International Insurers Department of the National Association of Insurance Commissioners.

(MISS. CODE § 83.21.17(1)(h))

Each nonadmitted insurer shall pay an annual filing fee of $500.

(MISS. CODE § 83.21.17)

Nonadmitted Insurer Eligibility List

Mississippi maintains a list of active surplus lines insurers at https://www.mid.ms.gov/licensing-search/company-search.aspx

(last visited July 15, 2020). When accessing the site, use the List Search section. Select Choose List: Company Type; Company Type: Surplus Lines – Alien or Surplus Lines – Foreign.

Types of Coverage Permitted or Prohibited

General Information

There are no prohibited coverages under Mississippi law.

Exempt Transactions

Mississippi statutes do not set forth any transactions exempt from surplus lines laws.

Service of Process

The commissioner is deemed to be the agent for service of process for surplus lines insurers.

(Miss. Code § 83-21-37)

Limitations on Actions Involving Judicial Proceedings

Before any unauthorized insurer files a pleading in any action, suit, or proceeding instituted against it, it must either procure a certificate of authority or deposit cash or securities with the clerk of the court in which such action, suit, or proceeding is pending, or file with such clerk a bond with good and sufficient sureties, to be approved by the court, in an amount to be fixed by the court sufficient to secure the payment of any final judgment that may be rendered in such actions.

(Miss. Code § 83-21-45)

Domestic Surplus Lines Insurers

Mississippi statutes have no provision allowing domestic surplus lines insurers.

Nonadmitted Insurer Filing Requirements

Nonadmitted insurers must submit data pertaining to the policies written and premiums collected during the prior year, as it appears on the policy's Declaration Page, to the Mississippi Surplus Lines Association. The following policy data is required:

- Policy number
- Insured name
- Premium
- Policy effective date
- Policy expiration date
- Transaction effective date
- Surplus lines insurance producer name, agency, or broker (person or entity responsible for reporting and paying the tax, stamping fee, and nonadmitted policy fee)

The annual policy data is due no later than March 15 for nonadmitted foreign insurers and June 1 for nonadmitted alien insurers.

See MSLA website, http://www.msla.org/insurers/insurer-procedures-manual/vi-annual-insurer-filings (last visited Aug. 26, 2020).

Surplus Lines Broker Licensing

The Commissioner of Insurance may, for a biennial fee of $100, issue a surplus lines insurance producer license to a qualified holder of an insurance producer license with a property, casualty, and/or personal lines line of authority, who is regularly commissioned to represent a casualty insurance company licensed to do business in the state. The license shall continue from the date of issuance until the last day of the month of the licensee's birthday in the second year following issuance or renewal of the license, with a minimum term of 12 months.

A nonresident person shall receive a surplus lines insurance producer license if:

a. The person is currently licensed as a surplus lines insurance producer or equivalent and in good standing in his or her home state;
b. The person has submitted the proper request for licensure and has paid the biennial fee of $100; and
c. The person's home state awards nonresident surplus lines licenses to residents of Mississippi on the same basis.

A nonresident person is not required to hold an insurance producer license with a property, casualty, and/or personal lines line of authority if the person is not required to perform a diligent search of admitted insurers. Note: Since Mississippi has eliminated the diligent search requirement, it would appear that a nonresident person is no longer required to obtain an insurance producer license with a property, casualty, and/or personal lines line of authority.

(Miss. Code § 83.21.19)

Due Care in Selecting Nonadmitted Insurer

Other than determining that an insurer meets the eligibility requirements, Mississippi statutes do not set forth any requirements with regard to the exercise of due care in selecting a nonadmitted insurer.

Diligent Effort/Diligent Search

The Mississippi diligent search requirement was repealed effective July 1, 2017.

See Bulletin 2017-3 at https://www.mid.ms.gov/legal/bulletins.aspx (last visited Sept. 23, 2020).

Export List

Mississippi does not maintain a list of coverages that may be exported to the surplus lines market without first making a diligent search of licensed insurers.

Exempt Commercial Purchasers

Although the NRRA (15 U.S.C. § 8201) exempts a broker from any applicable diligent search requirements when the insured is an exempt commercial purchaser, Mississippi statutes do not address this topic.

(MISS. CODE § 83.21.23)

Surplus Lines Broker Filing Requirements

Mississippi does not require annual reports. Surplus lines insurance producers must file all surplus lines business with the Mississippi Surplus Lines Association within 15 days following the end of the month in which a policy is procured.

See http://www.msla.org/producers/producer-faqs (last visited Oct. 25, 2021).

Each surplus lines insurance producer shall report under oath to the Commissioner of Insurance, within 30 days from the first of January and July of each year, the amount of gross premiums received by him for nonadmitted insurance, and shall pay to the Commissioner of Insurance a tax of 4 percent thereon.

(MISS. CODE § 83.21.25)

Notices

Every insurance policy written on a surplus line basis shall have stamped upon it in bold ten-point type, and bear the name of the surplus lines insurance producer who procured it, the following:

> NOTE: This insurance policy is issued pursuant to Mississippi law covering surplus lines insurance. The company issuing the policy is not licensed by the State of Mississippi, but is authorized to do business in Mississippi as a nonadmitted company. The policy is not protected by the Mississippi Insurance Guaranty Association in the event of the insurer's insolvency.

(MISS. CODE § 83.21.19)

When any policy of personal lines insurance is placed in the surplus lines market, the surplus lines insurance producer must furnish to the insured at the time of policy deliverance an informational notice as promulgated by the commissioner.

The form of the required notice is shown in Attachment "A" of MS DOI Bulletin 2017-3, which is available at https://www.mid.ms.gov/legal/bulletins.aspx (last visited Nov. 11, 2020).

Taxes, Stamping Fees, and Other Government-Imposed Charges

The surplus lines insurance producer must report to the Commissioner of Insurance, within 30 days from the first of January and July of each year, the amount of gross premiums received for such insurance in nonadmitted insurers, and shall pay to the Commissioner of Insurance a tax of 4 percent.

(Miss. Code § 83.21.25)

A stamping fee of .25 percent of gross premium and policy fees is due to the Mississippi Surplus Lines Association on January 30 and July 30.

(Miss. Code § 83.21.21)

A surplus lines insurance producer must collect from the insured and remit to the Mississippi Windstorm Underwriting Association a nonadmitted policy fee of 3 percent of gross premium and policy fees for business placed with a nonadmitted insurer, except that policies or portions thereof that cover residential earthquake risks or residential flood risks that are not written through the National Flood Insurance Program shall be exempt from the nonadmitted policy fee. Payments are due quarterly (April 20, July 20, October 20, and January 20).

(Miss. Code § 83.34.4)

Producer, Policy, Inspection, and Other Fees

The premium, plus any company or producer fees, are used when calculating taxes and other assessed fees.

See MS Bulletin 2012-3 at https://www.mid.ms.gov/legal/bulletins.aspx (last visited Dec. 9, 2020).

Industrial Insured Exemption

Mississippi statutes and regulations do not contain an industrial insured exemption with regard to surplus lines insurance.

Independent or Direct Procurement Law

Direct procurement is permitted under Mississippi law.

(Miss. Code § 83.34.4)

Each insured who directly procures or renews insurance with a nonadmitted insurer on properties, risks or exposures located or to be performed, in whole or in part, in Mississippi, other than insurance procured through a surplus lines licensee, shall, within 30 days after the date the insurance was so procured or renewed, file a written report with the commissioner, upon forms prescribed by the commissioner, showing the name and address of the insured or insureds, name and address of the insurer, the subject of the insurance, a general description of the coverage, the amount of premium currently charged, and additional pertinent information reasonably requested by the commissioner. Gross premiums charged for the independently procured insurance, less any return premiums, are subject to the same 4 percent premium tax as surplus lines placements. At the time of filing the report, the insured shall pay the tax to the commissioner.

(Miss. Code § 83.21.17(5))

MISSOURI

Missouri Department of Insurance, Financial Institutions
and Professional Registration
(DIFP)
Truman State Office Building
301 West High Street, Room 530
Jefferson City, MO 65101
(573) 751-4126

Alternate Address:
P.O. Box 690
Jefferson City, MO 65102-0690
(573) 751-1165 (fax)
www.insurance.mo.gov
surpluslines@insurance.mo.gov

Missouri does not have a stamping office.

Nonadmitted Insurer Eligibility

General Information

A surplus lines insurer must be authorized to write the kind of insurance in its domiciliary jurisdiction and meets one of these criteria:

1. Has capital and surplus of $15 million, except the director can approve an insurer with capital and surplus of at least $4.5 million; or
2. Appears on the list of eligible surplus lines insurers published by the director or on the Quarterly Listing of Alien Insurers maintained by the International Insurers Department of the National Association of Insurance Commissioners.

(Mo. Rev. Stat. § 384.021)

Nonadmitted Insurer Eligibility List

Missouri maintains a list of eligible domestic surplus lines insurers and relies on the Quarterly Listing of Alien Insurers maintained by the International Insurers Department of the National Association of Insurance Commissioners.

See https://insurance.mo.gov/industry/surplin/index.php (last visited July 15, 2020).

Types of Coverage Permitted or Prohibited

General Information

"Nonadmitted insurance" means any property and casualty insurance permitted to be placed directly or through a surplus lines licensee with a nonadmitted insurer eligible to accept such insurance. "Surplus lines insurance" means any insurance of risks resident, located or to be performed in this state, permitted to be placed through a surplus lines licensee with a nonadmitted insurer eligible to accept such insurance, other than reinsurance, and life and health insurance and annuities.

(Mo. Rev. Stat. § 384.015)

Exempt Transactions

Missouri statutes do not set forth any transactions exempt from surplus lines laws.

Service of Process

Any act of transacting insurance by any unauthorized insurer constitutes an appointment of the director as attorney of such insurer upon whom may be served all lawful process in any action, suit, or proceeding.

(Mo. Rev. Stat. § 375.256)

Limitations on Actions Involving Judicial Proceedings

Missouri statutes do not set forth any limitations on actions involving judicial proceedings that apply to the lawful transaction of surplus lines business.

Domestic Surplus Lines Insurers

Missouri permits a domestic insurer with at least $20 million minimum capital and surplus to be designated as a domestic surplus lines insurer upon the written approval of the director.

(Mo. Rev. Stat. § 384.018)

Nonadmitted Insurer Filing Requirements

1. Each insurer shall file with the NAIC a copy of the current annual statement and sworn, signed jurat page certified by such insurer no more than six months after the close of the period reported upon and which is either:
   a. Filed with and approved by the regulatory authority in the domicile of the nonadmitted insurer; or
   b. Certified by an accounting or auditing firm licensed in the jurisdiction of the insurer's domicile; or
   c. In the case of an insurance exchange, the statement may be an aggregate combined statement of all underwriting syndicates operating during the period reported.
2. Each nonadmitted insurer is to submit a listing of all Missouri business to the department. This listing is to include the name of the agency, producer name and address of the agency or producer, name and address of the insured, effective date, policy number, and total gross premium amount. There is a sample spreadsheet located at Missouri Surplus Lines Business Report for your use.
3. Each nonadmitted insurer must submit these documents by email to surpluslines@insurance.mo.gov and provide contact information.

See https://insurance.mo.gov/industry/surplin/index.php (last visited Aug. 26, 2020). When accessing the site, scroll down to "Notice to All Eligible Surplus Lines Carriers."

Surplus Lines Broker Licensing

The director shall issue a surplus lines license to any qualified holder of a current resident or nonresident property and casualty insurance producer license but only when the licensee has:

1. Remitted the $100 initial fee to the director;
2. Submitted a completed license application on a form supplied by the director; and
3. Passed a qualifying examination approved by the director, except that all holders of a license prior to July 1, 1987, shall be deemed to have passed such an examination.

Each surplus lines license shall be renewed for a term of two years on the biennial anniversary date of issuance and continue in effect until refused, revoked, or suspended by the director in accordance with § 384.065; except that if the biennial renewal fee for the license is not paid on or before the anniversary date, the license terminates. The biennial renewal fee is $100.

(Mo. Rev. Stat. § 384.043)

Due Care in Selecting Nonadmitted Insurer

Surplus lines insurance can only be placed by a surplus licensee if it is with an eligible surplus lines insurer and all other requirements of the surplus lines insurance laws of Missouri are met.

(Mo. Rev. Stat. §§ 384.017, 384.021(1)).

Diligent Effort/Diligent Search

Surplus lines insurance may be placed by a surplus lines licensee if the full amount or kind of insurance is not obtainable from admitted insurers who are actually transacting in this state the class of insurance required by the insured. Insurance shall be deemed obtainable within the meaning of this section if there is available a market with admitted insurers that can supply the insured's requirements both as to type of coverage and as to quality of service.

(Mo. Rev. Stat. § 384.017)

Export List

Missouri does not maintain a list of coverages that may be exported to the surplus lines market without first making a diligent search of licensed insurers.

Exempt Commercial Purchasers

Missouri has adopted the NRRA (15 U.S.C. § 8201) definition of exempt commercial purchasers. Coverage for these insureds may be exported to the surplus lines market without making a diligent effort to place the coverage with authorized insurers provided (i) the surplus lines broker has disclosed to the exempt commercial purchaser that coverage may or may not be available from an authorized insurer that may provide greater protection with more regulatory oversight, and (ii) such exempt commercial purchaser has subsequently requested such broker, in writing, to procure such policy from an unauthorized insurer.

(Mo. Rev. Stat. §§ 384.021, 384.015)

Surplus Lines Broker Filing Requirements

Within 45 days of the end of each calendar quarter ending each surplus lines broker must electronically report to the director a statement showing the gross amount charged for each surplus lines insurance risk for which the insured's home state is Missouri, exclusive of sums collected for the payment of federal, state, or local taxes, and the amount of net premiums for the insurance using the Appendix 1 form (Mo. Rev. Stat. § 384.057(2), 20 C.S.R. § 200-6.100(A)). Before March 2nd of each year, broker must prepare a statement on the Appendix 3 form (Mo. Rev. Stat. § 384.057(1), 20 C.S.R. § 200-6.100(B)).

Appendix 1 and Appendix 3 electronic instructions are available at http://insurance.mo.gov/industry/surplin/index.php (last visited Oct. 21, 2020). When accessing the site, click on "Appendix 1 Instructions" or "Appendix 3 instructions."

Notices

Every surplus lines producer is obligated to notify each insured in writing that:

> This is evidence of insurance procured and developed under the Missouri Surplus Lines Laws. It is NOT covered by the Missouri Insurance Guaranty Association. This insurer is not licensed by The State of Missouri and is not subject to its supervision.
>
> (Mo. Rev. Stat. § 384.036(6))

Taxes, Stamping Fees, and Other Government-Imposed Charges

Surplus lines insurance on risks located in this state are subject to a tax of 5 percent of the net premium received. "Net premiums" means the gross amount of charges for surplus lines insurance exclusive of sums collected for the payment of federal, state, and local taxes, less returned premiums. The tax shall be paid before April 16th of each year. The surplus lines broker may collect the tax from the insured.
(Mo. Rev. Stat. § 384.059)

Producer, Policy, Inspection, and Other Fees

1. For purposes of determining net premiums, the gross amount of charges for surplus lines insurance shall include any fee charged to the insured and paid to the surplus lines insurer or surplus lines licensee for the placement of the surplus lines insurance. Any compensation received by the surplus lines licensee will be

considered premium for purposes of the premium tax imposed by §§ 384.051 and 384.059, Mo. Rev. Stat., unless all the following conditions are met:

a. The surplus lines licensee is also the retail insurance producer (i.e., the surplus lines licensee has the primary direct relationship with the prospective policyholder); and
b. The surplus lines licensee's compensation is received pursuant to an insurance producer's agreement as permitted by 20 C.S.R. § 700-1.100; and
c. The amount of compensation excludable from the application of such premium tax does not exceed the amount of compensation such licensee would have received under such licensee's insurance producer service agreement if surplus lines insurance was not involved.

(20 C.S.R. § 200-6.300)

Industrial Insured Exemption

Missouri statutes and regulations do not contain an industrial insured exemption with regard to surplus lines insurance.

Independent or Direct Procurement Law

Every insured whose home state is this state who procures insurance in any surplus lines insurer, other than insurance procured through a surplus lines broker, shall file a written report on forms prescribed by the director of:

1. The name and address of the insured or insureds;
2. The name and address of the insurer or insurers;
3. The subject of the insurance;
4. A general description of the coverage;
5. The amount of premium currently charged therefor;
6. Such additional pertinent information as may be reasonably requested by the director.

For the general support of the government of this state there is levied upon the insured a tax at the rate of 5 percent of the gross amount of the premium.

(Mo. Rev. Stat. § 384.051)

MONTANA

Office of the Montana State Auditor, Commissioner of Securities and Insurance
840 Helena Avenue
Helena, MT 59601
(800) 332-6148
http://csimt.gov/insurance/

Montana does not have a stamping office.

Nonadmitted Insurer Eligibility

Foreign

An insurer domiciled in the United States is eligible to write nonadmitted insurance in Montana for risks whose home state is Montana if:

- It is eligible in its state of domicile to write the kinds of insurance that it intends to write in Montana; and
- It maintains minimum capital and surplus (or equivalent) requirements in the amount of $15 million or the minimum requirements of Mont. Code Ann. §§ 33-2-109 and 33-2-110, whichever requirements are greater. These requirements may be reduced, but not below $4.5 million, for an insurer as a result of an affirmative finding of acceptability by the commissioner based upon such factors as quality of management, capital and surplus of any parent company, company underwriting profit and investment income trends, market availability, and company record and reputation within the industry.

(Mont. Code Ann. § 33-2-307(1))

Alien

A surplus line broker may not place insurance with an alien insurer unless:

- The insurer is listed on the Quarterly Listing of Alien Insurers maintained by the International Insurers Department of the National Association of Insurance Commissioners.

(MONT. CODE ANN. § 33-2-307(2))

Nonadmitted Insurer Eligibility List

The Office of the Montana State Auditor, Commissioner of Securities and Insurance maintains a nonadmitted insurer eligibility list.

(MONT. CODE ANN. § 33-2-307(3) and Mont. Admin. Reg. 6.6.2808)

The list is available online at http://csimt.gov/insurance/surplus-lines/ (last visited July 15, 2020).

Types of Coverage Permitted or Prohibited

General Information

An eligible surplus lines insurer may provide coverage for lines of insurance if:

1. the line of the insurance or the full amount of the line of insurance cannot be obtained from authorized insurers, as evidenced by:
    a. the producing insurance producer making a diligent effort to place the business with a minimum of three insurers authorized and actually transacting that line of business in this state. If fewer than three insurers are authorized and actually transacting the line of business in this state, diligent effort must be met by searching this lesser market;
    b. the risk appears on the Approved Risk List (export list); or
    c. the insurance is natural disaster multiperil insurance;

AND

1. the insurance is not produced for the purpose of:
   a. securing a lower premium rate than would be accepted by an authorized insurer unless the premium rate quoted by the authorized insurer is at least 10 percent higher and at least $1,500 greater than the premium rate quoted by the unauthorized insurer; or
   b. an advantage in terms of the insurance contract.

(MONT. CODE ANN. § 33-2-302(2))

Exempt Transactions

Montana's surplus lines laws do not apply to the following kinds of insurance when placed by a licensed insurance producer:

- Reinsurance;
- Wet marine insurance;
- Insurance on property or operations of railroads; and
- Insurance of aircraft owned or operated by manufacturers of aircraft or aircraft operated in scheduled interstate flight or cargo of the aircraft or against liability, other than workers' compensation and employers' liability, arising out of the ownership, maintenance, or use of the aircraft.

(MONT. CODE ANN. § 33-2-317)

Service of Process

Before transacting surplus lines insurance in Montana, each surplus lines insurer must in writing appoint the commissioner as its true and lawful attorney upon whom legal process shall be served. (MONT. CODE ANN. § 33-2-315)

Limitations on Actions Involving Judicial Proceedings

Montana statutes do not set forth any limitations on actions involving judicial proceedings that apply to the lawful transaction of surplus lines business.

Domestic Surplus Lines Insurers

Montana statutes have no provision allowing domestic surplus lines insurers.

Nonadmitted Insurer Filing Requirements

Montana statutes do not set forth periodic filing requirements for nonadmitted insurers.

Surplus Lines Broker Licensing

An individual who holds a current Montana property and casualty insurance producer license may apply for a resident surplus lines insurance producer license by remitting the application fee to the commissioner and submitting a complete license application form.

(MONT. CODE ANN. § 33-2-305(3))

An individual who holds a current property and casualty insurance producer license in a state other than Montana may apply for a nonresident surplus lines insurance producer license the same way as a Montana-licensed producer applies, so long as the individual's home state awards noninsurance producer licenses to Montana residents on the same basis.

(MONT. CODE ANN. §§ 33-2-305(4), 33-17-401)

A business entity, whether resident or nonresident, is eligible to be licensed as a surplus lines insurance producer if the business entity license lists the individuals within the business entity who are Montana-licensed surplus lines producers and only those individuals transact surplus lines insurance.

(MONT. CODE ANN. § 33-2-305(6))

The application fee for the original license is $50 and the biennial renewal fee is $100. The fees are the same for residents, nonresidents, individuals, and business entities.

(MONT. CODE ANN. § 33-2-708(1)(b)(iii))

Due Care in Selecting Nonadmitted Insurer

Other than determining that an insurer meets the eligibility requirements, Montana statutes do not set forth any requirements with regard to the exercise of due care in selecting a nonadmitted insurer.

(MONT. CODE ANN. § 33-2-307)

Diligent Effort/Diligent Search

An eligible surplus lines insurer may provide coverage for lines of insurance if the line of the insurance or the full amount of the line of insurance cannot be obtained from authorized insurers, as evidenced by the producing insurance producer making a diligent effort to place the business with a minimum of three insurers authorized and actually transacting that line of business in this state. If fewer than three insurers are authorized and actually transacting the line of business in this state, diligent effort must be met by searching the available insurers.

(MONT. CODE ANN. § 33-2-302(2))

Export List

The commissioner maintains an approved risk list of risks that are presumed to be unobtainable from authorized insurers.

(Mont. Admin. Reg. 6.6.2809)

The approved risk list is available at https://csimt.gov/insurance/surplus-lines/ (last visited Sept. 30, 2020). When accessing the site, scroll the section titled Lists.

Exempt Commercial Purchasers

Montana has adopted the NRRA (15 U.S.C. § 8201) definition of exempt commercial purchasers. Coverage for these insureds may be exported to the surplus lines market without making a diligent effort to place the coverage with authorized insurers provided (1) the surplus lines broker has disclosed to the exempt commercial purchaser that coverage may or may not be available from an authorized insurer that may provide greater protection with more regulatory oversight, and (2) such exempt commercial purchaser has subsequently requested such broker, in writing, to procure such policy from an unauthorized insurer.

(MONT. CODE ANN. §§ 33-2-302(2)(c), 33-2-318)

Surplus Lines Broker Filing Requirements

The surplus lines producer must, within 60 calendar days of the surplus lines policy's effective date, file with the Department of Insurance a form reporting (a) information regarding the producing producer's diligent efforts to place the coverage with authorized insurers and the results of the efforts; and (b) the producing insurance producer's affirmation that the producer has expressly advised the insured prior to placing the insurance that (i) the surplus lines insurer with whom the insurance is placed is not authorized in this state and is not subject to the same supervision as an authorized insurer; and (ii) in the event of the insolvency of the surplus lines insurer, the property and casualty guaranty fund of the state will not pay losses under the surplus lines coverage.

(MONT. CODE ANN. § 33-2-303(2); Mont. Admin. Reg. 6.6.2803)

By April 1 of each year, surplus lines producers must file annual tax and fee statements with the commissioner on a form established by the commissioner. The filing must include (a) name and principal residence of the insured or the address at which the insured maintains its principal place of business; (b) a brief and general description of the risk or exposure insured and where located; (c) name and home office address of each insurer providing the surplus lines insurance; (d) amount of each surplus lines insurance policy, the premium rate, and the gross premium charged for the policy; (e) date and term of the policy; (f) amount of premium returned on each policy canceled or not taken; (g) amount of tax and other sums to be collected from the insured; (h) identity of the producing insurance producer; and (i) additional information that the commissioner may reasonably require.

(MONT. CODE ANN. § 33-2-310; Mont. Admin. Reg. 6.6.2810)

Notices

A surplus lines insurance producer who places a surplus lines policy must stamp or notate the first page of each insurance contract, cover note, declarations page, or certificate of insurance with the following completed statement:

> NOTICE: This coverage is issued by an unauthorized insurer that is an eligible surplus lines insurer. If this insurer becomes insolvent, there is no coverage by the Montana Insurance Guaranty Association under the Montana Insurance Guaranty Association Act.
>
> ______________________________________
>
> Printed Name of Surplus Lines Insurance Producer
>
> ______________________________________
>
> Montana License Number
>
> ______________________________________
>
> Signature of Surplus Lines Insurance Producer
>
> (Mont. Admin. Reg. 6.6.2803(6))

Taxes, Stamping Fees, and Other Government-Imposed Charges

Montana imposes a premium tax on surplus lines insurance of 2.75 percent of net premiums, which includes any inspection fees or charges billed to the insured, less any premiums returned to the insured. All premium taxes are payable to the commission.

(Mont. Code Ann. § 33-2-705)

In addition, Montana imposes a premium tax of 2.5 percent of the portion of the premium that pertains to fire coverage of the policy.

(Mont. Code Ann. § 50-3-109)

Producer, Policy, Inspection, and Other Fees

If the inspection fee is charged directly to the policyholder, the premium tax is charged on the inspection fee.

See Surplus Lines Filing Handbook at https://csimt.gov/insurance/surplus-lines/ (last visited Dec. 16, 2020).

Industrial Insured Exemption

Montana statutes and regulations do not contain an industrial insured exemption with regard to surplus lines insurance.

Independent or Direct Procurement Law

"Independently procured insurance" means surplus lines insurance procured directly by an insured from an eligible surplus lines insurer.

(MONT. CODE ANN. § 33-2-301(3)(k))

A surplus lines insurance producer license is not required for independently procured insurance.

(MONT. CODE ANN. § 33-2-305(8))

Every insured who independently procures insurance must submit to the Department of Insurance all information required to be filed by Montana surplus lines law § 33-2-301.

(Mont. Admin. Reg. 6.6.2803(1))

By April 1 of each year, surplus lines insurance producers and insureds who independently procured insurance must file with the commissioner the annual tax and fee statements for the preceding calendar year, and the insured must pay the taxes and fees.

(Mont. Admin. Reg. 6.6.2810(4); MONT. CODE ANN. § 33-2-310(3))

NEBRASKA

Nebraska Department of Insurance
P.O. Box 82089
Lincoln, NE 68501-2089
(402) 471-2201
http://Doi.nebraska.gov
Consumer affairs hotline for in-state only:
(877) 564-7323

Nebraska does not have a stamping office.

Nonadmitted Insurer Eligibility

Foreign

A foreign nonadmitted insurer must be authorized to write the type of insurance sought in its domiciliary jurisdiction, must have established satisfactory evidence of good repute and financial integrity, and must have capital and surplus that equals the greater of the minimum capital and surplus requirements under the laws of Nebraska or $15 million. If minimum capital and surplus does not meet these requirements, a surplus line licensee can place coverage with the insurer upon an affirmative finding of acceptability by the director. The director shall not make an affirmative finding of acceptability if the nonadmitted insurer's capital and surplus is less than $4.5 million.

(NEB. REV. STAT. § 44-5508(1))

Alien

No surplus lines licensee shall place nonadmitted insurance with or procure nonadmitted insurance from a nonadmitted insurer domiciled outside the United States unless the insurer is listed on the Quarterly Listing of Alien Insurers maintained by the

International Insurers Department of the National Association of Insurance Commissioners.

(NEB. REV. STAT. § 44-5508(2))

No nonadmitted alien insurer shall accept business under the Surplus Lines Insurance Act if it does not comply with the surplus and capital requirements of subsection (1) of § 44-5508 and the NAIC Quarter Listing requirements of subsection (2) of § 44-5508.

(NEB. REV. STAT. § 44-5508(4))

Nonadmitted Insurer Eligibility List

Nebraska does not maintain a nonadmitted insurer eligibility list.

Types of Coverage Permitted or Prohibited

General Information

Nonadmitted insurance means any property and casualty insurance permitted to be placed directly or through surplus lines licensees with a nonadmitted insurer eligible to accept such insurance; and the insurance procured shall not include any insurance described in subdivisions (1) through (4) of § 44-201, which are (1) life insurance; (2) variable life insurance; (3) variable annuities; (4) sickness and accident insurance. The law does not prohibit the procurement of disability insurance that has a benefit limit in excess of any benefit limit available from an admitted insurer.

(NEB. REV. STAT. §§ 44-5510(1)(b), 44-201)

Exempt Transactions

Nebraska statutes do not set forth any transactions exempt from surplus lines laws.

Service of Process

The issuance of contracts of insurance, solicitation of applications, collection of premiums, investigation or payment of claims, or any other transaction of business by any unauthorized foreign or alien insurer shall constitute sufficient contact with this state for the exercise of personal jurisdiction over such foreign or alien insurer in any action, suit, or proceeding instituted by or on behalf of an insured or beneficiary arising out of any such activities.

(NEB. REV. STAT. ANN. § 44-2011)

Limitations on Actions Involving Judicial Proceedings

Before any unauthorized insurer files or causes to be filed any pleading or other response in any court action, suit, or proceeding, they must post a bond or procure a certificate of authority. However, this shall not be construed to prevent an unauthorized insurer from filing a motion to quash a writ or to set aside service thereof made in the manner provided in § 44-2004, on the ground that such unauthorized insurer has not done any of the acts enumerated in § 44-2002.

(NEB. REV. STAT. ANN. § 44-2005)

Domestic Surplus Lines Insurers

Nebraska permits a domestic insurer with at least $15 million minimum capital and surplus to be designated as a domestic surplus lines insurer upon the written approval of the director.

(NEB. REV. STAT. ANN. § 44-5506.01)

Nonadmitted Insurer Filing Requirements

Nebraska statutes do not set forth periodic filing requirements for nonadmitted insurers.

Surplus Lines Broker Licensing

The department, in consideration of the payment of the license fee, may issue a surplus lines license, revocable at any time, to any individual who currently holds an insurance producer license or to a foreign or domestic corporation. The corporate surplus lines license shall list all officers or employees of the corporation who currently hold an insurance producer license or meet the requirements for an individual surplus lines license and who have authority to transact surplus lines business on behalf of the corporation. Only individuals listed on the corporate surplus lines license shall transact surplus lines business on behalf of the corporate licensee. If the applicant is an individual, the application for the license shall include the applicant's social security number.

(NEB. REV. STAT. ANN. § 44-5503)

Application shall be made on forms designated and furnished by the department and shall be accompanied by a license fee as established by the director not to exceed $250 for each individual and corporate surplus lines license. All corporate surplus lines licenses shall expire on April 30 of each year, and all individual surplus lines licenses shall expire on the licensee's birthday in the first year after issuance in which his or her age is divisible by two.

(NEB. REV. STAT. ANN. § 44-5504)

Due Care in Selecting Nonadmitted Insurer

A surplus lines licensee cannot place coverage with a nonadmitted insurer unless it meets the eligibility requirements in the statute.

(NEB. REV. STAT. ANN. §§ 44-5508(1), 44-5508(2))

Diligent Effort/Diligent Search

If an applicant for insurance is unable to procure such insurance as he or she deems reasonably necessary to insure a risk or exposure from an admitted insurer, such insurance may be procured from a nonadmitted insurer.

(NEB. REV. STAT. ANN. § 44-5510)

On or before March 1 for the quarter ending the preceding December 31, June 1 for the quarter ending the preceding March 31, September 1 for the quarter ending the preceding June 30, and December 1 for the quarter ending the preceding September 30 of each year, every surplus lines licensee shall file with the department a sworn statement by the licensee with regard to the coverages described in the quarterly report that, to the best of the licensee's knowledge and belief, the licensee could not reasonably procure such coverages from an admitted insurer.

(NEB. REV. STAT. ANN. § 44-5511)

Export List

Nebraska does not maintain a list of coverages that may be exported to the surplus lines market without first making a diligent search of licensed insurers.

Exempt Commercial Purchasers

Nebraska has adopted the NRRA (15 U.S.C. § 8201) definition of exempt commercial purchasers. Coverage for these insureds may be exported to the surplus lines market without making a diligent effort to place the coverage with authorized insurers provided (1) the surplus lines broker has disclosed to the exempt commercial purchaser that coverage may or may not be available from an authorized insurer that may provide greater protection with more regulatory oversight, and (2) such exempt commercial purchaser has subsequently requested such broker, in writing, to procure such policy from an unauthorized insurer.

(NEB. REV. STAT. §§ 44-5510(2), 44-5502)

Every exempt commercial purchaser whose home state is the state of Nebraska shall, on or before March 1 for the quarter ending the preceding December 31, June 1 for the quarter ending the preceding March 31, September 1 for the quarter ending the preceding June 30, and December 1 for the quarter ending the preceding September 30 of each year, pay to the department a tax in the amount required by subsection (2) of § 44-5506. The calculation of the taxes due pursuant to this section shall be based only on those premiums remitted for the placement or procurement of insurance by an exempt commercial purchaser whose home state is the state of Nebraska. The department shall prescribe a form for an exempt commercial purchaser tax filing.

(Neb. Rev. Stat. § 44-5515)

Surplus Lines Broker Filing Requirements

On or before March 1 for the quarter ending the preceding December 31, June 1 for the quarter ending the preceding March 31, September 1 for the quarter ending the preceding June 30, and December 1 for the quarter ending the preceding September 30 of each year every surplus lines licensee shall file with the department a report containing such information as the department may require, including (1) the name of the nonadmitted insurer; (2) the name of the licensee; (3) the number of policies issued by each nonadmitted insurer; (4) except for insurance placed or procured on behalf of an exempt commercial purchaser, a sworn statement by the licensee with regard to the coverages described in the quarterly report that, to the best of the licensee's knowledge and belief, the licensee could not reasonably procure such coverages from an admitted insurer; and (5) the premium volume for each nonadmitted insurer by line of business.

(Neb. Rev. Stat. § 44-5511)

A licensed individual or agency is required to file a quarterly report for each license separately, even if no business is written. Failure to file is subject to administrative action. No annual report is required.

See https://doi.nebraska.gov/producers/surplus-lines-information (last visited Oct. 21, 2020).

Notices

The surplus lines licensee shall stamp or type upon the declaration page of each policy procured and delivered under the Surplus Lines Insurance Act the following information: (1) the licensee's name, business address, and surplus lines license number; (2) the name under which the licensee transacts business if different than the licensee's own name; and (3) the language:

> This policy is issued by a nonadmitted insurer, and in the event of the insolvency of such insurer, this policy will not be covered by the Nebraska Property and Liability Insurance Guaranty Association.

Not later than 30 days after the effective date of such insurance, the insured shall provide, in writing, his or her permission for such insurance to be written in a nonadmitted insurer and his or her acknowledgment that, in the event of the insolvency of such insurer, the policy will not be covered by the Nebraska Property and Liability Insurance Guaranty Association.

(Neb. Rev. Stat. § 44-5509)

Taxes, Stamping Fees, and Other Government-Imposed Charges

Every surplus lines licensee transacting business under the Surplus Lines Insurance Act shall, on or before March 1 for the quarter ending the preceding December 31, June 1 for the quarter ending the preceding March 31, September 1 for the quarter ending the preceding June 30, and December 1 for the quarter ending the preceding September 30 of each year, make and file with the department a verified statement upon a form prescribed by the department or a designee of the director that shall exhibit the true amount of all such business transacted during that period.

The tax is 3 percent of the premiums for insurance that covers properties, risks, or exposures located or to be performed in the United States.

In no event shall such taxes be determined on a retaliatory basis pursuant to § 44-150. The surplus lines licensee is prohibited from rebating, for any reason, any portion of the tax.

(Neb. Rev. Stat. § 44-5506)

Producer, Policy, Inspection, and Other Fees

Premiums shall mean the consideration paid to insurance companies for insurance and shall include policy fees, assessments, dues, or other similar payments.

(NEB. REV. STAT. § 77-907)

Fees, assessments, dues, or other similar payments paid to the insurance company are included in the premium when calculating tax. Fees retained by the broker or a third party are not included in the calculation.

See Surplus Lines FAQ at https://doi.nebraska.gov/producers/surplus-lines-information (last visited Dec. 16, 2020).

Industrial Insured Exemption

Nebraska statutes and regulations do not contain an industrial insured exemption with regard to surplus lines insurance.

Independent or Direct Procurement Law

Nebraska statutes provide for independent procurement by exempt commercial purchasers. An exempt commercial purchaser is defined as any person purchasing commercial insurance that meets the requirements in the statute.

(NEB. REV. STAT. § 44-5502)

No person, other than an exempt commercial purchaser, shall place, procure, or effect insurance for or on behalf of an insured whose home state is the State of Nebraska in any nonadmitted insurer until such person has first been issued a surplus lines license from the department as provided in § 44-5503.

(NEB. REV. STAT. § 44-5504)

Every exempt commercial purchaser whose home state is the state of Nebraska shall, on or before March 1 for the quarter ending the preceding December 31, June 1 for the quarter ending the preceding March 31, September 1 for the quarter ending the preceding June 30, and December 1 for the quarter ending the preceding September 30 of each year, pay to the department a tax in the amount required by subsection (2) of § 44-5506.

The calculation of the taxes due pursuant to this section shall be based only on those premiums remitted for the placement or procurement of insurance by an exempt commercial purchaser whose home state is the state of Nebraska. The department shall prescribe a form for an exempt commercial purchaser tax filing.

(Neb. Rev. Stat. § 44-5515)

NEVADA

Nevada Division of Insurance
1818 East College Parkway, Suite 103
Carson City, NV 89706
(775) 687-0700
www.doi.nv.gov/
insinfo@doi.nv.gov

Alternate Address:
3300 West Sahara Avenue
Suite 275
Las Vegas, NV 89102

Nevada has a stamping office.

Nevada Surplus Lines Association
6490 S. McCarran Boulevard, Bldg. D-2 #39
Reno, NV 89509
(775) 826-7898
www.nsla.org

Nonadmitted Insurer Eligibility

Foreign

An insurer domiciled in the United States is eligible to write nonadmitted insurance in Nevada for risks whose home state is Nevada if:

1. It is eligible in its state of domicile to write the kinds of insurance that it intends to write in Nevada; and
2. It maintains minimum capital and surplus (or equivalent) requirements in the amount of $15 million or the minimum requirements of N.R.S. § 680A.120, whichever

requirements are greater. These requirements may be reduced for an insurer as a result of an affirmative finding of acceptability by the commissioner—based upon such factors as quality of management, capital and surplus of any parent company, company underwriting profit and investment income trends, market availability, and company record and reputation within the industry.

(NEV. REV. STAT. § 685A.070)

Alien

A surplus line broker may not place insurance with an alien insurer unless:

1. The insurer is listed on the Quarterly Listing of Alien Insurers maintained by the International Insurers Department of the National Association of Insurance Commissioners, or
2. The alien insurer has maintained a trust fund in a bank or trust company that is a member of the U.S. Federal Reserve in an amount that reasonably provides adequate protection to all of its policyholders in the United States.

Nonadmitted Insurer Eligibility List

Nevada does not maintain a nonadmitted insurer eligibility list.

Types of Coverage Permitted or Prohibited

General Information

There are no prohibited coverages under Nevada law.

Exempt Transactions

Lines of insurance exempt from surplus line regulations are:

- Reinsurance;
- Wet marine and transportation insurance;

- Insurance on subjects located outside of the state, or vehicles or aircraft owned and principally garaged outside of the state;
- Interstate railroad operations and property;
- Aircraft insurance of common carriers, or cargo of such aircraft, other than employer's liability, arising out of the ownership, maintenance, or use of the aircraft; and
- Automobile insurance of bodily injury and property damage liability written by Mexican insurers and occurring in Mexico.

(Nev. Rev. Stat. § 685A.020)

Service of Process

Any act of transacting insurance by any unauthorized insurer constitutes an appointment of the commissioner as attorney of such insurer upon whom may be served all lawful process in any action, suit, or proceeding.

(Nev. Rev. Stat. § 685B.050)

Limitations on Actions Involving Judicial Proceedings

Before any unauthorized insurer files or causes to be filed any pleading in any court action, suit, or proceeding or any notice, order, pleading, or process in an administrative proceeding before the commissioner, such insurer shall either post a bond or procure a certificate of authority to transact the business of insurance in Nevada. However, this shall not be construed to prevent an unauthorized insurer from filing a motion to quash a writ or to set aside service thereof, on the ground that such unauthorized insurer has not done any of the acts enumerated in N.R.S. § 685B.030 (unlawful transaction of business).

(Nev. Rev. Stat. § 685B.060)

An unauthorized insurer that is sued in a district court of this state has 40 days from the date of service of the summons and complaint upon the commissioner or an authorized representative of the commissioner within which to plead, answer, or defend any such suit.

(Nev. Rev. Stat. § 685A.200)

Domestic Surplus Lines Insurers

Nevada permits a domestic insurer with at least $15 million minimum capital and surplus to be designated as a domestic surplus lines insurer upon the written approval of the commissioner.

(Nev. Rev. Stat. § 685A.072)

Nonadmitted Insurer Filing Requirements

Nevada statutes do not set forth periodic filing requirements for nonadmitted insurers.

Surplus Lines Broker Licensing

Any resident person licensed by Nevada as an insurance producer for general lines for at least six months may be licensed as a surplus line broker. In addition, applicants must pass an examination on the subject of surplus lines.

Any nonresident person who has been licensed as a surplus line broker in another state and continues to be licensed in that state may be licensed as a surplus lines broker.

(Nev. Rev. Stat. § 685A.120)

Due Care in Selecting Nonadmitted Insurer

The broker must make a reasonable effort to determine the financial solvency of any surplus line insurer.

(Nev. Admin. Code § 685A.205)

A broker must not knowingly place insurance with a financially unsound or ineligible nonadmitted insurer.

(Nev. Rev. Stat. § 685A.070)

Diligent Effort/Diligent Search

If coverage cannot be obtained from admitted insurers after a diligent search is performed, insurance can be procured by a nonadmitted insurer. The surplus line broker must document the diligent search effort in a report detailing why the insurance was eligible for export under N.R.S. § 685A.040.

(Nev. Admin. Code § 685A.215 and Nev. Rev. Stat. § 685A.050)

Export List

Nevada maintains an export list that is available at http://www.nsla.org/export_list/export_list.aspx (last visited Sept. 30, 2020).

Exempt Commercial Purchasers

Nevada has adopted the NRRA (15 U.S.C. § 8201) definition of exempt commercial purchasers. Coverage for these insureds may be exported to the surplus lines market without making a diligent effort to place the coverage with authorized insurers provided (1) the surplus lines broker has disclosed to the exempt commercial purchaser that coverage may or may not be available from an authorized insurer that may provide greater protection with more regulatory oversight, and (2) such exempt commercial purchaser has subsequently requested such broker, in writing, to procure such policy from an unauthorized insurer.

(Nev. Rev. Stat. § 685A.040 (5)(a)(b))

Surplus Lines Broker Filing Requirements

Within 90 days of effecting surplus line insurance coverage, the broker must submit a report, in the form prescribed or accepted by the commissioner, setting forth facts from which it can be determined whether such insurance is eligible for export (N.R.S. § 685A.050). A separate report must be filed with the Association for renewals and extension of coverage and an amended report must be filed for each cancellation and endorsement which changes the insured name, description or location of risk, the coverage, conditions, terms, premium, or participating insurers.

(Nev. Admin. Code § 685A.240)

Reports are submitted to the Nevada Surplus Lines Association using the SLIP system. See http://www.nsla.org/ (last visited Oct. 21, 2020).

Notices

Each surplus line insurance contract must have conspicuously stamped upon it:

> This insurance contract is issued pursuant to the Nevada insurance laws by an insurer neither licensed by nor under the supervision of the Division of Insurance of the Department of Business and Industry of the State of Nevada. If the insurer is found insolvent, a claim under this contract is not covered by the Nevada Insurance Guaranty Association Act.

(Nev. Rev. Stat. § 685A.090)

Taxes, Stamping Fees, and Other Government-Imposed Charges

The broker must pay a 3.5 percent tax quarterly on the gross premium plus fees (minus return premium) on coverage written with a nonadmitted insurer. The tax filings and payments must be submitted by:

a. February 15th for the calendar quarter ending the preceding December 31st
b. May 15th for the calendar quarter ending the preceding March 31st
c. August 15th for the calendar quarter ending the preceding June 30th
d. November 15th for the calendar quarter ending the preceding September 30th

(Nev. Rev. Stat. § 685A.175)

Producer, Policy, Inspection, and Other Fees

A broker may charge a fee for procuring surplus line insurance but, unless otherwise agreed upon by the insurer and broker, the fee should not exceed 20 percent of the premium charged.
(NEV. REV. STAT. § 685A.155)

Industrial Insured Exemption

An unauthorized insurer may provide insurance, other than workers' compensation insurance, for industrial insurance provided pursuant to N.R.S. chapters 616A through 617, inclusive, involving the procurement of excess liability insurance above underlying liability coverage or self-insured retention of at least $25 million, if procured from an unauthorized alien or foreign insurer who does not solicit, negotiate, or enter into such transactions in this state by any means, and if procured by a person:

a. Whose total annual premiums for property and casualty insurance, not including workers' compensation or industrial insurance, is $1 million or more; and
b. Who employs 250 or more full-time employees.

A person who procures insurance in accordance with this subsection shall report and pay any premium tax on the insurance required pursuant to N.R.S. § 680B.040.
(NEV. REV. STAT. § 680A.070 (9)(a)(b))

Independent or Direct Procurement Law

For independent or directly procured insurance coverage, a report must be filed with the commissioner within 45 days after the end of the quarter the insurance was procured. The report must include:

a. The name and address of the insured or insureds;
b. The name and address of the insurer;
c. The subject of the insurance;
d. A general description of the coverage;

e. The premium currently charged therefor; and
f. Such additional pertinent information as is reasonably requested by the commissioner or the designee of the commissioner.

(Nev. Rev. Stat. § 680B.040)

A tax of 3.5 percent must be paid within 30 days of procuring the coverage.

(Nev. Rev. Stat. § 680B.027(1))

NEW HAMPSHIRE

New Hampshire Insurance Department
21 South Fruit Street, Suite 14
Concord, NH 03301
(603) 271-2261
https://www.nh.gov/insurance/

New Hampshire does not have a stamping office.

Nonadmitted Insurer Eligibility

Foreign

A foreign nonadmitted insurer must be licensed to write the same kind of insurance in its domiciliary jurisdiction and have the greater of $15 million in capital and surplus or surplus of not less than 25 percent of its capital stock in addition to paid up capital.

(N.H. Rev. Stat. Ann. § 405:24 (II)(a), (b)(1), (2))

Alien

An alien insurer must be listed on the Quarterly Listing of Alien Insurers maintained by the International Insurers Department of the National Association of Insurance Commissioners.

(N.H. Rev. Stat. Ann. § 405:24 (II)(b)(3))

Nonadmitted Insurer Eligibility List

The Insurance Department maintains a list of eligible surplus lines insurers at https://www.nh.gov/insurance/companies/surplus lines/index.htm (last visited July 15, 2020).

Types of Coverage Permitted or Prohibited

General Information

There are no prohibited coverages under New Hampshire law.

Exempt Transactions

Transactions in the state relative to a policy issued or to be issued outside New Hampshire involving insurance on vessels, craft or hulls, cargoes, marine builder's risk, marine protection and indemnity, or other risk, including strikes and war risks commonly insured under ocean or wet marine forms of policy are exempt from the unauthorized insurers law.

(N.H. Rev. Stat. Ann. § 406-B:16(VIII))

Service of Process

Any act of transacting insurance by any unauthorized insurer constitutes an appointment of the commissioner as attorney of such insurer upon whom may be served all lawful process in any action, suit, or proceeding.

(N.H. Rev. Stat. Ann. § 406-A:5)

Limitations on Actions Involving Judicial Proceedings

New Hampshire statutes do not set forth any limitations on actions involving judicial proceedings that apply to the lawful transaction of surplus lines business.

Domestic Surplus Lines Insurers

New Hampshire permits a domestic insurer with at least $15 million minimum capital and surplus to be designated as a domestic surplus lines insurer upon the written approval of the commissioner.

(N.H. Rev. Stat. Ann. § 405:24(IV))

Nonadmitted Insurer Filing Requirements

All approved surplus lines companies are asked to provide the Department of Insurance by May 1st with a detail list of all premiums written in New Hampshire summarized by the "broker's tax identification number."

See https://www.nh.gov/insurance/companies/surpluslines/index.htm (last visited Aug. 26, 2020).

Surplus Lines Broker Licensing

A person licensed as a surplus lines producer in his or her home state shall receive a nonresident surplus lines producer license provided:

a. The person is currently licensed as a resident and in good standing in his or her home state.
b. The person has submitted the proper request for licensure and has paid the required fees.
c. The person has submitted or transmitted to the commissioner the application for licensure that the person submitted to his or her home state or, in lieu of same, a completed uniform application.
d. The person's home state awards nonresident producer licenses to residents of New Hampshire on the same basis.

(N.H. Rev. Stat. Ann. § 402-J:8)

The commissioner may issue a surplus lines producer license to a resident of the state pursuant to R.S.A. § 402-J.

(N.H. Rev. Stat. Ann. § 405-24(III))

Due Care in Selecting Nonadmitted Insurer

A surplus lines agent shall not procure surplus lines insurance from any company that has not been approved by the insurance commissioner and does not possess and maintain a surplus to policyholders of at least $500,000, or from any company that has within the preceding 24 months been in an impaired condition.

(N.H. Rev. Stat. Ann. § 405:26)

Diligent Effort/Diligent Search

Insurance placed with an unadmitted surplus lines company shall be for such amount as the producer cannot place with an admitted company, and shall not be placed until the producer has first satisfied the insurance commissioner that the producer cannot procure such an insurance in an admitted company.

(N.H. Rev. Stat. Ann. § 405:24(III))

Export List

New Hampshire does not maintain a list of coverages that may be exported to the surplus lines market without first making a diligent search of licensed insurers.

Exempt Commercial Purchasers

New Hampshire has, by bulletin, adopted the NRRA (15 U.S.C. § 8201) definition of exempt commercial purchasers. Coverage for these insureds may be exported to the surplus lines market without making a diligent effort to place the coverage with authorized insurers provided (1) the surplus lines broker has disclosed to the exempt commercial purchaser that coverage may or may not be available from an authorized insurer that may provide greater protection with more regulatory oversight, and (2) such exempt commercial purchaser has subsequently requested such broker, in writing, to procure such policy from an unauthorized insurer.

(Ins. Dep't Bull. Docket No. 11-011-AB)

Surplus Lines Broker Filing Requirements

Every surplus lines licensee shall, on or before the tenth day of each month, execute and file with the commissioner a statement under oath covering all insurance policies and contracts of insurance or suretyship procured by him under his said license during the calendar month next preceding, giving the name of the company issuing each of said policies; the name and residence of the insured; and the amount, term, and premium of each policy and contract and the kind of property or risk insured thereby, and that he was unable to procure in companies admitted to do business in the state the amount of insurance necessary to protect said property or risk.

(N.H. Rev. Stat. Ann. § 405:25)

Surplus lines brokers shall keep a separate account of the business done under the license, a certified copy of which account he shall forthwith file with the commissioner, showing the exact amount of such insurance placed for any person, firm, or corporation the gross premium charged thereon, the companies in which the same is placed, the date of the policies and the term thereof; and he shall also file a report in the same detail of all such policies cancelled and the gross return premium thereon.

(N.H. Rev. Stat. Ann. § 405:28)

Notices

Before delivering to the insured a policy or binder of insurance written under the provisions of this section, every producer shall have stamped in a form approved by the commissioner on the face of the binder or policy the following:

> The company issuing this policy is an eligible surplus lines insurer in the state of New Hampshire and the rates charged and policy forms used have not been approved by the commissioner of insurance. If the company issuing this policy becomes insolvent, the New Hampshire insurance guaranty fund shall not be liable for any claims made against the policy.

(N.H. Rev. Stat. Ann. § 405:24 (III))

Taxes, Stamping Fees, and Other Government-Imposed Charges

The surplus line tax is 3 percent. Surplus lines brokers must file tax reports by January 31st of each year. Effective January 1, 2020, failure to file, or late filing and payment, carries a penalty based on the following schedule: 3 percent of the amount due for payments received 1–30 days after the due date, 6 percent for payments received 31–60 days after the due date, and 12 percent for payments received 60 days after the due date.

(N.H. Rev. Stat. Ann. § 405:29)

Producer, Policy, Inspection, and Other Fees

Producers may receive compensation in addition to commissions from either the insurer or insured, but a producer may not be compensated for the same service by both.

See Department Bulletin INS-15-003-AB at https://www.nh.gov/insurance/media/bulletins/2015/index.htm (last visited Dec. 16, 2020).

Industrial Insured Exemption

Any insurance company or underwriter issuing contracts of insurance to industrial insureds, or any contract of insurance issued to any one or more industrial insureds, is not subject to the unauthorized insurance provisions of state law. An "industrial insured" is:

1. An insured who procures the insurance of any risk or risks other than life and annuity contracts and health insurance contracts by use of the services of a full-time employee acting as an insurance manager or buyer or the services of a regularly and continuously retained qualified insurance consultant; and
2. An insured whose aggregate annual premiums for insurance on all risks total at least $15,000; and
3. An insured having at least 25 full-time employees.

(N.H. Rev. Stat. Ann. § 406-B:16(VI))

Independent or Direct Procurement Law

Direct procurement is permissible under New Hampshire law. A report must be filed with the Department of Insurance within 60 days of procurement. Any insurance placed with an unlicensed insurer on risks located or to be performed within New Hampshire, which is procured through negotiations or an application, in whole or in part occurring or made from within or outside of New Hampshire, shall be deemed to be insurance procured, or continued or renewed in New Hampshire.

(N.H. Rev. Stat. Ann. § 406-B:17)

NEW JERSEY

Department of Banking and Insurance (the "Department")
20 West State Street
P.O. Box 325
Trenton, NJ 08625-0325
(800) 446-7467
http://www.state.nj.us/dobi

New Jersey does not have a stamping office.

Nonadmitted Insurer Eligibility

General Information

Surplus lines insurers are not licensed but must meet eligibility standards in order to underwrite risks presented by surplus lines producers. Alien insurers listed on the Quarterly Listing of Alien Insurers maintained by the International Insurers Department of the National Association of Insurance Commissioners are considered eligible.

(N.J. Stat. Ann. § 17:22-6.45 & N.J. Admin. Code § 11:1-31.3)

Nonadmitted Insurer Eligibility List

New Jersey maintains a list of eligible surplus lines insurers that includes all insurers on the Quarterly Listing of Alien Insurers maintained by the International Insurers Department of the National Association of Insurance Commissioners.

See https://www.state.nj.us/dobi/division_insurance/sleo.htm (last visited July 15, 2020). When accessing the page, scroll to the link for "Eligible Surplus Lines Insurers (White List)."

Types of Coverage Permitted or Prohibited

Permitted

The following accident and health coverages are exportable provided they meet these requirements:

1. "Special Risk Disability and Personal Accident Coverage" means insurance providing coverage on a professional athlete, a professional musician or entertainer, or an executive essential to the insured's business operations obtained by a policyholder who procures insurance:
   i. For risk of financial loss caused by the cessation of earned income due to disability from sickness, ailment, or bodily injury;
   ii. For risk of financial loss caused by a contractual requirement to pay an executive or other person essential to the insured's business operations who can no longer perform his or her duties due to disability from sickness, ailment, or bodily injury;
   iii. For risk of accidental death in an amount equal to or exceeding $1 million in face amount only where no reasonable or adequate market exists among admitted insurers; or
   iv. For risk of financial loss caused by a contractual requirement to pay an executive or other person essential to the insured's business operations who can no longer perform his or her duties due to death. Such coverage, where no reasonable or adequate market exists among admitted insurers, must be purchased in an amount equal to or exceeding $1 million in face amount only and with a policy period not to exceed 24 months.
2. Insurance providing coverage on a person that is not a professional athlete, professional musician or entertainer, or executive or other person essential to a business operation, for any of the risks included in the definition of Special Risk Disability and Personal Accident Coverage, may be placed with an eligible surplus lines insurer

after a diligent search has been conducted. Note that the producer must report such transactions within 15 days after the end of the calendar quarter.

(N.J. ADMIN. CODE § 11:1-34.6)

Prohibited

The Department has declared that the following kinds of insurance are specifically not eligible for export:

1. Health insurance, including specific excess or aggregate excess purchased by self-funded health benefit plans, as defined by N.J.S.A. § 17B:17-4.
2. Annuities including Funding Agreements or Guaranteed Investment Contracts (GICs) as defined by N.J.S.A. § 17B:17-5.
3. Life insurance.

(N.J. ADMIN. CODE § 11:1-34.6)

Exempt Transactions

New Jersey exempts certain transactions by insurers not licensed in the state. In particular, the following risks are considered exempt and may be written by unauthorized insurers without regard to the surplus lines requirements:

- Railroad or aviation risks engaged in interstate or international commerce;
- Insurances of vessels, crafts or hulls, cargoes, marine builders' risks, marine protection and indemnity, or other risks including strikes and war risks commonly insured under ocean or wet marine forms of policy.

(N.J. STAT. ANN. § 17:22-6.37)

Service of Process

As part of the eligibility requirements, insurers must appoint the commissioner as agent for service of process.

(N.J. STAT. ANN. § 17:22-6.45(i))

Limitations on Actions Involving Judicial Proceedings

Before any insurer not authorized to transact business in this state shall file or cause to be filed any pleading or other paper in any action or proceeding instituted against it, such insurer shall either (1) deposit with the clerk of the court in which such action or proceeding is pending cash or securities or file with such clerk a bond with good and sufficient sureties, to be approved by the court, in an amount to be fixed by the court sufficient to secure the payment of any final judgment which may be rendered in such action; provided, however, that the court may in its discretion and after reasonable notice to the opposing party and upon a hearing make an order dispensing with such deposit or bond where the insurer shows to the satisfaction of the court that it maintains, in a state of the United States, funds or securities, in trust or otherwise, sufficient and available to satisfy any final judgment that may be entered in such action or proceeding; or (2) procure a certificate of authority to transact the business of insurance in this state.

(N.J. Stat. Ann. § 17:51-2)

Domestic Surplus Lines Insurers

New Jersey permits a domestic insurer with at least $15 million minimum capital and surplus to be designated as a domestic surplus lines insurer upon the written approval of the commissioner.

(N.J. Stat. Ann. § 17:22-6.69b & N.J. Admin. Code § 11:1-28.4A)

Nonadmitted Insurer Filing Requirements

Eligible surplus lines insurers are required to file a report electronically each year setting forth for each policy, the named insured, the transaction number, the producer's name and address, the policy number, the written premium amount, and the effective and expiration dates.

(N.J. Admin. Code § 11:19-3.4)

Surplus Lines Broker Licensing

In order to obtain surplus lines authority, a producer must first obtain a property and casualty producer license.

(N.J. STAT. ANN. § 17:22A-38)

If you are doing business as an agency and not solely as an individual, the business entity must be licensed. One or more licensed New Jersey producers must be designated as the responsible producer for the business entity.

(N.J. STAT. ANN. § 17:22A-32(b))

Due Care in Selecting Nonadmitted Insurer

No surplus lines agent shall place any coverage with any unauthorized insurer that is not an eligible surplus lines insurer.

(N.J. STAT. ANN. § 17:22-6.45)

Diligent Effort/Diligent Search

In order to export a risk to the surplus lines market, the surplus lines producer must first conduct a diligent search and attempt to procure the coverage from authorized insurers. Associated commercial general liability and commercial property coverages may be exported along with coverages for which a diligent search has be conducted.

(N.J. STAT. ANN. § 17:22-6.43)

The diligent search requirement is fulfilled by obtaining declinations from three insurers licensed in New Jersey to transact the class of insurance being procured.

(N.J. ADMIN. CODE § 11:1-33.2)

Export List

The insurance commissioner may declare eligible for export any class or classes of insurance coverage or risk for which there is no reasonable or adequate market among authorized insurers.

(N.J. STAT. ANN. § 17:22-6.43)

The export list is set forth in N.J.A.C. § 11:1-34.6.

Exempt Commercial Purchasers

New Jersey has adopted the NRRA (15 U.S.C. § 8201) definition of exempt commercial purchasers. Coverage for these insureds may be exported to the surplus lines market without making a diligent effort to place the coverage with authorized insurers provided (1) the surplus lines broker has disclosed to the exempt commercial purchaser that coverage may or may not be available from an authorized insurer that may provide greater protection with more regulatory oversight, and (2) such exempt commercial purchaser has subsequently requested such broker, in writing, to procure such policy from an unauthorized insurer.

(N.J. ADMIN. CODE § 11:1-33.3(g))

Surplus Lines Broker Filing Requirements

Surplus lines producers are required to file quarterly transaction reports along with the relevant taxes with the insurance commissioner within 45 calendar days of the end of the quarter.

(N.J. STAT. ANN. § 17:22-6.58)

If the producing broker obtained any declinations, the wholesale surplus lines producer must obtain a diligent search affidavit from the producing broker within 30 business days after the effectuation of coverage and maintain a copy of the affidavit in its files for five years.

(N.J. STAT. ANN. § 17:22-6.47)

New Jersey insurance law requires licensed surplus lines producers to number all surplus lines insurance policies in consecutive order. This is known as the transaction number. All subsequent documents or endorsements that pertain to the same surplus lines placement must bear the same transaction number. The New Jersey surplus lines producer quarterly tax return and instructions may be found at https://slip.njslasuite.com/ (last visited Oct. 21, 2020; you must have an account to access). General information is available without a login at http://www.njslasuite.com/ (last visited Oct. 21, 2020).

(N.J. ADMIN. CODE § 11:19-3.5)

Notices

At the time of quotation, the producer must provide the applicant with a copy of the following surplus lines policy notification:

> The undersigned solicited person has been advised by the undersigned insurance producer and understands that an insurance policy written by a surplus lines insurer is not subject to the filing or approval requirements of the New Jersey Department of Banking and Insurance. Such a policy may contain conditions, limitations, exclusions and less favorable terms than a policy issued by an insurer granted a Certificate of Authority by the New Jersey Department of Banking and Insurance.

The notice must be signed and dated by the producer and applicant and include the producer's license number.

The following notice must appear conspicuously on the face of all surplus lines policies, evidence of coverage, and renewal policies, or can be provided as a stand-alone notice:

> This policy is written by a surplus lines insurer and is not subject to the filing or approval requirements of the New Jersey Department of Banking and Insurance. Such a policy may contain conditions, limitations, exclusions and less favorable terms than a policy issued by an insurer granted a Certificate of Authority by the New Jersey Department of Banking and Insurance.

(N.J. Admin. Code § 11:1-33.3)

The surplus lines producer must write or print on the outside of the policy and on any certificate, cover note, or other confirmation of the insurance his name, address, and license number; the name of the New Jersey broker through whom the business originated; and the name, address, and code designation, if any, of the foreign or alien broker through whom the coverage was placed. Where such coverage is placed with an eligible surplus lines insurer there shall be stamped or written upon the first page of the policy or the certificate, cover note, or confirmation of insurance, the words:

This Insurance Is Issued Pursuant to the New Jersey Surplus Lines Law.

(N.J. STAT. ANN. § 17:22-6.52)

Taxes, Stamping Fees, and Other Government-Imposed Charges

Surplus lines premiums are subject to a tax of 5 percent of gross premiums. The surplus lines producer must collect the tax from the insured either directly or through the producing broker. Taxes must be filed along with the producer's quarterly transaction reports to the insurance commissioner. Where New Jersey is the home state, tax is due on the entire U.S. premium.

(N.J. Stat. Ann. § 17:22-6.59)

Producer, Policy, Inspection, and Other Fees

New Jersey permits a surplus lines producer to charge an insured for the actual cost incurred for any services performed by a person that is not associated with the surplus lines producer. In addition, the surplus lines producer may charge a fee to the originating producer, but such fees are limited as follows: (i) a fee of $50 for personal lines; and (ii) a fee equal to the greater of 2 percent of the premium for the applicable policy period or $100, but in no event in excess of $250 for commercial lines.

(N.J. STAT. ANN. § 17:22A-38 & N.J. ADMIN. CODE § 11:17B-3.2)

Industrial Insured Exemption

New Jersey statutes and regulations do not contain an industrial insured exemption with regard to surplus lines insurance.

Independent or Direct Procurement Law

New Jersey permits an insured to acquire insurance coverage directly from an insurer not authorized to do insurance business in the state. The transaction must take place substantially outside the state so that the insurer is not conducting business in New Jersey. The insured must report the transaction to the insurance commissioner and pay premium tax to New Jersey at the independently procured tax rate of 5 percent within 30 days of the transaction. The statute does not authorize independent procurement of life or disability insurances.

(N.J. Stat. Ann. § 17:22-6.64)

NEW MEXICO

New Mexico Office of Superintendent of Insurance
1120 Paseo de Peralta
Santa Fe, NM 87501
855-4-ASK-OSI
https://www.osi.state.nm.us/

New Mexico does not have a stamping office.

Nonadmitted Insurer Eligibility

General Information

Eligible surplus lines insurers transacting business in New Mexico are not otherwise authorized to transact insurance in this state. New Mexico surplus lines statutes are to be liberally construed to protect insureds and persons seeking insurance in this state; permit surplus lines insurance to be placed with reputable and financially sound eligible surplus lines insurers; establish a system of regulation that will permit controlled access to surplus lines insurance in this state; and assure collection of revenues and other amounts due to this state.

(N.M. Stat. § 59A-14-1)

Foreign

To qualify as an eligible surplus lines insurer, a nonadmitted insurer shall file information demonstrating to the superintendent's satisfaction that the insurer is authorized to write the particular line of business in the state in which it is domiciled.

(N.M. Stat. § 59A-14-4(C)(1)(a))

Additionally, a foreign eligible surplus lines insurer must maintain the greater of $15 million of capital and surplus or the minimum set by New Mexico for insurers in a particular line of business.

(N.M. Stat. § 59A-14-4(C)(1)(a))

A waiver of capital and surplus requirements, to a minimum of $4.5 million, may be granted by the superintendent in certain circumstances.

(N.M. Stat. § 59A-14-4(C)(1)(b))

A foreign surplus lines insurer must be licensed in its state of domicile for the lines of business it plans to write as surplus lines risks in New Mexico.

(N.M. Stat. § 59A-14-4(C)(1) & 15 U.S.C. § 8204(1))

For good cause shown, the superintendent may waive the eligibility requirements for a surplus lines insurer to permit insurance to be placed as to a particular risk and insurer if the insurance is not otherwise reasonably obtainable from an authorized insurer or eligible surplus lines insurer.

(N.M. Code R. § 13.19.2.13)

The superintendent may consider the following factors in determining good cause for this waiver:

a. the financial integrity, quality of management, record and reputation of the unauthorized insurer, including its management experience, A.M. Best's rating, IRIS reports, rate of growth, loss ratios, reserves, general financial condition, the length of time the insurer has been authorized in its state of domicile, the results of any previous regulatory action, and other related factors that the superintendent may determine are useful in making this assessment;
b. the capital and surplus of the unauthorized insurer's parent company, including the financial solidity of the parent company and the commitment by the parent company to support the unauthorized insurer through reinsurance;
c. the profitability of the unauthorized insurer, including its net income, stability, and consistency; and
d. the interests of the public and policyholders.

(N.M. Code R. § 13.19.2.13)

Alien

An alien surplus lines insurer writing risks in New Mexico must be listed on the Quarterly Listing of Alien Insurers maintained by the International Insurers Department of the National Association of Insurance Commissioners.

(N.M. Stat. § 59A-14-4(C)(3) and 15 U.S.C. § 8204(2))

Nonadmitted Insurer Eligibility List

The superintendent maintains a list of foreign insurers that qualify as eligible surplus lines insurers.

(N.M. Stat. § 59A-14-4(D))

See https://sbs.naic.org/solar-external-lookup/ (last visited July 15, 2020). When accessing the site, choose Jurisdiction: "New Mexico," Search Type: "Company," and Company Type: "Surplus Lines Insurer."

Types of Coverage Permitted or Prohibited

General Information

With limited exceptions, New Mexico law does not specify the types of risks eligible for surplus lines placement in the state. Automobile liability insurance must be written by an admitted insurer to comply with New Mexico Motor Vehicle Division regulations.

See N.M. Motor Vehicle Division website FAQ "Why did I receive a notice that my registration was suspended?" which indicates that vehicles must have "insurance through a New Mexico licensed insurance company" at https://www.mvd.newmexico.gov/vehicles/insurance/ (last visited July 15, 2020).

Exempt Transactions

Chapter 59A, Article 14 of the New Mexico statutes, relating to surplus lines insurance, does not apply to reinsurance transactions or to the following transaction:

1. any insurance where New Mexico is not the home state of the insured;
2. wet marine and transportation insurance, as defined in section 59A-7-5 NMSA 1978;
3. insurance on vehicles or aircraft owned and principally garaged outside this state;
4. insurance of property and operations of railroads engaged in interstate commerce;
5. insurance of aircraft of common carriers, or cargo of such aircraft, or against liability, other than employer's liability, arising out of ownership, maintenance, or use of such aircraft;
6. insurance of automobile bodily injury and property damage liability risks when written in Mexican insurers and covering in Mexico and not in the United States; or
7. insurance independently procured.

(N.M. Stat. § 59A-14-1)

Service of Process

Service of legal process against a surplus lines insurer may be made upon the superintendent as provided for in § 99 (N.M. Stat. § 59A-5-32) of the Insurance Code.

(N.M. Stat. § 59A-14-16(B))

Limitations on Actions Involving Judicial Proceedings

Before any unauthorized insurer files or causes to be filed any pleading or other response in any court action, suit, or proceeding, they must post a bond or procure a certificate of authority. However, this shall not be construed to prevent an unauthorized insurer from filing a motion to quash a writ or to set aside service thereof, on the ground that such unauthorized insurer has not transacted insurance in this state.

(N.M. Stat. § 59A-15-8)

Domestic Surplus Lines Insurers

New Mexico statutes have no provision allowing domestic surplus lines insurers.

Nonadmitted Insurer Filing Requirements

Alien insurers listed with the NAIC's International Insurer Department are not required to submit filings with the superintendent.

Eligible surplus lines insurers must file a certified and sworn copy of the insurer's most current annual statement. The statement shall be provided or made available at the same time it is provided to the insurer's domicile, but in no event more than nine months after the close of the period reported upon. No financial filings are required if the insurer's annual statement is available to the superintendent through the NAIC or from public sources.

(N.M. STAT. § 59A-14-4(D))

Surplus Lines Broker Licensing

The superintendent shall, upon due application and payment of the license fee, issue a license as surplus lines broker to a person qualified as follows:

1. if the applicant is an individual, the individual must have had experience or special training or education sufficient in duration and character to render the applicant, in the opinion of the superintendent, reasonably competent to engage in business as a surplus lines broker; and
2. if the applicant is a firm or corporation, all individuals to represent it as a surplus lines broker in this state must be licensed surplus lines brokers.

No surplus lines broker examination is required. An applicant for a surplus lines broker license shall file, as part of the application, documentation showing a combination of the following factors totaling at least five years:

a. experience as a licensed agent in the kind of insurance for which the surplus lines broker license is sought;
b. continuing education units of a type and quantity sufficient to satisfy the requirements for renewal of an agent's license; and
c. any other special experience, education, or training that the applicant offers to demonstrate that the applicant is reasonably competent to conduct surplus lines business in New Mexico.

A surplus line broker may accept and export surplus line business from and for any insurance agent or broker licensed by this state for the kind of insurance involved, and may compensate the agent or broker therefor.

A surplus line broker may not directly or indirectly compensate any person other than such a licensed agent or broker as to origination of such business. This provision does not prohibit payment of regular salaries to the surplus line broker's employees, or sharing of compensation with other persons pursuant to valid agency or business contracts. Violation of this provision is a misdemeanor.

(N.M. STAT. §§ 59A-14-7, 59A-14-9)

Due Care in Selecting Nonadmitted Insurer

Prior to placing insurance with an eligible surplus lines insurer, a surplus lines broker must ascertain that such insurer is in sound financial condition. To fulfill this requirement, the surplus lines broker must:

1. determine that the insurer is on the most recent list of eligible surplus lines insurers maintained by the superintendent; and
2. make inquiry sufficient to satisfy the surplus lines broker that the insurer is well managed, possesses financial capacity adequate to its business, and has a good reputation in the community.

A surplus lines broker shall not place any further business with an insurer, and shall promptly notify the superintendent if the broker becomes aware of a reasonable basis to doubt the financial condition of an insurer.

(N.M. Code R. § 13.19.2.10)

Diligent Effort/Diligent Search

New Mexico requires a diligent effort to place a risk in the admitted market prior to placement in surplus lines. No risk may be placed in surplus lines unless the full amount or type of insurance cannot be obtained from insurers authorized to do business in this state as determined after making a diligent search among insurers authorized to transact and actually writing the particular type and class of insurance in this state.

(N.M. Code R. § 13.19.2.8)

Artificial divisions of coverage in one class or any form of coverage under one class into two or more proposed contracts for the purpose of obtaining a marketing or rate advantage upon the entire risk is prohibited where the entire coverage sought in that class or form would be acceptable as a single contract to an authorized insurer. Combinations of primary coverage and excess coverage shall not be considered a violation of this section if the excess insurance is written by an eligible surplus lines insurer:

1. because of a refusal in writing by the primary authorized insurer to assume the limits of liability desired by the person seeking insurance; or
2. on a written demand, including specific reasons, by the person seeking insurance that the entire liability not be placed with one insurance company.

(N.M. Code R. § 13.19.2.9)

Export List

New Mexico OSI does maintain an export list. As of October 1, 2020, the latest list was published in OSI Bulletin 2015-007, which is available at https://www.osi.state.nm.us/news/bulletins/bulletin-2015-007 (last visited May 6, 2023).

Exempt Commercial Purchasers

New Mexico has adopted the NRRA (15 U.S.C. § 8201) definition of exempt commercial purchasers. Coverage for these insureds may be exported to the surplus lines market without making a diligent effort to place the coverage with authorized insurers provided (1) the surplus lines broker has disclosed to the exempt commercial purchaser that coverage may or may not be available from an authorized insurer that may provide greater protection with more regulatory oversight, and (2) such exempt commercial purchaser has subsequently requested such broker, in writing, to procure such policy from an unauthorized insurer.

(N.M. STAT. §§ 59A-14-3(C)(2), 59A-14-2(L))

Surplus Lines Broker Filing Requirements

Since the law was amended in 2017, surplus lines brokers are no longer required to file affidavits of diligent effort and declarations pages with the superintendent (N.M. STAT. § 59A-14-11). At the time of this writing, the regulation (N.M. Code R. § 13.19.2.17) has not been updated to reflect the change in the law and still references filing of these items and filing data on diskette. Surplus lines tax quarterly return filings are required. The form and instructions can be found at http://www.tax.newmexico.gov/insurance-premium-tax-program.aspx (last visited Oct. 28, 2020).

A surplus line broker must keep, in a publicly accessible office, complete records of surplus line insurance business transacted, including records of income and disbursements, copies of all policies, endorsements, cancellations, filing documents, reports, and other related records. The records shall be made available for examination by the superintendent at all times within seven years after issuance of a coverage to which the record relates.

(N.M. STAT. § 59A-14-10)

Notices

Every insurance contract procured and delivered as surplus lines insurance shall bear the name, address, and signature of the surplus lines broker who procured it.

(N.M. Stat. § 59A-14-5)

The policy must also contain a statement in boldface ten-point or larger type either upon its declarations page or by attachment of a promulgated endorsement, the following:

> This policy provides surplus lines insurance by an insurer not otherwise authorized to transact business in New Mexico. This policy is not subject to supervision, review or approval by the superintendent of insurance. The insurance so provided is not within the protection of any guaranty fund law of New Mexico designed to protect the public in the event of the insurer's insolvency.
>
> (N.M. Stat. § 59A-14-5)

Taxes, Stamping Fees, and Other Government-Imposed Charges

Within 60 days after expiration of a calendar quarter, the surplus lines broker shall pay to the superintendent a tax on gross premiums received, less returned premiums, on surplus lines business where New Mexico is the home state of the insured. The tax shall be at the same rate, currently 3.003 percent, as is applicable to premiums of authorized insurers.

(N.M. Stat. § 59A-14-12(A))

"Premiums" shall include any additional amount charged the insured, including policy fees, risk purchasing group fees, and inspection fees; but "premiums" shall not include any additional amount charged the insured for local, state, or federal tax; regulatory authority fee; or examination fee, if any.

(N.M. Stat. § 59A-14-12(B))

Effective January 1, 2020, filing of surplus lines tax was transferred to the New Mexico Taxation and Revenue Department. (HB 223, N.M. Leg. (2018))

Surplus Lines Tax Quarterly Return Form TRD-41397 is available at https://www.tax.newmexico.gov/businesses/insurance-premium-tax-program/ (last visited Aug. 2, 2021) and filing can be done online at https://tap.state.nm.us/TAP/_/ (last visited Aug. 2, 2021).

Producer, Policy, Inspection, and Other Fees

Surplus lines brokers may charge additional amounts to the insured, including policy fees, risk purchasing group fees, and inspection fees, but such fees are considered premiums for purposes of determining the applicable surplus lines tax.

(N.M. Stat. § 59A-14-12(B))

Industrial Insured Exemption

Transactions in New Mexico involving contracts of insurance to one or more industrial insureds are exempt from the general prohibition on placing insurance with unauthorized insurers. Such transactions are not subject to New Mexico surplus lines insurance laws or regulations.

An industrial insured is an insured:

a. which procures the insurance of any risk by the use of the services of a full-time employee acting as a risk manager or insurance manager or by utilizing the services of a regularly and continuously qualified insurance consultant;
b. which has aggregate annual premiums for insurance on all risks of at least $25,000; and
c. which has at least 25 full-time employees.

(N.M. Stat. § 59A-15-2(B)(5))

Independent or Direct Procurement Law

An insured who independently procures insurance, located in whole or in part within New Mexico, must file a written report of the same with the superintendent, upon forms prescribed by the superintendent, showing the name and address of the insured or insureds, name and address of the insurer, the subject of the insurance, a general description of the coverage, the amount of premium currently charged therefor, and such additional pertinent information as is reasonably requested by the superintendent. The statute does not apply to life insurance, health insurance, or annuities.

If an independently procured policy covers risks or exposures only partially located or to be performed in this state, the taxes, fees, and penalties imposed pursuant to the Insurance Code and the Insurance Premium Tax Act (N.M. Stat. §§ 7-40-1 to 7-40-10) shall be computed on the portion of the premium properly attributable to the risks or exposures located or to be performed in this state and reported to the secretary of taxation and revenue. In no event, however, shall a tax be payable solely because the risk in question, or any portion thereof, is located or to be performed in this state.

(N.M. Stat. § 59A-15-4)

NEW YORK

New York Department of Financial Services
One State Street
New York, NY 10004-1511
(212) 709-3500
www.dfs.ny.gov

New York has a stamping office.

Excess Line Association of New York
One Exchange Plaza
55 Broadway, 29th Floor
New York, NY 10006
(646) 292-5500
www.elany.org

Nonadmitted Insurer Eligibility

General Information

Surplus lines (known as excess lines in New York) insurers must meet eligibility standards in order to underwrite risks presented by specially licensed excess line brokers. These insurers need not be licensed by New York based on an exception to the insurer licensing requirements.

(N.Y. Ins. Law § 1101(b)(2)(F))

A nonadmitted eligible New York excess line insurer may operate from offices of an affiliated licensed insurer in New York state provided the excess line insurer only entertains risks submitted by excess line brokers and places a specific disclosure on each policy.

(N.Y. Ins. Law § 2117(i))

Nonadmitted eligible insurers are subject to limitations as to the activities in which they may engage.

(N.Y. INS. LAW § 2117)

A nonadmitted eligible New York excess line insurer may operate from offices of an affiliated licensed insurer in New York state provided the excess line insurer only entertains risks submitted by excess line brokers and places a specific disclosure on each policy and includes a notice, in no less than ten-point type, as follows: "This insurer is not licensed in the State of New York and is not subject to its supervision."

(N.Y. INS. LAW § 2117(i) & Reg. 41 (11 N.Y. COMP. CODES R. & REGS. 27) at § 27.16)

Foreign

Foreign insurers must maintain a minimum of $47 million policyholder surplus and be licensed in their state of domicile for the lines of business they plan to write as excess line risks in New York.

(11 N.Y. COMP. CODES R. & REGS. 27.13(2))

Alien

Alien insurers must be published on the most recent Quarterly Listing of Alien Insurers maintained by the International Insurers Department of the National Association of Insurance Commissioners to be eligible.

(15 U.S.C. § 8204 (2))

Nonadmitted Insurer Eligibility List

A voluntary list of insurers is maintained by the Excess Line Association of New York (also known as "ELANY"), a service provider and membership organization for excess line brokers. To apply for listing contact ELANY at 646-292-5500 and ask for the financial director.

ELANY's current list may be accessed online at http://www.elany.org/nyes.aspx?d=1006 (last visited July 15, 2020).

Types of Coverage Permitted or Prohibited

General Information

Excess line insurers may provide coverage for most of the kinds of insurance defined in Insurance Law § 1113(a) but not the following:

- Life Insurance
- Annuities
- Accident and Health
- Workers Compensation
- Title Insurance
- Mortgage Guaranty Insurance
- Credit Unemployment Insurance
- Financial Guaranty Insurance
- GAP Insurance
- Legal Services Insurance
- Involuntary Unemployment Insurance

Other specific types of coverage defined elsewhere in New York Insurance Law prohibit the sale of the following coverages in the excess line market:

- Identification Theft
- Group Credit Unemployment Insurance
- Credit Card, Debit Card, or Checking Account Group Policies
- Product or System Group Insurance Policies
- Identity Theft Group Insurance Policies
- Group Property Travel Insurance Policies
- Group Policies for Service Providers
- Self-Service Storage Company Group Insurance Policies
- Sponsored Group Personal Insurance (other than Employer Sponsored Group Excess)

Other coverages such as auto and medical malpractice can be written but primary coverage for those lines is partly restricted.

Finally, the Department of Financial Services interprets the law as prohibiting certain other types of coverage from being placed in the excess lines market.

Exempt Transactions

Certain transactions with unauthorized insurers are exempt from the affidavit filing and taxation requirements of New York Law. In particular, blue water ocean marine risks and tangible property risks located primarily or permanently outside the state of New York are exempt from the excess line law.

(N.Y. INS. LAW § 2117)

Service of Process

Any act of transacting insurance by any unauthorized insurer constitutes an appointment of the superintendent as attorney of such insurer upon whom may be served all lawful process in any action, suit, or proceeding.

(N.Y. INS. LAW § 1213)

Limitations on Actions Involving Judicial Proceedings

An unauthorized insurer shall deposit securities or a bond in any court proceeding prior to filing an answer or other responsive pleading in any proceeding against such insurer. Excess line transactions are exempted from these pre-answer security requirements provided the policy designates the superintendent and his successors as agent for service of process.

(N.Y. INS. LAW § 1213)

Domestic Surplus Lines Insurers

New York statutes have no provision allowing domestic surplus lines insurers.

Nonadmitted Insurer Filing Requirements

Insurance Regulation 41 at § 27.14 requires each eligible insurer to file a report electronically by March 15th each year, setting forth the prior calendar year's premiums, insureds, excess line broker, addresses, and other policy details.

(11 N.Y. COMP. CODES R. & REGS. § 27.14)

Surplus Lines Broker Licensing

An individual or entity, resident or nonresident, may obtain an excess line broker license in New York pursuant to Insurance Law § 2105. One must first be licensed as a broker under Insurance Law § 2104. The applications may be submitted simultaneously. If you operate as a corporation, LLC, or partnership and maintain the premium trust in the entity name and receive commission in the name of the entity, the entity must be licensed with one or more individuals licensed as "sublicensees" of the entity.

Only an excess line broker may procure insurance from an eligible excess line insurer. A licensed New York broker may obtain such insurance through a licensed excess line wholesale broker. A New York licensed agent (P/C license) may not procure excess line insurance through a licensed excess line broker.

Due Care in Selecting Nonadmitted Insurer

Excess line brokers are required to use due care when selecting an excess line insurer.

(N.Y. INS. LAW § 2118(a))

Insurance Regulation 41 at § 27.13 sets forth a list of requirements by which an excess line broker can meet the "due care" standard. Some of those requirements are waived if ELANY performs certain functions for all excess line licensees.

(11 N.Y. COMP. CODES R. & REGS. § 27.13)

Diligent Effort/Diligent Search

An excess line broker or a producing broker that has sought coverage through an excess line broker must conduct a search of the licensed market to attempt to procure the coverage from a licensed insurer that the broker has reason to believe might consider writing the type of coverage or class of insurance. Three declinations from licensed insurers are required to meet the diligent effort requirement.

(N.Y. Ins. Law § 2118(b))

Export List

The superintendent of the Department of Financial Services may waive the diligent effort in whole or part upon notice and a hearing, if the superintendent determines one or more coverages are generally unavailable from licensed insurers.

(N.Y. Ins. Law § 2118(b)(3)(E))

The list of coverages currently on the export list are set forth in Insurance Regulation 41 (11 N.Y. Comp. Codes R. & Regs. 27) at § 27.3(g) and is available at http://www.elany.org/coverage codes.aspx?d=1031 (last visited Oct. 7, 2020).

Exempt Commercial Purchasers

New York has adopted the NRRA (15 U.S.C. § 8201) definition of exempt commercial purchasers. Coverage for these insureds may be exported to the surplus lines market without making a diligent effort to place the coverage with authorized insurers provided (1) the surplus lines broker has disclosed to the exempt commercial purchaser that coverage may or may not be available from an authorized insurer that may provide greater protection with more regulatory oversight, and (2) such exempt commercial purchaser has subsequently requested such broker, in writing, to procure such policy from an unauthorized insurer.

(N.Y. Ins. Law §§ 2118(b)(3)(F), 2101(x)(2))

Surplus Lines Broker Filing Requirements

An excess line broker must file for each insurance policy procured:

1. an affidavit,
2. a notice of Excess Line Placement,
3. a copy of the declarations page or cover note (or binder if the declaration page or cover note are unavailable); such filing must be made within 45 days of policy inception.

A wholesale excess line broker must also file an affidavit of the producing broker if the producing broker obtained any declinations or delivers the Notice of Excess Line Placement to the insured. Subsequent premium bearing endorsements must also be filed. The filings are submitted to ELANY.

(N.Y. INS. LAW § 2118(b)(1),(2),(3) and (e)(2)(c))

It is unlawful for a broker to deliver in New York any declarations page of an insurance policy or cover note unless the insurance document is stamped by ELANY or exempt.

(N.Y. INS. LAW § 2118(b)(6))

Notices

There are two notices for which the excess line broker and or producing broker are responsible.

First, at the time of placement, a "Notice of Excess Line Placement" must be sent to the insured informing the insured that the placement was made with an insurer not licensed by New York State.

(N.Y. INS. LAW § 2118(e)(2)(C))

The second notice is required to be stamped on each policy document. The Notice of Excess Line Placement language mirrors the "Notice" language that must be stamped on a document which evidences coverage for delivery to the insured such as a binder, cover note or declarations page. The language must be in not less than ten-point bold type. It reads as follows:

> THE INSURER(S) NAMED HEREIN IS (ARE) NOT LICENSED BY THE STATE OF NEW YORK, NOT SUBJECT TO ITS SUPERVISION, AND IN THE EVENT OF THE INSOLVENCY OF THE INSURER(S), NOT PROTECTED BY THE NEW YORK STATE SECURITY FUNDS. THE POLICY MAY NOT BE SUBJECT TO ALL OF THE REGULATIONS OF THE DEPARTMENT OF FINANCIAL SERVICES PERTAINING TO POLICY FORMS.

(Regulation 41 (11 N.Y. COMP. CODES R. & REGS. 27) at § 27.15)

Taxes, Stamping Fees, and Other Government-Imposed Charges

An excess line broker must pay a tax of 3.6 percent on the gross premium less premiums returned to insureds when New York is the home state of the insured.

(N.Y. Ins. Law § 2118(d)(1))

When New York is the home state on a multistate risk there is no allocation of premium, the tax is on 100 percent of the gross premium with no reduction on premium for risk exposures outside of New York. However, when the risk contains exposures outside of the United States, the premium can be allocated as set forth in Regulation 41 (11 N.Y. Comp. Codes R. & Regs. 27) at § 27.9 and the Appendix of allocation formulas whereby New York only taxes the premium for exposures in the United States. Excess line brokers must file a tax statement on or before March 15 of the following year electronically with the Department of Financial Services and pay taxes due at that time. ELANY provides summary reports to each excess line licensee and to the Department of Financial Services to facilitate preparation of these tax statements.

(Regulation 41 (11 N.Y. Comp. Codes R. & Regs. 27) at § 27.8)

Though not a governmental entity, ELANY charges a stamping fee of .0017 percent on the taxable premium and bills the fee to each excess line broker monthly. The tax and stamping fees are owed by the excess line broker but can be charged back to the insured.

(N.Y. Ins. Law § 2119)

Producer, Policy, Inspection, and Other Fees

Brokers are permitted to charge producer service fees pursuant to Insurance Law § 2119. Other fees such as inspection fees and policy fees are also permitted. Policy fees payable to the insurer are subject to tax because they are considered to be a form of premium. Inspection fees are not taxable unless the insurer selects the inspection service and collects the fees from the insured directly. Any fees, taxes, or charges in excess of premium charged to an insured must be agreed to by the insured in writing.

(N.Y. INS. LAW § 2119)

Industrial Insured Exemption

New York statutes and regulations do not contain an industrial insured exemption with regard to surplus lines insurance.

Independent or Direct Procurement Law

An insured is permitted to acquire insurance coverage "directly" or "independently" from an insurer not authorized to do insurance business in New York. The transaction must take place substantially outside the borders of New York state so that the insurer is not conducting business in New York state for which a license is required.

(N.Y. INS. LAW § 1101(b)(2)(E))

The insured is subject to a tax of 3.6 percent upon the gross premium.

(N.Y. Tax Law § 1551)

The transaction must be reported and paid within 60 days of the end of the calendar quarter in which the policy became effective, to the commissioner of taxation and finance.

(N.Y. TAX LAW § 1554(a))

Certain entities are exempt from the tax. The tax is allocable on international risks in the same manner as the excess line premium tax is for international risks.

(N.Y. TAX LAW § 1553)

NORTH CAROLINA

North Carolina Department of Insurance
325 N. Salisbury Street
Raleigh, NC 27603
(855) 408-1212
http://www.ncdoi.com/

North Carolina has a stamping office.

North Carolina Surplus Lines Association
8412 Falls of Neuse, Suite 206
Raleigh, NC 27615
(919) 746-8415
https://www.ncsla.com/

Nonadmitted Insurer Eligibility

General Information

A Lloyd's plan or similar group of insurers may write surplus lines insurance if the group maintains a trust fund of at least $100 million as security to the full amount for all policyholders and creditors in the United States.

(N.C. Gen. Stat. § 58-21-20(a))

An insurance exchange created by the laws of individual states may write surplus lines insurance if the exchange maintains aggregate capital and surplus of at least $75 million.

(N.C. Gen. Stat. § 58-21-20(a))

A group of incorporated insurers under common administration that has continuously transacted insurance business outside the United States for at least three years may write surplus lines insurance if it maintains aggregate policyholders' surplus of least $10 billion and maintains in trust a surplus of at least

$100 million, and each insurer maintains capital and surplus of at least $25 million per company.

(N.C. GEN. STAT. § 58-21-20(a))

Foreign

An insurer domiciled in the United States is eligible to write nonadmitted insurance in North Carolina for risks whose home state is North Carolina if:

- It is eligible in its state of domicile to write the kinds of insurance that it intends to write in North Carolina; and
- It maintains minimum capital and surplus (or equivalent) requirements in the amount of $15 million or the minimum requirements of N.C. Gen. Stat. § 58-7-75, whichever requirements are greater.

These requirements may be reduced, but not below $4.5 million, for an insurer as a result of an affirmative finding of acceptability by the commissioner based upon such factors as quality of management, capital and surplus of any parent company, company underwriting profit and investment income trends, market availability, and company record and reputation within the industry.

(N.C. GEN. STAT. §§ 58-21-15(1a), 58-21-20(a))

Alien

A surplus line broker may not place insurance with an alien insurer unless the insurer is listed on the Quarterly Listing of Alien Insurers maintained by the International Insurers Department of the National Association of Insurance Commissioners.

(N.C. GEN. STAT. § 58-21-17)

Nonadmitted Insurer Eligibility List

The North Carolina Department of Insurance maintains a nonadmitted insurer eligibility list. North Carolina law does not specify the procedures or requirements for a company to be added to the list.

The list is available online at https://sbs.naic.org/solar-external-lookup/ (last visited May 6, 2023). When accessing the site, choose Jurisdiction: "North Carolina," Search Type: "Company," and Company Type: "SURPLUS LINES."

Types of Coverage Permitted or Prohibited

General Information

There are no prohibited coverages under North Carolina law.

Exempt Transactions

North Carolina's surplus lines laws do not apply to the following kinds of insurance when placed by a licensed insurance producer:

- Reinsurance;
- Commercial aircraft insurance;
- Wet marine and transportation insurance;
- Life and accident or health insurance; and
- Annuities.

(N.C. GEN. STAT. § 58-21-10(10))

Service of Process

Any act of transacting insurance by any unauthorized insurer constitutes an appointment of the commissioner as attorney of such insurer upon whom may be served all lawful process in any action, suit, or proceeding.

(N.C. GEN. STAT. § 58-21-100)

Limitations on Actions Involving Judicial Proceedings

Before any unauthorized foreign or alien insurer shall file or cause to be filed any pleading in any action, suit, or proceeding instituted against it, such unauthorized insurer shall either procure a bond or procure a license to transact the business of insurance in this North Carolina. However, this shall not be construed to prevent an unauthorized foreign or alien insurer from filing a motion to quash a writ or to set aside service thereof, on the ground that the insurer did not transact insurance in North Carolina.

(N.C. Gen. Stat. § 58-16-35(c))

Domestic Surplus Lines Insurers

North Carolina permits a domestic insurer with at least $15 million minimum capital and surplus to be designated as a domestic surplus lines insurer upon the written approval of the commissioner.

(N.C. Gen. Stat. § 58-21-21)

Nonadmitted Insurer Filing Requirements

Surplus lines insurers are required to file annual financial statements with the commissioner.

(N.C. Gen. Stat. § 58-21-20(a)(3))

Surplus Lines Broker Licensing

An individual holding a North Carolina residential property broker's or agent's license may obtain a surplus lines license by remitting $50 fee to the commissioner, submitting an application, and passing an exam.

(N.C. Gen. Stat. § 58-21-65(b))

An individual licensed as a surplus lines producer in the individual's home state may receive a nonresident surplus lines license if the home state awards nonresident licenses to North Carolina residents on a reciprocal basis.

(N.C. Gen. Stat. §§ 58-33-32(d), 58-21-65(e))

A resident business entity may obtain a surplus lines license by listing the individuals within the business entity who have satisfied the requirements to become surplus lines licensees. Only those individuals listed on the license may transact surplus lines business.

(N.C. Gen. Stat. § 58-21-65(c))

A business entity licensed as a surplus lines producer in its home state may receive a nonresident surplus lines license if the home state awards nonresident licenses to North Carolina business entities on a reciprocal basis. The business entity must list those individuals who have satisfied the requirements to become surplus lines licensees, and only those individuals listed on the license may transact surplus lines business.

(N.C. Gen. Stat. §§ 58-21-65(c), 58-33-32(d))

Due Care in Selecting Nonadmitted Insurer

A surplus lines licensee shall not place coverage with a nonadmitted insurer unless, at the time of placement, the surplus lines licensee has determined that the nonadmitted insurer meets the eligibility requirements.

(N.C. Gen. Stat. § 58-21-20)

Diligent Effort/Diligent Search

Surplus lines coverage may be procured when the full amount or kind of insurance cannot be obtained from insurers who are admitted to do business in this state. Such full amount or kind of insurance may be procured from eligible surplus lines insurers, provided that a diligent search is made among the insurers who are admitted to transact and are actually writing the particular kind and class of insurance in this state.

(N.C. Gen. Stat. § 58-21-15)

Export List

North Carolina does not maintain a list of coverages that may be exported to the surplus lines market without first making a diligent search of licensed insurers.

Exempt Commercial Purchasers

North Carolina has adopted the NRRA (15 U.S.C. § 8201) definition of exempt commercial purchasers. Coverage for these insureds may be exported to the surplus lines market without making a diligent effort to place the coverage with authorized insurers provided (1) the surplus lines broker has disclosed to the exempt commercial purchaser that coverage may or may not be available from an authorized insurer that may provide greater protection with more regulatory oversight, and (2) such exempt commercial purchaser has subsequently requested such broker, in writing, to procure such policy from an unauthorized insurer.

(N.C. GEN. STAT. § 58-21-16(a))

Surplus Lines Broker Filing Requirements

On or before the end of January, April, July, and October of each year, each surplus lines licensee must file with the commissioner a verified report of all surplus lines insurance transacted during the preceding three months, which must show the aggregate premiums written, the aggregate premiums returned, and the amount of aggregate tax to be remitted. The premium taxes are due and payable at the same time.

(N.C. GEN. STAT. § 58-21-80)

Within 30 days of placing surplus lines insurance, the surplus lines licensee must file with the commissioner a report, which must include the following:

- The name of the insured
- The identity of the insurer
- A description of the subject and location of the risk
- The amount of premium charged
- The amount of premium tax
- The policy period
- The policy number
- An acknowledgment that the surplus lines licensee has complied with § 58-21-15 or § 58-21-16
- The name, address, phone number, fax number, and email address of the licensee
- Any other relevant information the commissioner requires

(N.C. GEN. STAT. § 58-21-35(a))

Notices

Every evidence of insurance issued by a surplus lines licensee must state the name of the licensee and the following language in 12-point font in a contrasting color or in 12-point font and underlined and bold:

> The insurance company with which this coverage has been placed is not licensed by the State of North Carolina and is not subject to its supervision. In the event of the insolvency of the insurance company, losses under this policy will not be paid by any State insurance guaranty or solvency fund.
>
> (N.C. Gen. Stat. § 58-21-45(f))

Taxes, Stamping Fees, and Other Government-Imposed Charges

North Carolina imposes a premium tax on surplus lines insurance of 5.0 percent of gross premiums. The surplus lines licensee is prohibited from absorbing or rebating the premium tax. The surplus lines licensee shall remit the premium tax to the commissioner at the time the broker files his or her quarterly reports.

(N.C. Gen. Stat. §§ 58-21-85(a), 58-21-35, 58-21-80)

North Carolina imposes a stamping fee of 0.4 percent of gross premiums, payable to the North Carolina Surplus Lines Association.

See https://www.ncsla.com/announcements/surplus-lines-tax-stamping-fee-payment-information/ (last visited Nov. 18, 2020).

Producer, Policy, Inspection, and Other Fees

Company fees are those charged by the insurance company (insurer). The NCDOI considers all fees charged by the insurer part of the premium and subject to surplus lines tax and stamping fee. Any fees charged and retained by the broker are not considered company fees and are not subject to surplus lines tax or the stamping fee.

See "Taxable Fees" and "Non-Taxable Fees" on the stamping office website at https://www.ncsla.com/tax/tax-filing/taxes-fees (last visited Dec. 16, 2020).

Industrial Insured Exemption

North Carolina statutes and regulations do not contain an industrial insured exemption with regard to surplus lines insurance.

Independent or Direct Procurement Law

An insured may directly procure insurance with an eligible surplus lines insurer without the involvement of an agent, broker, or surplus lines licensee. Within 30 days of procuring or renewing such insurance, the insured must file with the commissioner a written report containing the name and address of the insured, the name and address of the insurer, the subject of insurance, a general description of the coverage, the amount of premium currently charged, and any other information required by the commissioner. The insured must also submit an affidavit stating that the full amount or kind of insurance cannot be obtained from licensed insurers and that the insured has made a diligent search among the licensed insurers. Gross premiums are subject to a 5.0 percent premium tax, which is due at the time of the filing of the report.

(N.C. GEN. STAT. § 58-28-5(b))

NORTH DAKOTA

North Dakota Insurance Department
600 E. Boulevard Avenue
Bismarck, ND 58505
(701) 328-2440
https://www.insurance.nd.gov/
insurance@nd.gov

North Dakota does not have a stamping office.

Nonadmitted Insurer Eligibility

General Information

To be eligible, a surplus lines insurer must be authorized to write the kind of insurance sought in its domiciliary jurisdiction, and must establish satisfactory evidence of good repute and financial integrity, including capital and surplus or its equivalent under the laws of its domiciliary jurisdiction, which equals the greater of North Dakota insurer capital and surplus requirements or $15 million. Alien insurers must be listed on the National Association of Insurance Commissioners (NAIC) Quarterly Listing of Alien Insurers. An insurer with less than the minimum capital and surplus can be eligible upon an affirmative finding of acceptability by the commissioner, provided the capital and surplus is not less than $4.5 million.

(N.D. Cent. Code § 26.1-44-03(4.a))

To be eligible, an insurer must also register with the department by submitting a request letter, an Agent for Service of Process form (SFN 8330), an Affidavit (SFN 4795), a Data Processing Questionnaire (SFN 4792), the most recently filed Annual Statement (not applicable to insurers on the NAIC Quarterly Listing of Alien Insurers), a financial examination report (not applicable to insurers on the NAIC Quarterly Listing of Alien Insurers), and a nonrefundable application fee of $100.

See department website at https://www.insurance.nd.gov/surplus-lines-application (last visited Mar. 22, 2021) for forms and further details.

Nonadmitted Insurer Eligibility List

North Dakota maintains a list of eligible surplus lines insurers. The list can be found on the NAIC State Based System (SBS) Lookup Search at https://sbs.naic.org/solar-external-lookup/ (last visited Mar. 22, 2021). For a complete list of registered surplus lines insurers, choose Jurisdiction: "North Dakota," Search Type: "Company," Company Type: "Surplus Lines Insurer," and leave all other fields blank.

Types of Coverage Permitted or Prohibited

General Information

Other than requiring a diligent effort search of licensed insurers, the surplus lines law of North Dakota does not place restrictions on the types of coverage permitted, however, it prohibits domestic surplus line insurers from issuing a policy designed to satisfy the motor vehicle financial responsibility requirements in chapter 26.1-41 or any other law mandating insurance coverage by a licensed insurance company.

(N.D. Cent. Code § 26.1-44-03.2(4))

Exempt Transactions

North Dakota laws consider the following to be separate from surplus lines insurance and not covered by surplus lines laws, and the insurer is not required to have a certificate of authority:

- Reinsurance;
- Policies covering risks outside of North Dakota at issuance;

- Life insurance, health insurance, or annuities provided to educational or religious or charitable institutions organized and operated without profit;
- Attorneys acting in the ordinary relation of attorney and client in the adjustment of claims or losses;
- Group life, accident, and health, or blanket accident and health insurance, or group annuities if the master policy of the group was lawfully issued and delivered in and pursuant to the laws of a state in which the insurance company was authorized;
- Policies issued outside North Dakota involving insurance on vessels, craft or hulls, cargoes, marine builder's risk, marine protection and indemnity or other risk, including strikes and war risks commonly insured under ocean or wet marine forms of policy;
- Industrial insureds transactions.

(N.D. Cent. Code § 26.1-02-05)

Service of Process

A North Dakota eligible surplus lines insurers must appoint the commissioner as its true and lawful "attorney" (agent) for service of process. Service on the commissioner in the event of legal proceedings is mandatory.

(N.D. Cent. Code § 26.1-44-04)

Limitations on Actions Involving Judicial Proceedings

Before any unauthorized insurance company files or causes to be filed any pleading in any court proceeding instituted against it, the company shall either file with the court a cash or other bond with good and sufficient sureties, or procure a certificate of authority to transact insurance in North Dakota.

(N.D. Cent. Code § 26.1-02-12)

Domestic Surplus Lines Insurers

The commissioner may designate a North Dakota domestic insurer as a domestic surplus lines insurer if the insurer has policyholder surplus of at least $15 million dollars and the insurer's board of directors has approved the designation. North Dakota domestic surplus lines insurers may not issue a policy, such as motor vehicle liability insurance, required by any law that mandates coverage by a licensed insurance company. A North Dakota domestic surplus lines insurer is subject to restrictions, such as diligent effort, and is subject to surplus lines premium tax. North Dakota domestic surplus lines insurers are subject to general domestic financial examination and solvency reporting and examination requirements, but are not subject to life or property and casualty guaranty fund statutes.

(N.D. CENT. CODE § 26.1-44-03.2)

Nonadmitted Insurer Filing Requirements

To become eligible, an insurer must register with the department by submitting a request letter, an Agent for Service of Process form (SFN 8330), an Affidavit (SFN 4795), a Data Processing Questionnaire (SFN 4792), the most recently filed Annual Statement (not applicable to insurers on the NAIC Quarterly Listing of Alien Insurers), a financial examination report (not applicable to insurers on the NAIC Quarterly Listing of Alien Insurers), and a nonrefundable application fee of $100.

Registration must be renewed by March 1 of each year via the Online Renewal System at https://apps.nd.gov/ins/core/index.aspx (last visited Mar. 22, 2021). The surplus lines insurer's Annual Statement must be filed with the National Association of Insurance Commissioners by March 1 of each year.

A written notification of any corporate changes, such as a name change, address change, merger, or re-domestication, must be sent to the North Dakota Insurance Department in a timely manner. The notification should include updated documents (Service of Process, Affidavit, Data Form) to reflect the change, as applicable.

See department website at https://www.insurance.nd.gov/surplus-lines-application (last visited Mar. 22, 2021) for forms and further details.

Surplus Lines Broker Licensing

North Dakota issues surplus lines producer licenses to both resident and nonresident individuals and business entities. Resident surplus lines agent applicants must first be licensed in North Dakota as an insurance producer for the appropriate lines of authority.

(N.D. CENT. CODE § 26.1-26-17)

A nonresident applicant must hold a surplus lines license in applicant's resident state.

(N.D. CENT. CODE § 26.1-26-20(4))

License applications can be submitted electronically through the National Insurance Producer Registry (NIPR) at www.nipr.com (last visited Mar. 22, 2021). The fee for the surplus lines license is $100. If the applicant is a business entity, it must also designate an individual principal insurance producer who holds a North Dakota surplus lines license and will be responsible for the filing of the annual report and payment of the premium tax.

See department website at https://www.insurance.nd.gov/surplus-lines (last visited Mar. 22, 2021).

Due Care in Selecting Nonadmitted Insurer

Surplus lines insurance to North Dakota home-state insured must be issued by surplus lines insurers that have established satisfactory evidence of good repute and financial integrity, and that otherwise meet the statutory eligibility requirements.

(N.D. CENT. CODE § 26.1-44-03)

Diligent Effort/Diligent Search

North Dakota requires a diligent search to ascertain whether the insurance, indemnity contract, or surety bond can be procured from an admitted insured. The surplus lines insurance producer may rely on a diligent search by a licensed insurance producer or the insured. The surplus lines agent must file an affidavit of diligent search with the commissioner within 60 days of placement.

(N.D. Cent. Code § 45-09-01-03)

The Surplus Lines Certified Diligent Search Statement is available at https://www.insurance.nd.gov/surplus-lines (last visited Sept. 30, 2020). When accessing the site, expand the section titled Quarterly Filings for Insurance Placement, Endorsement, Audit or Cancellation.

The affidavit is not required if the coverage is on North Dakota's export list (N.D. Cent. Code § 45-09-01-04) or if the insured is an exempt commercial purchaser (N.D. Cent. Code § 26.1-44-02).

Export List

North Dakota does maintain an export list. The list is set forth in Appendix I of Article 45-09 of N.D. Administrative Code.

(N.D. Admin. Code § 45-09-01-04)

A presumption exists that a diligent search has been made and that the insurance producer was unable to procure the insurance, indemnity contract, or surety bond desired from an admitted company authorized to do business if the coverage is in one of the categories set out in Appendix I of N.D. Administrative Code ch. 45-09-01.

Exempt Commercial Purchasers

North Carolina has adopted the NRRA (15 U.S.C. § 8201) definition of exempt commercial purchasers. Coverage for these insureds may be exported to the surplus lines market without making a diligent effort to place the coverage with authorized insurers provided (i) the surplus lines broker has disclosed to the exempt commercial purchaser that coverage may or may not be available from an authorized insurer that may provide greater protection with more regulatory oversight, and (ii) such exempt commercial purchaser has subsequently requested such broker, in writing, to procure such policy from an unauthorized insurer.

(N.D. Cent. Code §§ 26.1-44-02, 26.1-44-01-3)

Surplus Lines Broker Filing Requirements

Unless the coverage is on the export list or is issued to a commercial exempt insured, the surplus lines insurance producer must complete and file with the commissioner a surplus lines affidavit confirming such a search has been done within 60 days after placing of any surplus lines insurance.

(N.D. Admin. Code § 45-09-01-03)

Each surplus lines insurance producer must keep a full and true record of each surplus lines insurance contract placed by or through the producer, including a copy of the policy, certificate, cover note, or other evidence of insurance. The surplus lines producer must keep the record of each contract open at all reasonable times to examination by the insurance commissioner for a period of five years following the termination of the contract.

(N.D. Cent. Code § 26.1-44-06)

North Dakota's agent filing requirements are contained in the North Dakota Surplus Lines Systems User Guide available at https://www.insurance.nd.gov/surplus-lines (last visited Oct. 28, 2020).

Notices

North Dakota requires a notice to surplus lines insured in 16-point type on a separate document affixed to the application. The insured must sign and date a copy of the notice to acknowledge receipt. The surplus lines producer must maintain the signed notice in its file for a period of five years from the expiration of the policy. The surplus lines producer must deliver a copy of the signed notice to the insured at the time of delivery of the policy. The copy must be a separate document affixed to the policy.

The mandatory notice must state:

> Notice:
>
> An insurer that is not licensed in North Dakota is issuing the insurance policy that you have applied to purchase. These companies are called "nonadmitted" or "surplus lines" insurers.

The insurer is not subject to the financial solvency regulation and enforcement that applies to licensed insurers in this state.

These insurers generally do not participate in insurance guaranty funds created by state law. These guaranty funds will not pay your claims or protect your assets if the insurer becomes insolvent and is unable to make payments as promised.

Some states maintain lists of approved or eligible surplus lines insurers and surplus lines producers may use only insurers on the lists. Some states issue orders that particular surplus lines insurers cannot be used.

For additional information about the above matters and about the insurer, you should ask questions of your insurance producer or surplus lines producer. You may also contact the North Dakota Insurance Department.

(N.D. CENT. CODE § 26.1-44-05)

Taxes, Stamping Fees, and Other Government-Imposed Charges

If the insured's home state is North Dakota, a surplus lines premium tax of 1.75 percent is assessed on the gross premiums charged, assessments, membership fees, subscriber fees, policy fees, and service fees, less any return premiums. Each surplus lines producer shall pay the premium tax due at the time of filing the annual tax statement.

(N.D. CENT. CODE § 26.1-44-03.1)

Each surplus lines producer shall file with the commissioner no later than March 1st of each year an annual tax statement of all surplus lines insurance transacted during the preceding calendar year. An annual tax statement is not required to be filed if a surplus lines producer has transacted no surplus lines insurance during the preceding calendar year.

(N.D. CENT. CODE § 26.1-44-06.1)

The Surplus Lines Annual Placement Report (SFN 4824) form must be attached to the annual tax statement and can be generated using the North Dakota Insurance Department Surplus Lines application. Producers can also submit tax filings electronically through OPTins (Online Premium Tax for Insurance), a product of the National Association of Insurance Commissioners.

See https://www.insurance.nd.gov/surplus-lines (last visited Nov. 18, 2020).

Producer, Policy, Inspection, and Other Fees

North Dakota surplus lines agents may charge fees other than commissions under certain circumstances. Before rendering the services and accepting any payment, the insurance producer must disclose the fee to the party being charged, and the party being charged must be agree to the charge.

(N.D. CENT. CODE § 26.1-26-04.1)

The agent must also file an affidavit with the commissioner disclosing the services performed and the amount of the charges. The affidavit must be retained by the insurance producer for at least five years. A copy of the signed disclosure must be available to the insurance commissioner for inspection upon request.

See Insurance Producer Disclosure Notice—Fees for Insurance Services (SFN 61674) at https://www.insurance.nd.gov/forms (last visited Dec. 16, 2020).

Industrial Insured Exemption

Transactions involving insurance contracts issued to one or more industrial insureds for which independent procurement tax is paid are exempt from North Dakota surplus lines regulation. An industrial insured is an insured:

a. Which procures the insurance of any risk or risks other than life and annuity contracts by use of the services of a full-time employee acting as an insurance manager or buyer or the services of a regularly and continuously retained qualified insurance consultant;
b. Whose aggregate annual premiums for insurance on all risks total at least $25,000; and
c. Which has at least 25 full-time employees.

(N.D. CENT. CODE § 26.1-02-05-9)

Independent or Direct Procurement Law

"Independently procured insurance" means insurance procured directly by an insured from a nonadmitted insurer.

(N.D. Cent. Code § 26.1-44-01.1 (5))

If the insured's home state is North Dakota, in accordance with subsection 9 of § 26.1-02-05, each insured in North Dakota who independently procures or continues or renews insurance with a nonadmitted insurer on properties, risks, or exposures located or to be performed in whole or in part in this state, other than insurance procured through a surplus lines producer, is subject to the same requirements as apply to a surplus lines producer.

(N.D. Cent. Code § 26.1-44-10)

OHIO

Ohio Department of Insurance
50 W. Town Street, Third Floor, Suite 300
Columbus, OH 43215
(614) 644-2658
http://www.insurance.ohio.gov

Ohio does not have a stamping office.

Nonadmitted Insurer Eligibility

General Information

Ohio has adopted the eligibility requirements set forth in the NRRA (15 U.S.C. § 8201) stating that an insurer shall be considered eligible if the insurer meets the requirements and criteria in §§ 5A(2) and 5C(2)(a) of the Nonadmitted Insurance Model Act adopted by the National Association of Insurance Commissioners, and for an insurer domiciled outside the United States, if the insurer is listed on the Quarterly Listing of Alien Insurers maintained by the International Insurers Department of the National Association of Insurance Commissioners.

(39 Ohio Rev. Code § 3905.33(A))

Nonadmitted Insurer Eligibility List

Ohio does maintain a listing of eligible surplus lines insurers. The list is published online at https://ohioinsurance.force.com /community/s/surpluslinecompanies (last visited July 15, 2020).

Types of Coverage Permitted or Prohibited

General Information

An Ohio surplus lines broker's license permits the person named in the license to negotiate for and obtain insurance, other than life insurance, on property or persons in Ohio from unauthorized insurers.

(39 Ohio Rev. Code § 3905.30(C))

Exempt Transactions

Ocean marine insurance, when placed by licensed agents, is not subject to surplus lines tax and filing requirements.

(39 Ohio Rev. Code § 3905.38(B))

Service of Process

Any act of transacting insurance by any unauthorized insurer constitutes an appointment of the superintendent as attorney of such insurer upon whom may be served all lawful process in any action, suit, or proceeding.

(39 Ohio Rev. Code § 3901.26(A))

Limitations on Actions Involving Judicial Proceedings

Ohio statutes do not set forth any limitations on actions involving judicial proceedings that apply to the lawful transaction of surplus lines business.

Domestic Surplus Lines Insurers

Ohio permits a domestic insurer with at least $15 million minimum capital and surplus to be designated as a domestic surplus lines insurer upon the written approval of the superintendent.

(39 Ohio Rev. Code § 3905.332)

Nonadmitted Insurer Filing Requirements

Ohio statutes do not set forth periodic filing requirements for nonadmitted insurers.

Surplus Lines Broker Licensing

Individuals and business entities may be licensed. To be eligible for a resident surplus lines broker's license, a person must have both a property license and a casualty license. To be eligible for a nonresident surplus lines broker's license, a person must hold an active surplus lines broker license in the person's home state. A nonresident surplus lines broker must also obtain a nonresident license with a property and casualty line of authority in this state if the broker is or will be personally performing the due diligence requirements.

(39 OHIO REV. CODE § 3905.30(B))

To be eligible for a resident surplus lines license, it is further necessary for an individual or business entity to obtain a bond in the amount of $25,000 from an authorized insurer. The bond should be made payable to the State of Ohio (39 Ohio Rev. Code § 3905.35). Resident individual surplus lines applicants must submit to a state and federal criminal background check. The background check requirement, other helpful information, and links to applications and forms are on the Ohio Department of Insurance website at https://insurance.ohio.gov/companies/surplus-lines/resources/surplus-lines (last visited May 6, 2023).

A surplus lines broker's license is $100 annually (39 Ohio Rev. Code § 3905.30(C)) and expires on January 31st in the year after it is issued.

(39 OHIO REV. CODE § 3905.32)

Due Care in Selecting Nonadmitted Insurer

Other than determining that an insurer meets the eligibility requirements, Ohio statutes do not set forth any requirements with regard to the exercise of due care in selecting a nonadmitted insurer.

Diligent Effort/Diligent Search

Except when exempt, a diligent search of the admitted market must be made. An agent must get declinations from at least five of the authorized insurers the agent represents, or as many insurers as the agent represents, that customarily write the kind of insurance required by the insured. If any authorized insurer fails to respond within ten days after the initial contact, the agent may assume the insurer has declined to accept the risk.

(39 Ohio Rev. Code § 3905.33(B)(1–2))

Export List

Ohio does not maintain an list of coverages that may be exported to the surplus lines market without first making a diligent search of licensed insurers.

Exempt Commercial Purchasers

Ohio has adopted the NRRA (15 U.S.C. § 8201) definition of exempt commercial purchasers. Coverage for these insureds may be exported to the surplus lines market without making a diligent effort to place the coverage with authorized insurers provided (1) the surplus lines broker has disclosed to the exempt commercial purchaser that coverage may or may not be available from an authorized insurer that may provide greater protection with more regulatory oversight, and (2) such exempt commercial purchaser has subsequently requested such broker, in writing, to procure such policy from an unauthorized insurer.

(39 Ohio Rev. Code §§ 3905.33(B)(4), 3905.331)

Surplus Lines Broker Filing Requirements

A "Surplus Lines Statement" (affidavit) must be completed for every risk placed in the surplus lines market. The form does not need to be filed but must be kept on file for five years, and a copy of the completed form must be given to the insured and originating agent.

Surplus lines business must be reported using the On-Line Surplus Lines Reporting Application (https://insurance.ohio.gov/about-us/resources/surplus-lines-reporting-app). The application allows you to enter transactions at any time throughout the year. On midnight March 31 the application is locked and you may no longer enter or change any transactions for the preceding year.

See Ohio Department of Insurance website at https://insurance.ohio.gov/about-us/divisions/surplus-lines (last visited Oct. 28, 2020).

Notices

The Ohio Department of Insurance recommends language similar to the following to be prominently placed on the declaration page:

> THE INSURANCE HEREBY EVIDENCED IS WRITTEN BY AN APPROVED NON-LICENSED INSURER IN THE STATE OF OHIO AND IS NOT COVERED IN CASE OF INSOLVENCY BY THE OHIO INSURANCE GUARANTY ASSOCIATION.

This recommended wording, and the required "Surplus Lines Statement" that provides additional notices and must be signed by the insured, can be found on the department website at https://insurance.ohio.gov/companies/surplus-lines/resources/gen-info-surplus-agents-brokers (last visited Nov. 11, 2020).

(39 Ohio Rev. Code § 3905.33(c))

Taxes, Stamping Fees, and Other Government-Imposed Charges

By March 31 of each year taxes are due and the tax rate is 5 percent.

(39 Ohio Rev. Code § 3905.36(B)).

All tax payments should be accompanied by the Surplus Lines Premium Tax Summary Form INS 4001. The check and form are to be mailed to the Office of the Treasurer. Zero premium reports are not required.

See https://insurance.ohio.gov/companies/surplus-lines/resources/gen-info-surplus-agents-brokers (last visited Nov. 18, 2020), which also has a link to Form INS 4001.

The following are exempt from the surplus line tax:

1. An insured otherwise exempt from the payment of premium or franchise taxes under state or federal law;
2. Attorneys-at-law acting on behalf of their clients in the adjustment of claims or losses;
3. Transactions involving policies issued by a captive insurer;
4. Professional or medical liability insurance procured by a hospital organized under Chapter 3701 of the Revised Code;
5. Insurance with an initial policy period of more than three years and that is procured to cover known events related to environmental remediation that occurred prior to the effective date of that insurance;
6. Insurance procured on behalf of an entity that manufactures, packages, and sells, as more than 50 percent of the entity's business, pharmaceutical products for human use where the production, packaging, and sale of such products are subject to regulation by an agency of the United States;
7. A political subdivision or any combination or consortium of two or more political subdivisions.

(39 Ohio Rev. Code § 3905.36(C))

Producer, Policy, Inspection, and Other Fees

An agent may charge a consumer a fee if the fee is disclosed to the consumer in a manner that separately identifies the fee and the premium and the fee is not calculated as a percentage of the premium.

(39 Ohio Rev. Code § 3905.55(A))

Industrial Insured Exemption

Ohio statutes and regulations do not contain an industrial insured exemption with regard to surplus lines insurance.

Independent or Direct Procurement Law

Independent procurement is permitted in Ohio. Details of independent procurement transactions must be filed and a 5 percent premium tax paid, by March 31st of each year.

(39 Ohio Rev. Code § 3905.36(A))

OKLAHOMA

Oklahoma Insurance Department
Five Corporate Plaza
3625 NW 56th, Suite 100
Oklahoma City, OK 73112-4511
(405) 521-2828 (local)
(800) 522-0071 (in state toll free)
http://ok.gov/oid/

Alternate Address:
7645 E. 63rd Street, Suite 102
Tulsa, OK 74133
(918) 295-3700 (local)

Oklahoma does not have a stamping office.

Nonadmitted Insurer Eligibility

Foreign

To be eligible, a surplus lines insurer must meet the requirements of the Unauthorized Insurers and Surplus Lines Insurance Act (36 Okla. Stat. §§ 36-1100, *et seq.*) and have capital and surplus that equals the greater of the minimum capital and surplus requirements under the laws of Oklahoma for nonadmitted insurers, or $15 million. The requirements may be satisfied by an insurer's possessing less than the minimum capital and surplus upon an affirmative finding of acceptability by the insurance commissioner. The finding shall be based upon such factors as quality of management, capital and surplus of any parent company, company underwriting profit and investment income trends, market availability and company record and reputation within the industry. In no event shall the insurance commissioner make an affirmative finding of acceptability when the nonadmitted insurer's capital and surplus is less than $4.5 million.

(36 OKLA. STAT. § 36-1106(1)(a) & (b))

Alien

An alien surplus line insurer is eligible if it is listed on the Quarterly Listing of Alien Insurers maintained by the International Insurers Department of the National Association of Insurance Commissioners.

(36 OKLA. STAT. § 36-1106(1)(c))

Nonadmitted Insurer Eligibility List

Oklahoma maintains a list of eligible nonadmitted insurers at https://www.oid.ok.gov/regulated-entities/surplus-lines/#1584971868535-95f6ab2f-f0ed (last visited July 15, 2020).

Types of Coverage Permitted or Prohibited

Permitted

Under Oklahoma surplus lines insurance law, any property and casualty insurance permitted to be placed through a surplus lines licensee or broker with a nonadmitted insurer eligible to accept such insurance is considered nonadmitted insurance, and this can include independently procured insurance and surplus lines insurance.

(36 OKLA. STAT. § 36-1100.1(6))

Permitted types, classes, or kinds of coverage allowed under Oklahoma surplus lines insurance law are those that are not readily procurable from authorized insurers in Oklahoma.

(36 OKLA. STAT. § 36-1108)

Prohibited

Oklahoma surplus lines insurance law does not apply to reinsurance.

(36 OKLA. STAT. § 36-1119)

Exempt Transactions

The provisions relative to surplus line coverages do not apply to reinsurance.

(36 Okla. Stat. § 36-1119)

Service of Process

Any act of transacting insurance by any unauthorized insurer constitutes an appointment of the commissioner as attorney of such insurer upon whom may be served all lawful process in any action, suit, or proceeding. There are certain exemptions from the service of process provisions in § 1104.

(36 Okla. Stat. § 36-1118)

Limitations on Actions Involving Judicial Proceedings

An insurer that has been served with process pursuant to § 36-1103 shall have the right to appear in and defend the action and employ attorneys and other persons in this state to assist in its defense or settlement.

(36 Okla. Stat. § 36-1103(F))

Domestic Surplus Lines Insurers

Oklahoma permits a domestic insurer with at least $15 million minimum capital and surplus to be designated as a domestic surplus lines insurer upon the written approval of the commissioner.

(36 Okla. Stat. § 36-1101.1)

Nonadmitted Insurer Filing Requirements

Oklahoma statutes do not set forth periodic filing requirements for nonadmitted insurers.

Surplus Lines Broker Licensing

To obtain a surplus lines license, an individual must hold an underlying producer license with property and casualty lines and pay a fee of $100. No separate exam is required for the surplus lines license.

See https://nipr.com/licensing-center/state-requirements/oklahoma-resident-licensing-individual (last visited Sept. 9, 2020).

Business entities may be licensed as surplus lines brokers. The business entity must designate a licensed producer responsible for the business entity's compliance with the insurance laws, rules, and regulations of Oklahoma and pay a fee of $100.

See https://nipr.com/licensing-center/state-requirements/oklahoma-resident-licensing-business (last visited Sept. 9, 2020).

A person licensed as a surplus lines producer in the person's home state may receive a nonresident surplus lines producer license in this state if the person's home state awards nonresident surplus lines license to residents of Oklahoma on the same basis.

(36 Okla. Stat. § 36-1435.9(E))

Due Care in Selecting Nonadmitted Insurer

Insurance may be procured from surplus lines insurers if they meet the eligibility requirements of the statute.

(36 Okla. Stat. § 36-1106)

Diligent Effort/Diligent Search

If insurance required to protect the interest of the insured for the amount of insurance, coverage terms, and solvency requirements of the insured cannot be procured from admitted insurers, after inquiry in the market available to the producer, then insurance may be procured through a licensed surplus lines broker from surplus lines insurers that meet all Oklahoma surplus lines statutory requirements.

(36 Okla. Stat. § 36-1106)

A surplus lines licensee or broker is not required to make a due diligence search to determine whether the full amount or type of insurance can be obtained from admitted insurers when the surplus lines licensee or broker is seeking to procure or place flood insurance with a nonadmitted insurer.

(36 Okla. Stat. § 36-1106.2)

Export List

Oklahoma does not maintain a list of coverages that may be exported to the surplus lines market without first making a diligent search of licensed insurers.

Exempt Commercial Purchasers

Oklahoma has adopted the NRRA (15 U.S.C. § 8201) definition of exempt commercial purchasers. Coverage for these insureds may be exported to the surplus lines market without making a diligent effort to place the coverage with authorized insurers provided (1) the surplus lines broker has disclosed to the exempt commercial purchaser that coverage may or may not be available from an authorized insurer that may provide greater protection with more regulatory oversight, and (2) such exempt commercial purchaser has subsequently requested such broker, in writing, to procure such policy from an unauthorized insurer.

(36 Okla. Stat. § 36-1106.1(A))

Surplus Lines Broker Filing Requirements

After procuring any surplus lines insurance, surplus line brokers shall execute and file reports with the insurance commissioner as required pursuant to § 1107 of title 36 on Form SL-3(a–d). All Forms SL 3 (a–d) shall be retained in the files of the brokers, to support the policy issued thereunder, for a period of not less than three years.

All applications (Form SL-3) shall be completely filled out and verified under oath by the broker submitted for each policy for which approval for issuance is sought; provided, that in the event any group insurance is determined to constitute a surplus line of insurance, a specific method of reporting additional individual certificates issued or cancelled under such group policy shall be agreed upon between the insurance commissioner and the broker concerned.

Each surplus lines licensee or broker licensed or transacting business in Oklahoma shall on or before April 1 of each year file with the insurance commissioner a verified statement of all surplus lines insurance transacted by the broker during the preceding calendar year where Oklahoma is the home state of the insured. The statement shall be on a form prescribed and furnished by the insurance commissioner and shall show such information required to be submitted as established by the insurance commissioner. The information shall be provided to the insurance commissioner until and unless, in the exercise of his or her sole discretion and judgment, the insurance commissioner decides to enter or join the Nonadmitted Insurance Multi-State Agreement or any other multistate agreement or compact with the same function and purpose and other transaction reporting requirements are thereby established.

Also, filings are made using the OPTins system.

See instructions on the department website at https://www.oid.ok.gov/regulated-entities/surplus-lines/ (last visited Oct. 28, 2020).

Notices

Insurance contracts procured as surplus line coverage shall contain in boldface type notification stamped by the surplus lines licensee or broker or surplus lines insurer on the declaration page of the policy that the contracts are not subject to the protection of any guaranty association in the event of liquidation or receivership of the surplus lines insurer. The commissioner is authorized to promulgate rules to establish further disclosure requirements for the purpose of protecting consumers of surplus line coverage.

(36 Okla. Stat. § 36-1109(B))

Taxes, Stamping Fees, and Other Government-Imposed Charges

Where Oklahoma is the home state of the insured, surplus line tax is 6 percent of the total gross premiums. The surplus lines licensee or broker is prohibited from rebating, for any reason, any part of the tax.

Policies sold to federally recognized Indian tribes shall be exempt from the surplus line premium tax to the extent that the insurance commissioner can identify that coverage is for risks that are wholly owned by a tribe and located within Indian Country, as defined in § 1151 of title 18 of the United States Code.

The surplus line premium tax on insurance on motor transit operations conducted between this and other states shall be paid on the total premium charged on all surplus line insurance less the portion of the premium charged for operations in other states taxing the premium of an insured where Oklahoma is the home state; or the premium for operations outside of this state of an insured maintaining its headquarters office outside of this state and branch office in this state.

Flood insurance policies and policies sold to any city or town in Oklahoma, incorporated pursuant to law are exempt from the surplus lines premium tax.

(36 Okla. Stat. § 36-1115)

The Oklahoma Insurance Department (OID) requires Surplus Lines Brokers and all accompanying premium tax payments and each quarterly remittance electronically per 36 O.S. § 350, 36 O.S. § 1115, and per order No. 16-353-PRJ. Effective April 1, 2017, the Oklahoma Insurance Department (OID) requires all Surplus Lines Annual Statements to be filed by electronic format pursuant to 36 O.S. § 350, 36 § 1114, and per order No. 16-353-PRJ. All surplus lines tax filing and payment instructions can be found on the OID website at https://www.oid.ok.gov/regulated-entities/surplus-lines/ (last visited Nov. 18, 2020).

Producer, Policy, Inspection, and Other Fees

Any policy, broker, or service fee charged to the insured is considered to be part of the premium and therefore subject to the surplus lines premium tax.

According to § 365:25-3-12(b)(3) of the Ohio Administrative Code, "Gross Fee" means the total of all fees received by an insurance consultant derived by offering any advice, counsel, opinion, or service with respect to the advantages, disadvantages promised under any policy of insurance that could be issued or delivered in this state.

See "FAQ: SL Broker Quarterly Summary Reports" and "FAQ: Surplus Lines Brokers Premium Tax Annual Reports" at https://www.oid.ok.gov/regulated-entities/surplus-lines/ (last visited Dec. 16, 2020).

Industrial Insured Exemption

Oklahoma statutes and regulations do not contain an industrial insured exemption with regard to surplus lines insurance.

Independent or Direct Procurement Law

Independently procured insurance means insurance procured by an insured directly from a nonadmitted insurer.

(36 Okla. Stat. § 36-1100.1(3))

Where Oklahoma is the home state of the insured, gross premiums charged for independently procured insurance, less any return premiums, are subject to a premium tax at the rate of 6 percent payable to the Oklahoma insurance commissioner, whether the properties, risks, or exposures are located or to be performed inside or outside Oklahoma.

(36 Okla. Stat. § 36-1115(C))

Other information and forms are available in the Direct Placement Entities section of the Oklahoma insurance department website at https://www.oid.ok.gov/regulated-entities/financial/premium-tax/ (last visited Jan. 13, 2021).

OREGON

Insurance Commissioner
Oregon Department of Consumer and Business Services
Division of Financial Regulation
350 Winter Street, NE
Salem, OR 97301-3883
(503) 947-7980
Alternate Address:
P.O. Box 14480
Salem, OR 97309-0405
https://dfr.oregon.gov/Pages/index.aspx
DFR.InsuranceHelp@oregon.gov

Oregon has a stamping office.

Surplus Line Association of Oregon
7360 SW Hunziker Street, Suite 105
Portland, OR 97223-2305
(503) 718-6700
www.oregonsla.org

Nonadmitted Insurer Eligibility

General Information

Surplus line insurers must be authorized by the insurance supervisory official in the insurer's domiciliary jurisdiction to write the kind of insurance to be placed with them by the surplus lines licensee. They must also meet financial requirements. Alien insurers must meet these requirements and maintain in the United States an irrevocable trust fund that adheres to certain capital and duration criteria. They may also be listed on the Quarterly Listing of Alien Insurers maintained by the International

Insurers Department of the National Association of Insurance Commissioners. Groups of insurers must also maintain a trust fund and insurance exchanges must meet capital and surplus requirements.

(OR. REV. STAT. § 735.415)

Nonadmitted Insurer Eligibility List

Oregon does not maintain a nonadmitted insurer eligibility list. Each licensee bears the responsibility for qualifying the surplus line insurer at the time of each placement. The Oregon SLA does, however, maintain a list of insurers that it believes met the financial requirements on the date of their last annual report and will probably not be found ineligible by the state. The list is available at http://www.oregonsla.org/resources/insurer-listing (last visited July 15, 2020).

Alien insurers currently on the National Association of Insurance Commissioner's International Insurers Department's Quarterly Listing of Alien Insurers are automatically eligible in Oregon.

(OR. REV. STAT. § 735.415)

Types of Coverage Permitted or Prohibited

Prohibited

Reinsurance, wet marine and transportation insurance, independently procured insurance, life insurance, and health insurance and annuities cannot be placed through a surplus lines licensee with a nonadmitted insurer.

(OR. REV. STAT. § 731.144)

Exempt Transactions

Oregon law exempts reinsurance and insurers writing wet marine and transportation insurance from the requirement to have a certificate of authority.

(OR. REV. STAT. § 731.374)

Service of Process

Any act of transacting insurance by any unauthorized insurer constitutes an appointment of the secretary of state as attorney of such insurer upon whom may be served all lawful process in any action, suit, or proceeding.

(OR. REV. STAT. § 731.324)

Limitations on Actions Involving Judicial Proceedings

Before an unauthorized insurer files or causes to be filed any pleading, notice, order, or process in any court action or administrative proceeding, such insurer shall post cash, securities, or a bond. However, this shall not be construed to prevent an unauthorized insurer from filing a motion to quash a writ or to set aside service thereof.

(OR. REV. STAT. § 731.328)

When an insurer transacting insurance on an Oregon home state risk under the provisions of ORS 735.400 to 735.495 is sued upon any cause of action, arising under any policy of insurance so issued, the insurer shall have 40 days from the date of the service of the summons and complaint upon the insurance producer in which to plead, answer, or defend any such cause.

(OR. REV. STAT. § 731.490(3))

Domestic Surplus Lines Insurers

Oregon statutes have no provision allowing domestic surplus lines insurers.

Nonadmitted Insurer Filing Requirements

For an insurer to maintain surplus lines eligibility in Oregon, either a surplus lines licensee or the insurer must file the insurer's annual statement by June 30 each year. The annual statement can be filed electronically with the National Association of Insurance Commissioners (NAIC). The insurer also must file a hard copy of the signed jurat page in Oregon as proof of filing.

See https://dfr.oregon.gov/business/reg/insurer/instructions/Pages/surplus.aspx (last visited Sept. 2, 2020).

Surplus Lines Broker Licensing

Resident licensing requirements:
A person may not procure any contract of surplus lines insurance with any nonadmitted insurer for an Oregon home state risk unless the person is licensed under ORS chapter 744 to transact surplus lines insurance. A person may obtain a license to transact surplus lines insurance only if the person is licensed as an insurance producer under ORS chapter 744 to transact property and casualty insurance.

(OR. REV. STAT. § 735.450)

Nonresident licensing requirements:

1. Current resident insurance producer's license in good standing in the applicant's home state;
2. Submission of a request for a nonresident insurance producer license;
3. Payment of fees;
4. Submission of the resident insurance producer license application that the applicant submitted to the applicant's home state or a complete Uniform Application; and
5. Documentation showing that the person's home state grants nonresident insurance producer licenses to residents of Oregon on the same basis.

(OR. REV. STAT. § 744.063)

Due Care in Selecting Nonadmitted Insurer

A surplus lines licensee may not place any coverage with a nonadmitted insurer unless at the time of placement the nonadmitted insurer meets the eligibility requirements in the statute.

(OR. REV. STAT. § 735.415(1))

Diligent Effort/Diligent Search

Oregon requires a diligent search of the admitted market before placement with a nonadmitted insurer. Insurance procured on behalf of exempt commercial purchasers is not subject to the diligent search requirement.

(OR. REV. STAT. § 735.410)

Effective January 1, 2017, it is no longer required that the Diligent Search Statement be filed with the SLA of Oregon. Instead, the filer simply acknowledges that they have received a properly completed and signed Diligent Search Statement from the producer and will retain the Diligent Search Statement for no less than five years following contract termination.

See SLA of Oregon website https://www.oregonsla.org/node/68 (last visited June 7, 2023).

Export List

Oregon does not maintain an list of coverages that may be exported to the surplus lines market without first making a diligent search of licensed insurers.

Exempt Commercial Purchasers

Oregon has adopted a modified version of the NRRA (15 U.S.C. § 8201) definition of exempt commercial purchasers, with some different criteria. Oregon's definition only requires $10 million in net worth, $20 million in annual revenues, and 50 full-time employees. Coverage for these insureds may be exported to the surplus lines market without making a diligent effort to place the coverage with authorized insurers provided (1) the surplus lines broker has disclosed to the exempt commercial purchaser that coverage may or may not be available from an authorized insurer that may provide greater protection with more regulatory oversight, and (2) such exempt commercial purchaser has subsequently requested such broker, in writing, to procure such policy from an unauthorized insurer.

(OR. REV. STAT. § 735.410(2), 735.405(6))

Surplus Lines Broker Filing Requirements

Anyone placing surplus line business on a policy for which Oregon is the "home state" must complete a filing form, file the form, and pay appropriate taxes and fees to the state of Oregon via the Surplus Line Association of Oregon.

Within 90 days after the placing of any surplus lines insurance on an Oregon home state risk, each surplus lines licensee must file with the director of the Department of Consumer and Business Services a statement signed by the licensee regarding the insurance, which must be kept confidential, including the following information:

1. The name and address of the insured;
2. The identity of the insurer or insurers;
3. A description of the subject and location of the risk;
4. The amount of premium charged;
5. Other pertinent information as reasonably required by the director.

(OR. REV. STAT. § 735.425)

The surplus lines licensee must also file a monthly report with the director of the Department of Consumer and Business Services. This report must be filed on or before the end of each month and must contain an account of all surplus lines insurance transacted on Oregon home state risks during the preceding 90 days. Insurance shown on a previous report need not be shown. The report must show the following information:

1. Aggregate amount of gross premium written;
2. Aggregate amount of return premiums;
3. Aggregate amount of tax.

(OR. REV. STAT. § 735.465)

Notices

All surplus lines contracts must bear the name of the licensee and the following legend in bold typeface:

This evidence of insurance was procured and developed under the Oregon Surplus Lines laws. It is not covered by the provisions of ORS 734.510 to 734.710 relating to the Oregon Insurance Guaranty Association. If the insurer issuing this insurance becomes insolvent, the Oregon Insurance Guaranty Association has no obligation to pay claims under this evidence of insurance.

(OR. REV. STAT. § 735.435)

Taxes, Stamping Fees, and Other Government-Imposed Charges

The surplus lines licensee is responsible for paying a surplus lines premium tax equal to 2 percent of the gross amount of premiums received on Oregon home state risks and a fire marshal tax equal to 0.3 percent of the premium or fees charged by the insurer or the insurer's insurance producer and other intermediaries. Taxes are due quarterly on the 45th day following the calendar quarter in which the premium is collected.

(OR. REV. STAT. § 735.470)

An insurance producer shall pay to the director of the Department of Consumer and Business Services a premium tax that is equal to three-fourths of 1 percent of the gross amount of premiums the insurance producer receives for wet marine and transportation insurance that the insurance producer places with unauthorized or nonadmitted insurers if the insured's home state is Oregon. Brokers are prohibited from absorbing or rebating any taxes. The producer must also file with the director of the Department of Consumer and Business Services, in accordance with the director's prescription, a verified report of any Oregon home state risk nonadmitted wet marine and transportation insurance the producer transacted during the previous 90 days and shall accompany the report with payment of the tax due on each transaction.

(OR. REV. STAT. § 735.808)

In addition to the 2.3 percent in taxes, the broker must pay a $15 flat stamping fee for each new or renewal transaction.

The stamping fee is not applicable to endorsements. See http://www.oregonsla.org/resources/tax-calculator (last visited Nov. 18, 2020).

Although not directly addressed in Oregon statutes, federal government entities, state, or federal chartered credit unions and Native American tribes are exempt from surplus line tax as described in notices available on the SLA of Oregon website at http://www.oregonsla.org/publications/other-publications (last visited Nov. 18, 2020).

Producer, Policy, Inspection, and Other Fees

A surplus lines licensee may charge a producer a fee or a combination of a fee and commission. The licensee must obtain written agreement from the producer regarding this fee prior to the binding or issuance of the policy. The licensee, when transacting directly for a prospective insured, may charge the prospective insured a fee or a combination of a fee and commission if the licensee has a written agreement with the prospective insured prior to the binding or issuance of the policy.

(OR. REV. STAT. § 735.455)

Industrial Insured Exemption

Oregon statutes and regulations do not contain an industrial insured exemption with regard to surplus lines insurance.

Independent or Direct Procurement Law

Oregon permits an insured to acquire coverage directly from a nonadmitted insurer provided that the insured files a written report with and pays taxes to the director of the Department of Consumer and Business Services. The report must show the name and address of the insurer, the subject of the insurance, the amount of premium, and additional pertinent information reasonably requested by the director. The taxes must equal the amount that would be imposed on identical insurance premiums for policies acquired through a surplus line intermediary under ORS 735.470.

(OR. REV. STAT. § 735.417)

PENNSYLVANIA

Insurance Commissioner
Pennsylvania Insurance Department
1326 Strawberry Square
Harrisburg, PA 17120
(877) 881-6388
http://www.insurance.pa.gov/Pages/default.aspx

Pennsylvania has a stamping office.

Pennsylvania Surplus Lines Association
180 Sheree Boulevard
Suite 3100
Exton, PA 19341
(610) 594-1340
www.pasla.org

Nonadmitted Insurer Eligibility

General Information

Surplus lines insurers are not licensed but must meet eligibility standards in order to underwrite risks presented by surplus lines producers. Alien insurers listed on the Quarterly Listing of Alien Insurers maintained by the International Insurers Department of the National Association of Insurance Commissioners are considered eligible.

(40 PA. STAT. § 991.1605)

Nonadmitted Insurer Eligibility List

The department maintains a list of eligible surplus lines insurers that includes alien insurers that appear on the Quarterly

Listing of Alien Insurers maintained by the International Insurers Department of the National Association of Insurance Commissioners. A link to the list can be found on the Pennsylvania Surplus Lines Association website at http://pasla.org/eligible_insurers_overview.htm (last visited July 15, 2020). A searchable list is also available on the department's website at https://www.insurance.state.pa.us/dsf/slasearch.html (last visited July 15, 2020).

Types of Coverage Permitted or Prohibited

Prohibited

The definition of surplus lines insurance excludes life insurance and annuities.

(40 PA. STAT. § 991.1602)

Exempt Transactions

Pennsylvania law creates an exemption from the insurer licensing law for certain transactions. In particular, the following risks are considered exempt and may be written by unauthorized insurers without regard to the surplus lines law:

- Insurance on the property and operation of railroads or aircraft engaged in interstate or foreign commerce, and
- Insurance of vessels, crafts or hulls, cargoes, marine builders' risks, marine protection and indemnity, lessees and charterers' liability, or other risks including strikes and war risks commonly insured under ocean or wet marine forms of policies.

(40 PA. STAT. § 46(8))

In addition, wet marine and transportation insurance is excluded from the definition of surplus lines insurance and therefore are not subject to the surplus lines law.

(40 PA. STAT. § 991.1602)

Service of Process

Pennsylvania regulations require that all surplus lines contracts contain a clause subjecting the insurer to jurisdiction of U.S. courts and naming an agent for service of process. The clause must also state that process may be served on the commissioner.

(31 Pa. Code § 124.4(c))

Limitations on Actions Involving Judicial Proceedings

Before any company, association, or exchange of another state or foreign government shall file or cause to be filed any pleading in any action, suit, or proceeding instituted against it under this section, such company, association, or exchange shall, if the court in its discretion shall require, deposit with the prothonotary of the court in which such action, suit, or proceeding is pending, cash or securities, or file with such prothonotary or clerk a bond with good and sufficient sureties to be approved by the court. Said deposit or bond shall be in such amount as the court in its sole discretion, after taking into account the financial condition of such company, association, or exchange and such other factors as the court considers pertinent, may deem sufficient to secure the payment of any final judgment that may be rendered in such action, suit, or proceeding.

(40 Pa. Stat. Ann. § 46)

Domestic Surplus Lines Insurers

Pennsylvania statutes have no provision allowing domestic surplus lines insurers.

Nonadmitted Insurer Filing Requirements

Surplus lines insurers are required to file a financial statement with the department on an annual basis.

(31 Pa. Code § 124.10(b))

Surplus Lines Broker Licensing

In order to obtain surplus lines authority, a producer must first obtain a Pennsylvania property and casualty producer license. Business entities must be separately licensed and must designate an officer or partner licensed as a producer to be responsible for compliance with all reporting and recordkeeping requirements.
(40 PA. STAT. § 991.1615)

Due Care in Selecting Nonadmitted Insurer

No surplus lines licensee shall place any coverage with a nonadmitted insurer unless it meets the eligibility requirements.
(40 PA. STAT. § 991.1605)

Diligent Effort/Diligent Search

In order to export a risk to the surplus lines market, the surplus lines producer must first conduct a diligent search and attempt to procure the coverage from authorized insurers (40 Pa. Stat. § 991.1604). In Pennsylvania the diligent search requirement is fulfilled by obtaining declinations from three insurers licensed in Pennsylvania to transact the class of insurance being procured.
(31 PA. CODE § 124.5(1))

Export List

The insurance commissioner maintains an export list of insurance coverages for which the full amount or kind of insurance cannot be obtained from admitted insurers. A diligent search is not required for placement of these risks.
(31 PA. CODE § 124.6)
The export list is available at http://www.pabulletin.com/secure/data/vol47/47-19/837.html (last visited Oct. 7, 2020).

Exempt Commercial Purchasers

Pennsylvania has adopted the NRRA (15 U.S.C. § 8201) definition of exempt commercial purchasers. Coverage for these insureds may be exported to the surplus lines market without making a diligent effort to place the coverage with authorized insurers provided (1) the surplus lines broker has disclosed to the exempt commercial purchaser that coverage may or may not be available from an authorized insurer that may provide greater protection with more regulatory oversight, and (2) such exempt commercial purchaser has subsequently requested such broker, in writing, to procure such policy from an unauthorized insurer.

(40 Pa. Stat. § 991.1610)

The surplus lines producer must report the transaction to the department.

(31 Pa. Code § 124.11)

Surplus Lines Broker Filing Requirements

Within 30 days of placement, the writing producer must execute and forward to the surplus lines producer a written statement declaring that (1) a diligent search was conducted, and (2) the insured was provided with the required disclosure notice (see notice requirement in the next section). Surplus lines producers must file an affidavit with regard to each policy placed with the department within 45 days.

(40 Pa. Stat. § 991.1609(a))

Surplus lines brokers must file a monthly transactional report with the department within 30 days of the end of the month.

(40 Pa. Stat. § 991.1620)

A premium tax report and payment must be filed on an annual basis with the Department of Revenue and a copy of the report must be filed with the department.

(40 Pa. Stat. § 991.1621)

In the event that a portion of a risk is permissibly placed with an unauthorized insurer that is not an eligible surplus lines insurer, the surplus lines producer must make a filing specifying the amount and percentage placed, along with a full explanation of why the risk could not be placed with admitted or eligible surplus lines insurers and naming the nonadmitted insurer with which placement was made.

(40 Pa. Stat. § 991.1606)

Notices

At the time of quotation, the surplus lines producer must present to the insured or to the writing producer written notice, prominently printed on the first page of the quotation, that the insurance or a portion thereof involves placement with nonadmitted insurers. The surplus lines producer must, either directly or through the writing producer, give notice to the insured that:

1. The insurer with which the licensee places the insurance is not licensed by the department and is subject to its limited regulation; and
2. in the event of the insolvency of an eligible surplus lines insurer, losses will not be paid by the Pennsylvania Property and Casualty Insurance Guaranty Association.

(40 PA. STAT. § 991.1608)

Every evidence of insurance negotiated, placed, or procured by the surplus lines licensee must bear the name of the surplus lines producer and the following legend in ten-point type:

> The insurer which has issued this insurance is not licensed by the Pennsylvania Insurance Department and is subject to limited regulation. This insurance is NOT covered by the Pennsylvania Property and Casualty Insurance Guaranty Association.

(40 PA. STAT. § 991.1612)

Taxes, Stamping Fees, and Other Government-Imposed Charges

Surplus lines premiums are subject to a tax of 3 percent of gross premiums less any returns. There is also a stamping fee of 0.5 percent of gross premium. A premium tax report and payment must be filed on an annual basis with the Department of Revenue and a copy of the report must be filed with the department.

(40 PA. STAT. § 991.1621)

Producer, Policy, Inspection, and Other Fees

A licensee may charge a fee in addition to a commission to a person for the sale, solicitation, or negotiation of a contract of insurance for commercial business. The fee charged by the licensee shall be disclosed in advance in writing to the person and shall be reasonable in relationship to the services provided. No insurance producer shall charge a fee for the completion of an application for a contract of insurance.

(40 PA. STAT. § 310.74)

Industrial Insured Exemption

Pennsylvania permits an insured that meets the definition of an industrial insured to acquire insurance coverage directly from an insurer not authorized to do an insurance business in the state. Industrial insured is defined as an insured:

1. who procures the insurance of any risk or risks by use of the services of a full-time employee acting as an insurance manager or buyer or the services of a regularly and continuously retained qualified insurance consultant; and
2. whose aggregate annual premiums for insurance on all risks total at least $25,000; and who has a least 25 full-time employees.

(40 PA. STAT. § 46(e)(6))

Independent or Direct Procurement Law

Pennsylvania permits an insured to acquire insurance coverage directly from an insurer not authorized to do an insurance business in the state.

(40 PA. STAT. § 991.1602)

The insured must report the transaction on forms prescribed by the Department of Revenue and pay premium tax at the rate of 3 percent within 30 days from the last day of the month in which the insurance was independently procured, continued, or renewed. The report must contain all information that would be required of a surplus lines producer.

(40 Pa. Stat. § 991.1622)

RHODE ISLAND

Department of Business Regulation—Insurance Division
1511 Pontiac Avenue
Cranston, RI 02920
(401) 462-9500
https://dbr.ri.gov/insurance-banking-securities-and-charitable-organizations/insurance

Rhode Island does not have a stamping office.

Nonadmitted Insurer Eligibility

Foreign

To be eligible, a foreign surplus lines insurer must be authorized to write the type of insurance in its domiciliary jurisdiction; must have established satisfactory evidence of good repute and financial integrity; and must have capital and surplus that equals the greater of the minimum capital and surplus requirements under the law of Rhode Island, or $15 million.

(R.I. GEN. LAWS § 27-3-40)

Alien

To be eligible, an alien surplus lines insurer must be authorized to write the type of insurance in its domiciliary jurisdiction; must have established satisfactory evidence of good repute and financial integrity; and must be listed on the Quarterly Listing of Alien Insurers maintained by the International Insurers Department of the National Association of Insurance Commissioners.

(R.I. GEN. LAWS § 27-3-40)

Nonadmitted Insurer Eligibility List

Rhode Island maintains a list of eligible surplus lines insurers (foreign companies only), which is available at https://dbr.ri.gov/insurance-banking-securities-and-charitable-organizations/insurance/insurance-companies/licensed (last visited May 7, 2023).

Types of Coverage Permitted or Prohibited

General Information

Surplus lines insurers may generally provide insurance coverage except for life and health and accident.

(R.I. Gen. Laws § 27-3-38(a))

Prohibited

The surplus lines laws do not apply to life and health and accident, as noted in § 27-3-38(a), and surplus lines brokers may not place insurance in those lines in the surplus market. However, for disability insurance with a benefit limit in excess of a benefit limit available from an admitted insurer, a broker may obtain insurance from the surplus market.

(R.I. Gen. Laws § 27-3-38.3)

Exempt Transactions

Rhode Island statutes do not set forth any transactions exempt from surplus lines laws.

Service of Process

Before writing coverage for any unauthorized insurer, a licensed broker in Rhode Island must ensure that such insurer has previously, in writing, appointed the broker as an agent for the acceptance of service of process, or that the unauthorized insurer has designated a Rhode Island representative as an agent for the service of process.

(R.I. GEN. LAWS § 27-3-41)

Limitations on Actions Involving Judicial Proceedings

Rhode Island statutes do not set forth any limitations on actions involving judicial proceedings that apply to the lawful transaction of surplus lines business.

Domestic Surplus Lines Insurers

Rhode Island statutes have no provision allowing domestic surplus lines insurers.

Nonadmitted Insurer Filing Requirements

There are some filing requirements for surplus line insurers regarding professional liability for licensed healthcare professionals and facilities (due March 1) and professional liability claims settlement for licensed healthcare professionals and facilities (due 30 days after notice of the claim, settlement, judgment or arbitration award).

See Department of Business Regulation website at https://dbr.ri.gov/insurance-banking-securities-and-charitable-organizations/insurance/insurance-companies (last visited May 7, 2023) and scroll down to "Annual/Quarterly Statement Filing Instructions" for Property and Casualty Insurers.

Annual renewal invoices are mailed to surplus lines insurers March 1 of each year.

See Department of Business Regulation website at https://dbr.ri.gov/insurance-banking-securities-and-charitable-organizations/insurance/insurance-companies (last visited May 7, 2023), click on "Initial and Renewal Licensing" and scroll down to "Surplus Lines Insurer Instructions."

Surplus Lines Broker Licensing

To obtain a surplus lines broker license, residents of this state must hold a property and casualty insurance producer license and submit an application.

A Rhode Island resident business entity acting as a surplus line broker may elect to obtain a surplus line broker license. Application shall be made using the uniform business entity application and the business entity must pay the appropriate fees and designate a licensed surplus line broker responsible for the business entity's compliance with the insurance laws and rules of this state.

(R.I. Gen. Laws § 27-3-38)

Rhode Island participates in the National Insurance Producer Registry (NIPR) with respect to broker licensing and payment of applicable fees.

See https://www.nipr.com (last visited Sept. 9, 2020).

Due Care in Selecting Nonadmitted Insurer

Surplus lines insurance may be placed by a surplus lines broker if the insurer has established satisfactory evidence of good repute and financial integrity and otherwise meets he eligibility requirements in the statute.

(R.I. Gen. Laws § 27-3-40)

Diligent Effort/Diligent Search

For all policies subject to Rhode Island law, affidavits must be executed setting forth facts showing that the insured or a Rhode Island producer were unable, after diligent effort, to procure from no less than three authorized insurers the full amount of insurance required to protect the property owned or controlled by the insured or the risks insured. Such affidavit is not required when insuring the following interest: amusement parks and devices, environmental improvement and/or remediation sites, vacant property or property under renovation, demolition operations, event cancellation due to weather, railroad liability,

discontinued products, fireworks and pyrotechnics, warehouseman's legal liability, excess property coverage, and contingent liability
(R.I. GEN. LAWS § 27-3-38(c))

Export List

Rhode Island does not maintain a list of coverages that may be exported to the surplus lines market without first making a diligent search of licensed insurers.

Exempt Commercial Purchasers

Rhode Island has adopted the NRRA (15 U.S.C. § 8201) definition of exempt commercial purchasers. Coverage for these insureds may be exported to the surplus lines market without making a diligent effort to place the coverage with authorized insurers provided (1) the surplus lines broker has disclosed to the exempt commercial purchaser that coverage may or may not be available from an authorized insurer that may provide greater protection with more regulatory oversight, and (2) such exempt commercial purchaser has subsequently requested such broker, in writing, to procure such policy from an unauthorized insurer.

(R.I. GEN. LAWS § 27-3-38(c))

Surplus Lines Broker Filing Requirements

A surplus lines licensee must file a yearly report with the insurance commissioner on a form prescribed by the insurance commissioner showing the business procured under the surplus line license for the preceding calendar year, and the report shall be due annually on or before April 1.

(R.I. GEN. LAWS § 27-3-38(d))

Notices

The Rhode Island statutes and regulations do not address disclosure or notice requirements for placement of surplus lines coverage.

Taxes, Stamping Fees, and Other Government-Imposed Charges

The Rhode Island tax rate is 4 percent on the gross premiums charged the insured by the insurers, less the amount of premiums returned to the insured.

(R.I. GEN. LAWS § 27-3-38(e))

Producer, Policy, Inspection, and Other Fees

Brokers may charge fees in addition to commissions only when such fees are not included in premium, provided that such fees are reasonable and appropriate in order to cover underwriting expenses that are unique to a surplus lines agency. Such fees must be fully disclosed in detail to the insured, whether directly or through another licensed producer, in writing prior to the sale. Documentation evidencing the disclosure of fees must be retained by the broker or licensed producer for a period of three years following the expiration of the policy sold. The department may, at the expense of the broker, examine the operations of a broker to determine that fees charged are reasonable and appropriate for the services performed or the expenses incurred.

(230 R.I CODE R. 20-50-1.5(I))

According to the Division of Taxation, carrier/broker/inspection fees are not taxable.

See https://www.tax.ri.gov/guidance/notices/ (last visited May 7, 2023). Click on "2016 Notices" to expand the section. Then scroll down to "Notice 2016-09 - Guide for surplus lines" and see the applicable frequently asked question on page 16.

Industrial Insured Exemption

Rhode Island statutes and regulations do not contain an industrial insured exemption with regard to surplus lines insurance.

Independent or Direct Procurement Law

Each insured who procures or continues or renews insurance with an insurer not licensed to do an insurance business in Rhode Island, other than insurance procured through a surplus lines licensee, file a written report within 30 days of such procurement with the tax administrator showing the name and address of the insured or insured's, name and address of the insurer, the subject of the insurance, a general description of the coverage, the amount of premium currently charged, and additional pertinent information reasonably requested by the tax administrator. The Rhode Island independent procurement tax rate is 4 percent on the gross premiums charged the insured by the insurers, less the amount of premiums returned to the insured.

(R.I. Gen. Laws § 27-3-38.1)

SOUTH CAROLINA

South Carolina Department of Insurance
P.O. Box 100105
Columbia, SC 29202
(803) 737-6160
https://doi.sc.gov/

South Carolina does not have a stamping office.

Nonadmitted Insurer Eligibility

Foreign

A nonadmitted insurer may be approved as an eligible surplus lines insurer to write certain risks located in the state if one or more insurers licensed in this state have declined those risks, in circumstances where the insurer:

a. Is licensed in its domiciliary state or jurisdiction; and
b. Meets at least the minimum capital and surplus requirements of this state.

(S.C. Code § 38-45-90)

Form 1000 and Form 1027 SL are required with the application.

See https://www.doi.sc.gov/473/Company-Licensing (last visited July 15, 2020).

Alien

A non-U.S. insurer is considered eligible to write insurance on an unauthorized basis in South Carolina if the insurance broker placing the insurance meets the requirements of § 38-45-90.

According to the website of the Department of Insurance, a nonadmitted insurer must be listed on the Quarterly Listing of Alien Insurers maintained by the International Insurers

Department of the National Association of Insurance Commissioners. Also, once approved to be added to the Quarterly Listing of Alien Insurers, it must remain on the list. Finally, an application is required that must include a description of the business to be written in South Carolina and the names of the surplus lines brokers that the alien insurer intends to have place the business. Form 1000 and Form 1027 SL are required with the application.

See https://www.doi.sc.gov/473/Company-Licensing (last visited July 15, 2020).

Nonadmitted Insurer Eligibility List

South Carolina maintains a list of eligible surplus lines insurers online at https://doi.sc.gov/581/Company-Information (last visited July 15, 2020). When accessing the site, scroll to "List of Approved Eligible Surplus Lines Insurers."

Types of Coverage Permitted or Prohibited

General Information

"Surplus lines insurance" means any property and casualty insurance permitted to be placed directly or through a surplus lines broker, or an insurance producer as provided in sub-item (b)(ii), with a surplus lines insurer eligible to accept the insurance as defined in § 38-1-20(56).

(S.C. Code § 38-45-10(10)).

Permitted

Excess and stop-loss insurance coverage upon group life, accident, and health insurance or upon a self-insured's life, accident, and health benefits program, disability insurance in excess of any benefit limit available from an admitted insurer, and international major medical insurance may be approved as surplus lines insurance.

(S.C. Code § 38-1-20(56))

Prohibited

"Surplus lines insurance" means insurance in this state of risks located or to be performed in this state, permitted to be placed through a licensed broker, or a licensed broker as provided in § 38-45-10(8)(b)(ii), with a nonadmitted insurer eligible to accept the insurance, other than reinsurance, wet marine, and transportation insurance; insurance independently procured; and life and health insurance and annuities.

(S.C. CODE § 38-1-10(56))

In addition, workers' compensation forms shall be approved by the director.

(S.C. CODE § 42-5-60)

Exempt Transactions

Surplus lines producers may procure the following kinds of insurance from eligible surplus lines insurers without otherwise adhering to the surplus lines procedures:

a. Wet marine and transportation insurance; and
b. Insurance on subjects located, resident, or to be performed wholly outside of South Carolina.

(S.C. CODE § 38-25-150(3), (7))

Service of Process

A nonadmitted insurer must appoint the director as agent for service of process.

(S.C. CODE § 38-45-170)

Limitations on Actions Involving Judicial Proceedings

An unauthorized insurer is not permitted to maintain any action, suit, or proceeding in this state to enforce a right, claim, or demand arising out of the transaction of insurance business until the insurer has obtained a certificate of authority to transact insurance business in this state. The unauthorized insurer may maintain an action, suit, or proceeding in connection with its investments in this state or in connection with a contract issued by it at a time when it was authorized to do business in the state where the contract was issued. This section does not prevent the insurer from defending an action in the courts of this state. The failure of an insurer transacting insurance business in this state to obtain a certificate of authority does not impair the validity of any act or contract of the insurer. This section does not apply to an eligible surplus lines insurer that maintains the deposit required by § 38-9-80 or that has on file with the department a surety bond issued by an admitted insurer in an amount determined by the director or his designee to be sufficient to meet the security requirements of § 38-9-80. Before an eligible surplus lines insurer files or causes to be filed any action, suit, or proceeding in this state to enforce a right, claim, or demand arising out of the transaction of insurance, it shall produce evidence that the security deposit is presently on file or that the required surety bond is then in force and effect.

(S.C. Code § 38-25-540)

Domestic Surplus Lines Insurers

South Carolina statutes have no provision allowing domestic surplus lines insurers.

Nonadmitted Insurer Filing Requirements

South Carolina statutes do not set forth periodic filing requirements for nonadmitted insurers.

Surplus Lines Broker Licensing

A resident property and casualty-licensed insurance producer may be licensed as an insurance broker if the following requirements are met:

1. Licensure of the resident as an insurance producer for the same lines of insurance for which he proposes to apply as a broker of the state;
2. Successfully passed the South Carolina broker licensing examination;
3. Payment of a biennial license fee of $200, which is earned fully when received, not refundable; and
4. Filing of a bond with the department in a form approved by the attorney general in favor of South Carolina of $10,000 executed by a corporate surety licensed to transact surety insurance in the state and personally countersigned by a licensed resident agent of the surety.

(S.C. Code § 38-45-20)

A nonresident may be licensed as an insurance broker if the following requirements are met:

1. Filing an application on a form prescribed by the director or his designee; and
2. Paying a biennial license fee of $200 fully earned when received, not refundable.

(S.C. Code § 38-45-30)

Due Care in Selecting Nonadmitted Insurer

A duly licensed broker may place business with an eligible surplus lines insurer and must exercise due care in the placing of surplus lines insurance.

(S.C. Code § 38-45-90(A))

Diligent Effort/Diligent Search

An insurance broker shall exercise due care in the placing of surplus lines insurance.

(S.C. Code § 38-45-90)

When filing with the Department of Insurance, brokers must provide the complete name(s) of at least one, but not more than three, insurers declining to write the indicated coverage for an insured.

See Surplus Line Broker Tax Filing Instructions at https://www.doi.sc.gov/979/Premium-Taxes (last visited Sept. 30, 2020).

Export List

South Carolina does not maintain a list of coverages that may be exported to the surplus lines market without first making a diligent search of licensed insurers.

Exempt Commercial Purchasers

South Carolina has adopted the NRRA (15 U.S.C. § 8201) definition of exempt commercial purchasers. Coverage for these insureds may be exported to the surplus lines market without making a diligent effort to place the coverage with authorized insurers provided (1) the surplus lines broker has disclosed to the exempt commercial purchaser that coverage may or may not be available from an authorized insurer that may provide greater protection with more regulatory oversight, and (2) such exempt commercial purchaser has subsequently requested such broker, in writing, to procure such policy from an unauthorized insurer.

(S.C. Code § 38-45-90(B))

Surplus Lines Broker Filing Requirements

All brokers doing insurance business in the state shall make and keep a record of the business done by them, showing the number, date, term, amount insured, premiums, and the person to whom issued of every policy or certificate of renewal. The information from these records must be furnished to the director or his designee on demand, and the original books or records are open to the inspection of the director or his designee on demand. These records must be kept for a minimum of five years.

(S.C. Code § 38-45-80)

In respect to placements with eligible surplus lines insurers, the director or his designee may require the broker to submit, on behalf of the insurer, documents necessary to satisfy him that the insurer is licensed in its domiciliary state, that it meets at least the minimum capital and surplus requirements of South Carolina, and that its operation is not hazardous to the policyholders. Each broker transacting business in South Carolina during a calendar year shall file annually with the department within 30 days after December 31st a detailed report of this business. The report must be in the form prescribed. The broker's books, papers, and accounts must be open at all times to inspection.

(S.C. CODE § 38-45-90)

Notices

Surplus lines policies in South Carolina must contain the following disclosure statement:

> This company has been approved by the director or his designee of the South Carolina Department of Insurance to write business in this State as an eligible surplus lines insurer, but it is not afforded guaranty fund protection.

(S.C. CODE § 38-45-110)

Taxes, Stamping Fees, and Other Government-Imposed Charges

A premium tax may also be placed on surplus lines, which is defined as:

> with respect to surplus lines or independently procured insurance coverage, any tax, fee, assessment, or other charge imposed by a governmental entity directly or indirectly based on any payment made as consideration for an insurance contract, including premium deposits, assessments, registration fees, and any other compensation given in consideration for a contract of insurance.

Every licensed surplus lines broker is subject to a broker's premium tax rate of 6 percent. The rate is composed of a 4 percent state broker's premium tax and a 2 percent municipal broker's premium tax.

(S.C. CODE § 38-45(12))

Producer, Policy, Inspection, and Other Fees

Premium tax for surplus lines or independently procured insurance coverage is based on any payment made as consideration for an insurance contract, including premium deposits, assessments, registration fees, and any other compensation given in consideration for a contract of insurance.

(S.C. CODE § 38-45-10(12))

Industrial Insured Exemption

South Carolina permits an insured that meets the definition of an industrial insured to acquire insurance coverage directly from an insurer not authorized to do an insurance business in the state. An industrial insured means an insured

1. Which procures insurance by use of the services of a full-time employee acting as a risk manager or insurance manager or utilizing the services of a regularly and continuously qualified insurance consultant;
2. Whose aggregate annual premiums for insurance on all risks total at least $25,000; and
3. Which has at least 25 full-time employees.

(S.C. CODE § 38-25-150(8))

Independent or Direct Procurement Law

South Carolina statutes and regulations do not contain provisions addressing independently procured insurance.

SOUTH DAKOTA

South Dakota Department of Labor & Regulation—Division of Insurance
124 S. Euclid Avenue
2nd Floor
Pierre, SD 57501
(605) 773-3563
https://dlr.sd.gov/insurance/
sdinsurance@state.sd.us

South Dakota does not have a stamping office.

Nonadmitted Insurer Eligibility

General Information

Surplus lines insurance may be placed by a licensee in South Dakota where the insurer is authorized to write the type of insurance in its domiciliary jurisdiction and either meets criteria established through a multi-state agreement or meets one of the following criteria:

1. Has capital and surplus or its equivalent under the laws of its domiciliary jurisdiction that equals the greater of the minimum capital and surplus requirements under South Dakota statute § 58-6-23 or $15 million dollars; or
2. The insurer is a nonadmitted insurer domiciled outside the United States and appears on the Quarterly Listing of Alien Insurers maintained by the International Insurers Department of the National Association of Insurance Commissioners.

These requirements may be satisfied by the insurer's possessing less than the minimum capital and surplus upon an affirmative finding of acceptability by the director. The finding shall be based upon such factors as quality of management and capital and surplus of a parent company, but in no event may the director make a finding of acceptability if the insurer's capital and surplus is less than $4.5 million.

(S.D. CODIFIED LAWS § 58-32-22)

Nonadmitted Insurer Eligibility List

South Dakota does not maintain a list of eligible surplus lines insurers.

See https://dlr.sd.gov/insurance/ (last visited Dec. 9, 2020) and search for surplus lines insurer packet.

Types of Coverage Permitted or Prohibited

General Information

There are no prohibited coverages under South Dakota law.

Exempt Transactions

The provisions of the surplus lines law do not apply to life and health insurance, annuities, or reinsurance. In addition, the following coverages are not prohibited when the export requirements of the surplus lines law are met:

1. Disability insurance that has a benefit limit in excess of any benefit limit available from an admitted insurer;
2. Health insurance for an individual traveling or temporarily living outside the United States for health care costs incurred abroad.

(S.D. CODIFIED LAWS § 58-32-4)

Service of Process

Service of process against an unauthorized insurer may be made by service upon the director in accordance with South Dakota law applicable to service of process, by which the insurer must appoint the director as agent for service of process, on a form designated and furnished by the director. The director shall mail a copy of the process served to the person designated by the insurer for the purpose, by prepaid, registered, or certified mail by return receipt requested.

(S.D. Codified Laws §§ 58-6-39, 58-32-37)

Limitations on Actions Involving Judicial Proceedings

Before any unauthorized foreign or alien insurer shall file or cause to be filed any pleading in any action, suit, or proceeding instituted against it, such unauthorized insurer shall in addition to any other requirement that may be imposed by law either:

1. Deposit with the clerk of the court in which such action, suit, or proceeding is pending cash or securities or file with such clerk a bond with good and sufficient sureties, to be approved by the court, in an amount to be fixed by the court sufficient to secure the payment of any final judgment that may be rendered in such action; provided, however, that the court may in its discretion make an order dispensing with such deposit or bond where the insurer makes a showing satisfactory to such court that it maintains in a state of the United States funds or securities, in trust or otherwise, sufficient and available to satisfy any final judgment that may be entered in such action, suit, or proceedings; or
2. Procure a certificate of authority to transact the business of insurance in this state.

(S.D. Codified Laws § 58-8-13)

However, nothing in § 58-8-13 is to be construed to prevent an unauthorized foreign or alien insurer from filing a motion to quash any process or to set aside service thereof made in the manner provided in §§ 58-8-8 to 58-8-10, inclusive, on the ground either (1) that such unauthorized insurer has not done any of the acts enumerated in § 58-8-7; or (2) that the person on whom service was made pursuant to § 58-8-10 was not doing any of the acts therein enumerated.

(S.D. Codified Laws § 58-8-14)

Domestic Surplus Lines Insurers

South Dakota statutes have no provision allowing domestic surplus lines insurers.

Nonadmitted Insurer Filing Requirements

South Dakota statutes do not set forth periodic filing requirements for nonadmitted insurers. However, the Division of Insurance website lists the following requirements:

1. Surplus lines insurer business written and premium tax report
2. Spreadsheet of all policies placed showing the name and address of all South Dakota licensed surplus line brokers responsible for placing the direct business written on South Dakota resident risks, the name and address of the insured, date effective, policy number, and amount of the premium
3. Schedule T
4. South Dakota state page

See https://dlr.sd.gov/insurance/surplus_lines.aspx (last visited Dec. 9, 2020).

Surplus Lines Broker Licensing

Any individual who is licensed in this state as an insurance producer and who is determined by the director to be competent and trustworthy with respect to the handling of surplus lines may be licensed as a surplus line broker. No individual is required to be licensed pursuant to this chapter as a surplus lines broker if the selling, soliciting, or negotiating of surplus lines insurance takes place in an insured's home state and the home state of the insured is a state other than South Dakota.

(S.D. Codified Laws § 58-32-7)

Application for license as a surplus lines broker shall be made to the director on forms furnished by the director. The license fee shall be as specified in § 58-2-29.

(S.D. Codified Laws § 58-32-8)

A nonresident original insurance producer license is $30.

(S.D. Codified Laws § 58-2-29(e)(i))

Nonresident producers should complete a licensing application via Sircon (Vertafore), accessed at https://www.sircon.com, or the National Association of Insurance Commissioners' National Insurance Producer Registry (NIPR), accessed at https://nipr.com. The fee of $30 and applicable service fee will be due at the time an electronic application is submitted.

See https://dlr.sd.gov/insurance/producers/forms.aspx (last visited May 7, 2023).

Within 30 days of issuance of a license as a resident surplus line broker and before procuring any insurance coverage for an insured, the broker shall file with the director, and thereafter for as long as the license remains in effect the broker shall keep in force, a bond in favor of the state of South Dakota in the penal sum of $2,000 dollars with an authorized corporate surety approved by the director. The bond shall be conditioned upon the broker conducting business under the license in accordance with the provisions of this chapter and promptly remitting the taxes pursuant to §§ 58-32-44 and 58-32-45. No such bond may be terminated unless at least 30 days' prior written notice of the termination is given to the broker and filed with the director.

(S.D. Codified Laws § 58-32-10.1)

Due Care in Selecting Nonadmitted Insurer

Surplus lines insurance may be placed by a surplus lines licensee if the insurer is authorized to write the type of insurance in its domiciliary jurisdiction and meets the eligibility criteria set forth in the statute.

(S.D. Codified Laws § 58-32-22)

Diligent Effort/Diligent Search

If certain insurance coverages cannot be procured from authorized insurers, the coverages, hereinafter designated, surplus lines, may be procured from unauthorized insurers, subject to the conditions set forth in S.D. Codified Laws §§ 58-32-17 to 58-32-19, inclusive.

(S.D. Codified Laws § 58-32-16)

The surplus lines insurer registration packet on the website of the department of insurance explains that the onus is on the surplus line broker to confirm that the nonadmitted company is financially solvent and meets the eligibility requirements of S.D. Codified Laws § 58-32-22.

See https://dlr.sd.gov/insurance/surplus_lines.aspx (last visited May 7, 2023).

Export List

South Dakota does/not maintain a list of coverages that may be exported to the surplus lines market. Insurance must not be exported pursuant to § 58-32-16 if there is coverage readily available from an authorized insurer, unless the authorized insurer quotes a premium or terms not competitive with the premium or terms quoted by an unauthorized insurer. If one portion of the risk is acceptable to an authorized insurer, but another portion of the same risk is not acceptable, the entire coverage may be placed with an eligible unauthorized insurer, if it can be shown that an eligible unauthorized insurer will accept the entire coverage but not the rejected portion alone.

(S.D. Codified Laws § 58-32-18)

Exempt Commercial Purchasers

For the purposes of §§ 58-24-68 to 58-24-74, inclusive, the term "exempt commercial policyholder" means any person who applies for or procures any kind of property casualty insurance, except title or workers' compensation insurance, through the use of a risk manager employed or retained by such person, and meets at least two of the following qualifications:

1. Has purchased the insurance with aggregate premiums in the sum of at least $100,000 during the most recently completed calendar year;
2. Has a net worth of at least $10 million as reported in the policyholder's most recently issued financial statement, reviewed or audited by an independent certified public accountant;
3. Has annual net revenues or net sales of at least $10 million as reported in the policyholder's most recently issued financial statement, reviewed or audited by an independent certified public accountant;
4. Employs at least 100 full-time employees, either individually or, if the policyholder is a member of an affiliated group, collectively with all members of the affiliated group;
5. Has, if the policyholder is a nonprofit organization, an annual operating budget of at least $2.5 million for the most recently completed calendar or fiscal year, whichever applies;
6. Has, if the policyholder is a public entity, an operating budget of at least $10 million for the most recently completed calendar or fiscal year, whichever applies; or
7. Has, if the policyholder is a municipality, a population of at least 20,000.

(S.D. Codified Laws § 58-24-68)

For the purposes of §§ 58-24-68 to 58-24-74, inclusive, the term "risk manager" means an employee of the exempt commercial policyholder, or a third-party consultant retained by the policyholder who provides skilled services in loss prevention, loss reduction, or risk and insurance coverage analysis, and the purchase of insurance, and who possesses at least one of the following credentials:

1. A bachelor's or higher degree in risk management issued by an accredited college or university;
2. A designation as a chartered property and casualty underwriter issued by the American Institute for Chartered Property and Casualty Underwriters and Insurance Institute of America;
3. A designation as an associate in risk management issued by the American Institute for Chartered Property and Casualty Underwriters and Insurance Institute of America;
4. A designation as a certified risk manager issued by the National Alliance for Insurance Education and Research;
5. A designation as a fellow in risk management or RIMS fellow issued by the Global Risk Management Institute; or
6. At least seven years of experience in one or more of the following areas of commercial property and casualty insurance:
   a. Risk financing;
   b. Claims administration;
   c. Loss prevention; or
   d. Risk and insurance coverage analysis.

(S.D. Codified Laws § 58-24-69)

Surplus Lines Broker Filing Requirements

Premium and tax forms are due April 1. Annual and quarterly tax reports are not required with policies filed through the SL Clearinghouse, https://www.slasclearinghouse.com (last visited May 7, 2023). Zero filings are not required.

Notices

Upon placing a surplus lines insurance policy, a broker must promptly deliver to the insured evidence of the insurance consisting of either the policy as issued by the insurer, or if the policy is not then available, the surplus lines broker's certificate of insurance. Such a certificate shall be executed by the broker and shall show the description and the location of the subject of the insurance, coverage, conditions and term of insurance, the premium and rate charged and taxes collected from the insured, and the name and address of the insured and the insurer. If the direct risk is assumed by more than one insurer, the certificate shall state the name and address and the proportion of the entire risk assumed by each such insurer.

(S.D. CODIFIED LAWS § 58-32-27)

Taxes, Stamping Fees, and Other Government-Imposed Charges

The surplus lines tax is 2.5 percent. In addition, there is a tax of 3.0 percent for fire policies.

(S.D. CODIFIED LAWS § 10-44-2(3)(b))

Producer, Policy, Inspection, and Other Fees

A consultant may collect a fee from an insurance customer for services provided as a consultant but may not collect a fee for any insurance placed with that insurance customer if a commission is payable to that consultant. A consultant may act as a consultant and collect a fee from an insurance customer and also receive a commission for insurance sold, solicited, or negotiated with that same insurance customer provided that the fee and commission are for separate and distinct insurance products. The term "fee," as used in this section, does not include a fee that is payable pursuant to the terms or conditions of an insurance policy, contract, or certificate or that are required to be paid for reasons other than the services provided by the consultant.

Any consultant collecting a fee from an insurance customer shall set forth the fee to be charged to that insurance customer and the terms and conditions of the services provided to that insurance customer in the form of a written agreement with that insurance customer.

(S.D. CODIFIED LAWS § 58-30-144.1)

Premium is the consideration for insurance by whatever name called. Any assessment, or any membership, policy, survey, inspection, service, or similar fee or other charge in consideration for an insurance contract is deemed part of the premium. Fees not specified in the insurance product are prohibited, and consulting fees on policies for which producers collect a commission are prohibited. Consultant fees are not subject to premium tax.

(S.D. Codified Laws § 58-11-1)

See also Department Bulletin 13-04, available at https://dlr.sd.gov/insurance/laws.aspx (last visited Dec. 16, 2020).

Industrial Insured Exemption

South Dakota statutes and regulations do not contain an industrial insured exemption with regard to surplus lines insurance.

Independent or Direct Procurement Law

Insureds who independently procure insurance from an unauthorized insurer shall file a written report of the same with the director within 30 days on forms furnished by the director to the insured, giving the name and address of the insurer, the subject of the insurance, a general description of the coverage, the amount of premium currently charged therefor, and such additional pertinent information as the director reasonably requests. If the insurance covers also a subject of insurance resident, located or to be performed outside this state, a proper pro rata portion of the entire premium payable for all such insurance shall be allocated to this state for the purposes of § 58-32-50.

(S.D. Codified Laws § 58-32-47)

Independently procured insurance is subject to a 2.5 percent tax. The tax and report are due within 30 days of procurement.

(S.D. Codified Laws § 58-32-50)

TENNESSEE

Tennessee Department of Commerce and Insurance
Insurance Division
500 James Robertson Parkway
Nashville, TN 37243
(615) 741-2241
https://www.tn.gov/commerce/section/insurance

Tennessee does not have a stamping office.

Nonadmitted Insurer Eligibility

Foreign

No unauthorized insurer shall be or become an eligible surplus lines insurer, unless the unauthorized insurer is a United States domiciled insurer and it is authorized to write the type of insurance in its domiciliary jurisdiction and one of the following criteria is met:

1. The unauthorized insurer has capital and surplus or its equivalent under the laws of its domiciliary jurisdiction that equals the greater of:
   a. The minimum capital and surplus requirements under the law of this state; or
   b. $15 million; or
2. If the unauthorized insurer does not satisfy the preceding requirements, the commissioner may make an affirmative finding that the unauthorized insurer is acceptable. The commissioner's finding shall be based upon such facts as quality of management, capital and surplus of any parent company, company underwriting profit and investment income trends, market availability and company record, and reputation within the industry. In no

event shall the commissioner make an affirmative finding of acceptability when the unauthorized insurer's capital and surplus is less than $4.5 million.

(TENN. CODE § 56-14-109(b)(1))

Alien

For an alien unauthorized insurer to be eligible, it must be listed on the Quarterly Listing of Alien Insurers maintained by the International Insurers Department of the National Association of Insurance Commissioners.

(TENN. CODE § 56-14-109(b)(2))

Nonadmitted Insurer Eligibility List

A list of eligible surplus lines insurers may be found at the Tennessee Department of Commerce and Insurance surplus lines webpage at https://sbs-tn.naic.org/Lion-Web/jsp/sbsreports/CompanySearchLookup.jsp (last visited July 15, 2020). When accessing the site, choose Company Type: "SURPLUS LINES."

Types of Coverage Permitted or Prohibited

General Information

The following types of coverage are not permitted to be written with a surplus lines insurer: primary personal automobile liability, surety, and workers' compensation, except workers' compensation may be written if the full amount of insurance required is not procurable, after a diligent effort has been made to do so, from among the authorized companies licensed to transact and actually writing such kind and class of insurance in this state, and the amount of insurance eligible for surplus lines shall be only the amount in excess of the amount procurable from licensed insurers.

(TENN. CODE § 56-14-105)

Exempt Transactions

The following transactions can be procured from an unauthorized insurer, separate from the surplus lines law:

- Reinsurance;
- Transactions in Tennessee involving policies lawfully solicited, written, and delivered outside of the state covering only subjects of insurance not resident, located, or expressly to be performed in Tennessee at the time of issuance or covering property in the course of transportation by land, air, or water, to, from, or through the state and including any preparation or storage incidental thereto, and which transactions are subsequent to the issuance of those policies.

(TENN. CODE § 56-2-105(2) and (3))

Service of Process

An unauthorized insurer must appoint the commissioner as agent for service of process. Any enumerated actions constituting doing business in Tennessee shall signify the insurer's acceptance of the commissioner as agent for service of process. The policy issued by the insurer, or any certificate of insurance issued by the surplus lines agent, shall contain a provision stating the substance of § 56-14-112(a) and designating the person to whom the commissioner shall mail process.

(TENN. CODE §§ 56-2-602, 56-14-112(a))

Limitations on Actions Involving Judicial Proceedings

Before any unauthorized foreign or alien insurer files or causes to be filed any pleading in any action, suit, or proceeding instituted against it, the unauthorized insurer shall deposit with the clerk of the court in which the action, suit, or proceeding is pending cash or securities or file with the clerk a bond with good and sufficient sureties, to be approved by the court, in an amount to be fixed by the court sufficient to secure the payment of any final judgment that may be rendered in the action.

(TENN. CODE § 56-2-607)

Domestic Surplus Lines Insurers

Tennessee statutes have no provision allowing domestic surplus lines insurers.

Nonadmitted Insurer Filing Requirements

The Insurance Division requires foreign surplus lines insurers to submit an eligibility form and fees annually. The form sets forth foreign insurer filing requirements.

See https://www.tn.gov/commerce/insurance/types-of-insurance-companies/surplus-lines.html (last visited Sept. 2, 2020). When accessing the site, scroll down to the "Surplus Lines Specific Information" section and look for "Foreign Surplus Lines Continuing Eligibility Review and Filing Fees."

Surplus Lines Broker Licensing

Tennessee-licensed agents who are licensed to write in the admitted market the lines of coverage authorized for surplus lines may apply for a surplus lines agent's license. Licenses are issued for a 24-month term and the license fee is $120 for the term.

(TENN. CODE § 56-14-104)

Due Care in Selecting Nonadmitted Insurer

Other than determining that an insurer meets the eligibility requirements, Tennessee statutes do not set forth any requirements with regard to the exercise of due care in selecting a nonadmitted insurer.

(TENN. CODE § 56-14-103)

Diligent Effort/Diligent Search

Coverage may be obtained from surplus lines insurers if, after a diligent effort, the full amount cannot be procured from licensed insurers that actually write the type of coverage sought, and then only the amount in excess of the amount procurable from licensed insurers.

(TENN. CODE § 56-14-105(a))

Export List

Tennessee does not maintain a list of coverages that may be exported to the surplus lines market without first making a diligent search of licensed insurers.

Exempt Commercial Purchasers

Tennessee has adopted the NRRA (15 U.S.C. § 8201) definition of exempt commercial purchasers. Coverage for these insureds may be exported to the surplus lines market without making a diligent effort to place the coverage with authorized insurers provided (1) the surplus lines broker has disclosed to the exempt commercial purchaser that coverage may or may not be available from an authorized insurer that may provide greater protection with more regulatory oversight, and (2) such exempt commercial purchaser has subsequently requested such broker, in writing, to procure such policy from an unauthorized insurer.

(TENN. CODE § 56-14-105(b))

Surplus Lines Broker Filing Requirements

Surplus lines agents must file quarterly a verified report of all surplus lines insurance transactions during the preceding quarter placed, procured, or effected for, or on behalf of, an insured whose home state is Tennessee, showing:

- Aggregate gross premiums written;
- Aggregate return premiums;
- Amount of tax remitted to this state; and

- Except for insurance placed or procured on behalf of an exempt commercial purchaser, a sworn statement by the agent with regard to the coverages described in the report that, to the best of the agent's knowledge and belief, the agent could not reasonably procure such coverages from an admitted insurer.

Within 30 days of placing any new or renewal surplus lines contracts or endorsements, the surplus lines agent shall make an affidavit for every new or renewed surplus lines insurance contract placed, procured, or effected for, or on behalf of, an insured whose home state is Tennessee. The affidavit shall be promptly filed with the insurance department and shall include an affirmation that the agent is, after diligent effort, unable to procure from an admitted company or admitted companies the full amount of insurance required to protect the interest of the insured for each surplus lines insurance transaction except those procured or placed for exempt commercial purchasers.

(TENN. CODE § 56-14-106(a), (b))

Notices

Every insurance policy written on a surplus line basis must contain the name and address of the writing agent and the following:

> This insurance contract is with an insurer not licensed to transact insurance in this state and is issued and delivered as a surplus lines coverage pursuant to the Tennessee insurance statutes.

(TENN. CODE § 56-14-107(a))

Taxes, Stamping Fees, and Other Government-Imposed Charges

The surplus line tax is 5 percent. Surplus lines agents must pay taxes quarterly. The surplus lines agent shall collect from the insured the amount of the tax at the time of delivery of the cover note, certificate of insurance, policy, or other initial confirmation of insurance, in addition to the full amount of the gross premium charged by the insurer for the insurance. No agent shall absorb the tax nor shall any agent, as an inducement for insurance or for any other reason, rebate all or any part of the tax or the agent's commission.

(TENN. CODE § 56-14-113(b))

Producer, Policy, Inspection, and Other Fees

An insurance producer may charge fees for services not connected with the sale, solicitation, and negotiation of insurance by the insurance producer if the fees are based upon a qualified written agreement, signed by the party to be charged in advance of the performance of the services under the agreement. A copy of the qualifying agreement must be provided to the party to be charged at the time the agreement is signed by the party.

(TENN. CODE § 56-6-125(3))

For the purposes of premium tax, premium includes all premiums, membership fees, assessments, dues, or any other consideration for insurance.

(TENN. CODE § 56-14-113)

Industrial Insured Exemption

Tennessee permits an insured that meets the definition of an industrial insured to acquire insurance coverage directly from an insurer not authorized to do an insurance business in the state. Industrial insured means an insured:

a. who procures the insurance of any risk or risks by use of the services of a full-time employee acting as an insurance manager or buyer; and
b. whose aggregate annual premiums for insurance on all risks total at least $25,000; and
c. who has at least 25 full-time employees.

(TENN. CODE § 56-2-105(7))

Independent or Direct Procurement Law

Tennessee statutes and regulations do not contain provisions addressing independently procured insurance.

TEXAS

Texas Department of Insurance
PO Box 149104
Austin, TX 78714-9104
(800) 578-4677
Alternate Address:
333 Guadalupe Street
Austin, TX 78701
https://www.tdi.texas.gov

Texas has a stamping office.

Surplus Lines Stamping Office of Texas (SLTX)
805 Las Cimas Parkway Suite 300
Austin, TX 78746
(512) 531-1880
(800) 681-5848
https://www.sltx.org

Nonadmitted Insurer Eligibility

General Information

Eligible surplus lines insurers in Texas may place surplus lines risks pursuant to an exemption from Texas unauthorized insurance prohibition.

(TEX. INS. CODE § 101.053)

Before an insurer may issue surplus lines insurance, the insurer must hold an authorization to engage in the business of insurance from its domiciliary state or country. The authorization from the domiciliary state or country must be for the same kind or class of insurance to be written in this state as surplus lines insurance. The surplus lines insurer must provide to the commissioner satisfactory evidence that the insurer holds the authorization.

(TEX. INS. CODE § 981.051)

Foreign

A foreign eligible surplus lines insurer must maintain a minimum of $15 million of capital and surplus and be licensed in its state of domicile for the lines of business it plans to write as surplus lines risks in Texas.

(TEX. INS. CODE §§ 981.051, 981.057)

Alien

An alien surplus lines insurer writing risks in Texas must be listed on the Quarterly Listing of Alien Insurers maintained by the International Insurers Department of the National Association of Insurance Commissioners.

(TEX. INS. CODE §§ 981.057(b), 981.058)

Nonadmitted Insurer Eligibility List

The eligibility of the foreign insurers is determined by requirements listed in subchapter B of Texas Insurance Code Ch. 981. The Texas Department of Insurance (TDI) provides a list of eligible surplus lines insurers in Texas at https://appscenter.tdi.texas.gov/tdireports/p/externalReports (last visited July 15, 2020). When accessing the site, from the Company Licensing drop down on the left, choose "Surplus Lines" then click "Run Report."

That list is also available from the Surplus Lines Stamping Office of Texas (SLTX) at https://www.sltx.org/insurers/eligible-insurer-list/eligible-insurers/ (last visited on July 15, 2020).

Neither TDI nor SLTX officially approve foreign surplus lines insurers for eligibility, nor do these entities have the duty or responsibility to determine the actual financial condition or claims practices of such foreign surplus lines insurers.

(Tex. Ins. Code § 981.063)

Types of Coverage Permitted or Prohibited

General Information

With limited exceptions, Texas law does not specify the types of risks eligible for surplus lines placement in the state. Exceptions to this general guideline include prohibitions on placing automobile liability insurance (Tex. Trans. Code § 601.071(a)), workers' compensation insurance (Tex. Labor Code § 406.003), and title insurance (Tex. Ins. Code § 2501.003(14)) in surplus lines. In any event, the department interprets Texas insurance laws as restricting, if not prohibiting, certain other types of coverage, such as life, accident, and health insurance, from being placed in the surplus lines market.

Exempt Transactions

Texas statutes do not set forth any transactions exempt from surplus lines laws. Texas does recognize exemptions in federal law.

See Texas comptroller's website at https://comptroller.texas.gov/taxes/publications/94-142.php (last visited July 15, 2020).

Service of Process

Any act of transacting insurance by any unauthorized insurer constitutes an appointment of the Secretary of State as attorney of such insurer upon whom may be served all lawful process in any action, suit, or proceeding.

(Tex. Ins. Code § 804.106)

Policies issued by an eligible surplus lines insurer and certificates of insurance issued by a surplus lines agent must state the irrevocable appointment of the secretary of state by the subject surplus lines insurer and designate the person to whom the commissioner is to mail process.

(Tex. Ins. Code § 804.106(d))

Service of process on an eligible surplus lines insurer may also be effected by serving the commissioner, which is deemed service on the principal.

(Tex. Ins. Code § 804.202)

Surplus lines documents must include a statement designating the name and address of the individual to whom the commissioner will mail service of process in accordance with the Insurance Code and a stamping fee.

(28 Tex. Admin. Code § 15.5(a))

Limitations on Actions Involving Judicial Proceedings

Texas statutes do not set forth any limitations on actions involving judicial proceedings that apply to the lawful transaction of surplus lines business.

Domestic Surplus Lines Insurers

Texas permits a domestic insurer with at least $15 million minimum capital and surplus to be designated as a domestic surplus lines insurer upon the written approval of the commissioner.

(Tex. Ins. Code § 981.072)

Nonadmitted Insurer Filing Requirements

Foreign surplus lines insurers are required to file financial statements with the National Association of Insurance Commissioners (NAIC) on an annual and quarterly basis, including CPA reports, actuarial opinions, and management discussion and analysis information by the due dates prescribed by the NAIC. To remain eligible, foreign surplus lines insurers must maintain the minimum level of capitalization as required by TIC § 981.057. Financial documents filed with the NAIC are not required to be filed directly with this department if they are timely filed with the NAIC. The insurer should notify the department within 30 days of any changes to its status, name, or address and provide evidence of the change such as the Certificate of Authority.

Alien surplus lines insurers are required to file annual financial statements with the NAIC International Insurance Department (IID) and do not file anything directly with this department.

Grandfathered non-IID alien insurers are required to file in accordance with TIC § 981.058 as it existed prior to the enactment of Senate Bill 951. See TDI Form FIN 423, Alien Insurers Filing Requirements Checklist.

See https://www.tdi.texas.gov/insurer/surpluslines.html (last visited Sept. 2, 2020). When accessing the site, search for or scroll down to "Annual and Quarterly Filing Requirements for Surplus Lines Insurers."

Surplus Lines Broker Licensing

The department may issue a surplus lines license to an individual, a corporation, a limited liability company, or a partnership. Individual applicants must pass a surplus lines examination under Texas Insurance Code Ch. 4002 and department rules. An individual applicant must also hold a current license as either a Texas licensed general property and casualty agent or a managing general agent. A surplus lines agent applicant that is a corporation, limited liability company, or partnership must have at least one officer or director or at least one active partner who has passed the required surplus lines license examination. The designated individual must also hold a current license as a general property and casualty agent authorized under subchapter B, chapter 4051 or a managing general agent. Texas does not require nonresident surplus lines agent license applicants to obtain a general property and casualty agent license if the home state of each insured is Texas and the individual is licensed as a surplus lines agent in the individual's state of residence. The individual nonresident applicant must submit information acceptable to the commissioner as evidence of meeting statutory requirement for a nonresident surplus lines agent license.

(Tex. Ins. Code § 981.203(a))

Due Care in Selecting Nonadmitted Insurer

A surplus lines agent may not place surplus lines coverage with a surplus lines insurer unless the insurer meets statutory eligibility requirements and the stamping office provides evidence to the department that the insurer meets those requirements.

(Tex. Ins. Code § 981.210)

Additionally, a surplus lines agent may not knowingly place surplus lines insurance with a financially unsound insurer. A surplus lines agent must make a reasonable effort to determine the financial condition of an eligible surplus lines insurer before placing insurance with that insurer.

(Tex. Ins. Code § 981.211)

Furthermore, a surplus lines agent must make a reasonable inquiry into the financial condition and operating history of the insurer before placing insurance with an eligible surplus lines insurer. The surplus lines agent has a continuous duty during the course of placing a surplus lines risk to stay informed of the insurer's solvency and the soundness of its financial strength, as well as the insurer's ability to process claims and pay losses expeditiously.

(28 Tex. Admin. Code § 15.104)

Diligent Effort/Diligent Search

An eligible surplus lines insurer may provide surplus lines insurance only if the full amount of required insurance cannot be obtained, after a diligent effort, from an insurer authorized to write and actually writing that kind of insurance in this state. An eligible surplus lines insurer may provide surplus lines insurance only in the amount that exceeds the amount of insurance obtainable from authorized insurers.

(Tex. Ins. Code § 981.004)

Export List

Texas does not maintain a list of coverages that may be exported to the surplus lines market without first making a diligent search of licensed insurers.

Exempt Commercial Purchasers

Texas has adopted the NRRA (15 U.S.C. § 8201) definition of exempt commercial purchasers. Coverage for these insureds may be exported to the surplus lines market without making a diligent effort to place the coverage with authorized insurers provided (1) the surplus lines broker has disclosed to the exempt commercial purchaser that coverage may or may not be available from an authorized insurer that may provide greater protection with more regulatory oversight, and (2) such exempt commercial purchaser has subsequently requested such broker, in writing, to procure such policy from an unauthorized insurer.

(Tex. Ins. Code § 981.004(c))

The surplus lines agent must maintain the agent's disclosure and the exempt commercial purchaser's request for surplus lines coverage in the contract file. The documentation must also include a signed statement by the ECP identifying the qualifying criteria for the ECP and the qualified risk manager.

(28 Tex. Admin. Code § 15.111)

Surplus Lines Broker Filing Requirements

A Texas licensed surplus lines agent responsible for surplus lines premium tax filings must file surplus lines policies and renewal documents with SLTX not later than the 60th day after the later of the effective date or the issue date of new or renewal surplus lines insurance.

Documents to be filed with SLTX within 60 days of effective date or issue date include a copy of the policy issued or, if the policy has not been issued, a copy of the certificate, cover note, or other confirmation of insurance delivered to the insured.

(Tex. Ins. Code § 981.105)

Additionally, a surplus lines agent responsible for surplus lines tax filings is also required to "promptly" file with the stamping office the following documents:

1. A copy of each substitute certificate, cover note, or other confirmation of insurance delivered to an insured;

2. A copy of each endorsement of an original policy, certificate, cover note, or other confirmation of insurance delivered to an insured; and
3. A memorandum from the agent informing the stamping office of the substance of any change from the original coverage represented by the document(s).

The commissioner may assess a fee against an agent who files a surplus lines policy after the 60-day filing deadline for policies and renewals. The criteria for imposition of late-filing fees and for determining the amount of such fees are listed in Texas Insurance Code § 105(d)–(i). Late-filing violations incurring fees under the statute are not subject to official sanctions. In general, a late-filing violation is subject to a sanction instead of a fee if the agent fails to pay a late-filing fee, files after 365 days of a policy's effective date or renewal, or files after 180 but before 365 days of a policy's effective date or renewal and late-filed more than 2 percent of the agent's policies in the preceding calendar year.

(TEX. INS. CODE § 981.105)

TDI rules establish procedures for resolving disputes concerning the timing of filings.

(TEX. ADMIN. CODE § 114)

Notices

A surplus lines document issued by an eligible surplus lines insurer must state, in 11-point type, the following:

> This insurance contract is with an insurer not licensed to transact insurance in this state and is issued and delivered as surplus line coverage under the Texas insurance statutes. The Texas Department of Insurance does not audit the finances or review the solvency of the surplus lines insurer providing this coverage, and the insurer is not a member of the property and casualty insurance guaranty association created under Chapter 462, Insurance Code. Chapter 225, Insurance Code, requires payment of a __________ (insert appropriate tax rate) percent tax on gross premium.

(TEX. INS. CODE § 981.101(b))

A surplus lines document issued by a domestic surplus lines insurer must include the following statement:

> This insurance contract is issued and delivered as surplus line coverage under the Texas Insurance Code. The insurer is not a member of the property and casualty insurance guaranty association created under Insurance Code Chapter 462. Insurance Code Chapter 225 requires payment of a ________ (insert appropriate tax rate) percent tax on gross premium.

(Tex. Ins. Code § 981.076 & 28 Tex. Admin. Code § 15.5(c))

The term "surplus lines document" means each new or renewal insurance contract, certificate, cover note, or other confirmation of insurance obtained and delivered as surplus line coverage under this chapter.

(Tex. Ins. Code § 981.101(a))

Taxes, Stamping Fees, and Other Government-Imposed Charges

A surplus lines agent who collects gross premiums for surplus lines insurance for any risk in which Texas is the home state of the insured is responsible for payment of a surplus lines premium tax at a rate of 4.85 percent of gross premiums. Taxable gross premiums under this section are based on gross premiums written or received for surplus lines insurance placed through an eligible surplus lines insurer during a calendar year.

(Tex. Ins. Code §§ 225.003, 225.004)

"Premium" means any payment made in consideration for insurance and includes a premium, premium deposits, membership fees, registration fees, assessments, dues, and any other compensation given in consideration for surplus lines insurance.

(Tex. Ins. Code § 225.001(5))

Surplus lines premium taxes are due on March 1 for the previous calendar year (for example, March 1, 2024, for premiums received in 2023). Prepayments are due by the 15th of the month in which the agent accrues $70,000 or more. Additional information concerning payments and penalties is available from the

Texas Comptroller of Public Accounts at https://comptroller.texas.gov/taxes/insurance/surplus-lines.php (last visited Dec. 2, 2020).

A surplus lines agent must submit a stamping fee to SLTX for each surplus lines policy, contract, or other detailed evidence of coverage issued on Texas risks, including additions or deletions to, or cancellations. The current stamping fee rate and procedures for paying stamping fee invoices are available from SLTX at https://www.sltx.org/brokers/billing-information/stamping-fees-taxes (last visited Dec. 2, 2020).

Premiums on risks or exposures that are properly allocated to federal or international waters or that are under the jurisdiction of a foreign government are not taxable in Texas. However, this exemption is for the surplus lines premium tax only, and surplus lines policies must comply with Texas surplus lines laws and regulations unless 100 percent of the risk is allocated to federal or international waters, under the jurisdiction of a foreign government, or located outside of Texas.

(Tex. Ins. Code § 225.04(e))

Producer, Policy, Inspection, and Other Fees

Under certain conditions, a Texas insurance agent may charge fees in lieu of or in addition to the commission for services the agent agrees to perform in connection with the sale or service of a particular policy.
(Tex. Ins. Code § 4005 & 28 Tex. Admin. Code § 19.1502)
Texas Insurance Code § 4005.003, which regulates permissible fees in addition to commissions, does not apply to a surplus lines agent placing surplus lines insurance.
(Tex. Ins. Code § 4005.003(c)(2))

Industrial Insured Exemption

Industrial insured means a person who purchases commercial insurance and, at the time of placement:

1. Employs or retains a qualified risk manager to negotiate insurance coverage; and
2. Either:
   a. Has paid aggregate nationwide commercial property and casualty insurance premiums of more than $25,000 in the immediately preceding 12 months; or
   b. Employs at least 25 full-time employees.

(Tex. Ins. Code § 981.0033)

The diligent search requirement in § 981.004(a)(1) does not apply to insurance procured for an industrial insured if:

1. The agent procuring or placing the insurance discloses to the industrial insured that:
   a. Comparable insurance may be available from the admitted market that is subject to more regulatory oversight than the surplus lines market; and
   b. A policy purchased in the admitted market may provide greater protection than the surplus lines insurance policy;
2. The surplus lines company offering the coverage has a financial strength rating of A- or better from the A. M. Best Company; and
3. After receiving the notice described by subdivision (1), the industrial insured requests in writing that the agent procure the insurance from or place the insurance with an eligible surplus lines insurer.

(Tex. Ins. Code § 981.004(d))

Independent or Direct Procurement Law

Independently procured insurance is exempt from the Texas prohibition of doing business with an unauthorized insurer.

(Tex. Ins. Code §§ 101.053, 101.102)

To qualify for this exemption, an insurance transaction on a Texas risk must be independently procured by the insured from an insurance company not authorized to do insurance business in this state through negotiations occurring entirely outside this state. Furthermore, the transaction must be reported to the Texas comptroller of public accounts (comptroller), and the insured must pay the independently procured insurance tax.

(Tex. Ins. Code §§ 101.053, 226.052)

"Premium" means any payment made in consideration for insurance and includes a premium, premium deposits, membership fees, registration fees, assessments, dues, and any other compensation given in consideration for surplus lines insurance.

(Tex. Ins. Code § 225.051(6))

A tax is imposed on each insured at the rate of 4.85 percent of the premium paid for the insurance contract.

(Tex. Ins. Code § 226.052)

However, if an independently procured insurance policy covers risks or exposures only partially located in this state and this state has not joined a cooperative agreement, reciprocal agreement, or compact with another state for the allocation of non-admitted insurance taxes as authorized by Texas Insurance Code Chapter 229, the tax is computed on the entire policy premium for any policy in which this state is the home state of the insured. The insured purchasing independently procured insurance is responsible for filing a tax report and for paying the tax, but the insured may designate another person to file the report and pay the tax. An insured who fails to withhold from the premium the amount of tax imposed by this subchapter is liable for the amount of the tax and shall pay the tax due.

(Tex. Ins. Code § 226.053(b))

Independently procured insurance tax owed by a corporation that files a franchise tax report must be reported directly to the comptroller and is due at the time the franchise tax report is due or on another date prescribed by the comptroller.

(Tex. Ins. Code § 226.054)

UTAH

Utah Insurance Department
4315 South 2700 West, Suite 2300
Taylorsville, UT 84129
(801) 957-9200
https://insurance.utah.gov
prop-cas.uid@utah.gov

Utah has a stamping office.

Surplus Line Association of Utah
6711 South 1300 East
Salt Lake City, UT 84121
(801) 944-0114
www.slaut.org

Nonadmitted Insurer Eligibility

General Information

Utah maintains a list of recognized surplus lines insurers. New applications for foreign and alien insurers are available on the department website at https://insurance.utah.gov/licensee/insurers/excess-surplus-lines (last visited July 15, 2020). Renewal instructions are available at https://insurance.utah.gov/licensee/insurers/renewals/surplus-lines (last visited July 15, 2020).

Foreign

Foreign nonadmitted insurers must establish satisfactory evidence of good reputation and financial integrity.

They must submit annual financial statements directly to the commissioner or through the NAIC. They must comply with the risk-based capital standards in UCA chapter 17, part 6, or maintain capital and surplus of at least $15 million, whichever is greater.

(UTAH CODE ANN. § 31A-15-103(6)(e))

Alien

An alien insurers must be on the Quarterly Listing of Alien Insurers maintained by the International Insurers Department of the National Association of Insurance Commissioners. A "Lloyd's" or other similar incorporated or unincorporated group of alien individual insurers can be eligible if it maintains a trust fund of not less than $50 million.

(UTAH CODE ANN. § 31A-15-103(6)(e))

Nonadmitted Insurer Eligibility List

The Surplus Line Association of Utah maintains a list of eligible surplus lines insurers on their website at https://www.slaut.org/insurers-list (last visited July 15, 2020).

Types of Coverage Permitted or Prohibited

Prohibited

Workers' compensation insurance coverage is not eligible for export to the surplus lines market where the employer is located in Utah, except for stop loss coverage issued to an employer securing workers' compensation coverage under UCA § 34A-2-2013(3).

(UTAH CODE ANN. § 31A-15-103)

The commissioner may by rule prohibit contracts for specified coverages if authorized insurers establish a market for that type of insurance that is adequate and reasonably competitive.

(UTAH CODE ANN. § 31A-15-103)

Exempt Transactions

The following types of insurance are exempt from surplus line taxes:

a. Ocean marine insurance;
b. Insurance premiums paid by institutions within the state system of higher education as specified in § 53B-1-102; or
c. Annuities.

(Utah Code Ann. § 31A-3-301)

Service of Process

The commissioner is the agent for receipt of service process for surplus lines insurers.
(Utah Code Ann. § 31A-2-309)

Limitations on Actions Involving Judicial Proceedings

No pleading, notice, order, or process in any action in court or in any administrative proceeding against an unauthorized person may be filed unless the unauthorized person posts a bond or procures proper authorization to do an insurance business in Utah. However, this does not prevent an unauthorized person from filing a motion to quash a writ or to set aside service on the ground that the person has not done any of the acts specified under subsection 31A-15-102(2), which lists prohibited acts that constitute transaction of insurance by an unauthorized insurer.
(Utah Code Ann. § 31A-15-107)

Domestic Surplus Lines Insurers

Utah statutes have no provision allowing domestic surplus lines insurers.

Nonadmitted Insurer Filing Requirements

File its annual statements in each subsequent year within 60 days of the day on which it is filed with the insurance regulatory authority in their domiciliary jurisdiction.

(UTAH CODE ANN. § 31A-15-103(6)(e))

Surplus Lines Broker Licensing

Resident licensing requirements:

1. Have been a property and casualty insurance producer for at least three of the past four years
2. Pass the Surplus Lines Producer examination
3. Submit an application and appropriate fees

(UTAH CODE ANN. §§ 31A-23a-203(1), 31A-23a-106)

Nonresident licensing requirements:

1. Be licensed and in good standing in home state for all lines for which applying in Utah
2. Submit an application and appropriate fees

(UTAH CODE ANN. § 31A-23a-109(1))

Due Care in Selecting Nonadmitted Insurer

A Utah surplus line producer may not knowingly place insurance with a financially unsound insurer, an insurer engaged in unfair practices, or an otherwise substandard insurer.

(UTAH CODE ANN. § 31A-15-103(7)(a))

Diligent Effort/Diligent Search

The insurance producer must make a good faith effort to place insurance with admitted carriers that write the type of coverage involved before placing the risk in the nonadmitted market. Placing coverage for a lower rate does not constitute a good faith effort. The producer must document his/her diligent effort with a written explanation that the effort was in good faith. The document must be maintained in the producer's records for at minimum three years from coverage inception.

(UTAH CODE ANN. R590-171-6)

Export List

Utah does maintain a list of coverages that are exempt from the diligent search requirement. This list is available at https://www.slaut.org/export-list (last visited Oct. 7, 2020).

Exempt Commercial Purchasers

Utah has adopted the NRRA (15 U.S.C. § 8201) definition of exempt commercial purchasers. Coverage for these insureds may be exported to the surplus lines market without making a diligent effort to place the coverage with authorized insurers provided (1) the surplus lines broker has disclosed to the exempt commercial purchaser that coverage may or may not be available from an authorized insurer that may provide greater protection with more regulatory oversight, and (2) such exempt commercial purchaser has subsequently requested such broker, in writing, to procure such policy from an unauthorized insurer. (R590-171-3(B), Ins. Dep't Bull. 2011-4)

Surplus Lines Broker Filing Requirements

Utah does not require annual or quarterly reports. Surplus lines transactions with exposures in Utah must be submitted to the Surplus Lines Association of Utah within 60 days of the effective date of the transaction. Late submissions will be assessed a penalty. Submitted transactions must include the following:

1. A complete copy of the policy, certificate, or endorsement. A binder with full specifics of the coverage is acceptable in lieu of the policy if the policy is not available within the 60 days allowed.
2. Submission forms

(UTAH CODE ANN. § 31A-15-103(11))

Information about filing and forms is available at https://www.slaut.org/ and Utah Insurance Department website https://insurance.utah.gov/licensee/insurers/excess-surplus-lines (last visited Oct. 28, 2020).

Notices

All surplus lines policies must have the following statement attached or affixed to them:

> The insurer issuing this policy does not hold a certificate of authority to do business in this state and thus is not fully subject to regulation by the Utah insurance commissioner. This policy receives no protection from any of the guaranty associations created under Chapter 28, Title 31A.
>
> (UTAH CODE ANN. § 31A-15-103(8)(c))

Taxes, Stamping Fees, and Other Government-Imposed Charges

Utah charges a 4.25 percent tax and a 0.15 percent stamping office fee. These are assessed on gross premiums less return premiums due to cancellations or premium reductions. Gross premiums include all policy fess, but do not include the stamping office fee. The insurer, broker(s), and policy holder are jointly and severally liable for these charges; however, it is the surplus lines producer who is responsible for remitting the tax to the SLA.

(UTAH CODE ANN. § 31A-3-301)

See Utah Insurance Department website at https://insurance.utah.gov/licensee/insurers/excess-surplus-lines (last visited Dec. 2, 2020).

See also SLA of Utah website at https://www.slaut.org/faq (last visited Dec. 2, 2020).

Producer, Policy, Inspection, and Other Fees

Gross premium subject to surplus lines tax means the monetary consideration for a surplus lines insurance policy including the fees charged to the insured, however designated.

(Utah Code Ann. 1953 § 31A-3-301)

Surplus lines premium means the monetary consideration for an insurance policy procured from an unauthorized insurer, and includes policy fees, membership fees, required contributions, or monetary considerations, however designated.

(Utah Code Ann. R590-157-3)

Industrial Insured Exemption

Utah statutes and regulations do not contain an industrial insured exemption with regard to surplus lines insurance.

Independent or Direct Procurement Law

Any person may directly procure insurance with a nonadmitted insurer providing no resident producer licensed in Utah is involved in the transaction and the negotiations occur outside of the state of Utah.

Within 60 days of procuring or renewing the contract, a report of the transaction must be made to the commissioner and taxes paid as specified under § 31A-3-301.

(Utah Code Ann. § 31A-15-104)

VERMONT

Department of Financial Regulation—Insurance Division
89 Main Street
Montpelier, VT 05620-3101
(802) 828-2470
dfr.complic@vermont.gov

Vermont does not have a stamping office.

Nonadmitted Insurer Eligibility

Foreign

A nonadmitted insurer must maintain capital and surplus that equals the greater of the minimum capital and surplus requirements under the laws of Vermont or $15 million, whichever is greater. A surplus lines insurer that does not meet these capital and surplus requirements may receive approval upon an affirmative finding of acceptability by the commissioner.

(8 Vt. Stat. Ann. § 5026(a) & (b))

Additionally, nonadmitted insurers domiciled in the United States must be authorized to write the desired coverage in their state of domicile.

See Department of Financial Regulation Insurance Bulletin #163 available at https://dfr.vermont.gov/reg-bul-ord/nonadmitted-insurance-reform-bulletin (last visited July 15, 2020) and department website at https://dfr.vermont.gov/industry/insurance/company-licensing/how-apply/surplus-lines-insurers (last visited July 15, 2020).

Alien

A nonadmitted alien insurer must be listed on the Quarterly Listing of Alien Insurers maintained by the International Insurers Department of the National Association of Insurance Commissioners.

(8 VT. STAT. ANN. § 5026(a)(2))

Nonadmitted Insurer Eligibility List

Although the Department of Financial Regulation (DFR) is permitted to publish a list of insurers meeting the eligibility qualifications, DFR does not currently maintain such a list.

Types of Coverage Permitted or Prohibited

Prohibited

Surplus line insurers cannot provide life insurance, health insurance, annuities, or reinsurance, nor the following insurance when so placed by any licensed producer in this state:

1. Insurance on subjects whose home state is other than Vermont;
2. Insurance on the property or operations of aircraft or railroads engaged in transportation in interstate and foreign commerce; or
3. Insurance of vessels, crafts or hulls, cargoes, marine builder's risks, marine protection and indemnity, or other risks, including strikes and war risks commonly insured under ocean or wet marine forms of policy.

(8 VT. STAT. ANN. § 5025)

Exempt Transactions

The provisions controlling the placement of insurance with nonadmitted insurers shall not apply to life insurance, health insurance, annuities, or reinsurance, nor to the following insurance when so placed by any licensed producer in this state:

1. Insurance on subjects whose home state is other than Vermont;
2. Insurance on the property or operations of aircraft or railroads engaged in transportation in interstate and foreign commerce; or
3. Insurance of vessels, crafts or hulls, cargoes, marine builder's risks, marine protection and indemnity, or other risks, including strikes and war risks commonly insured under ocean or wet marine forms of policy.

(8 Vt. Stat. Ann. § 5025)

Service of Process

Any act of transacting insurance by any unauthorized insurer constitutes an appointment of the secretary of state as attorney of such insurer upon whom may be served all lawful process in any action, suit, or proceeding.

(8 Vt. Stat. Ann. § 3370)

Limitations on Actions Involving Judicial Proceedings

Vermont statutes do not set forth any limitations on actions involving judicial proceedings that apply to the lawful transaction of surplus lines business.

Domestic Surplus Lines Insurers

Vermont permits a domestic insurer with at least $15 million minimum capital and surplus to be designated as a domestic surplus lines insurer upon the written approval of the commissioner.

(8 Vt. Stat. Ann. § 5023a)

Nonadmitted Insurer Filing Requirements

Vermont statutes do not set forth periodic filing requirements for nonadmitted insurers.

See https://dfr.vermont.gov/industry/insurance/company-licensing/how-apply/surplus-lines-insurers (last visited Sept. 2, 2020).

Surplus Lines Broker Licensing

After written application on a form supplied by the commissioner, any licensed producer who is deemed by the commissioner to be trustworthy and competent may be licensed as a surplus lines broker, pursuant to the provisions related to insurance producer licensing in Vermont.

(8 Vt. Stat. Ann. §§ 4791, *et seq.*)

Due Care in Selecting Nonadmitted Insurer

Other than determining that an insurer meets the eligibility requirements, Vermont statutes do not set forth any requirements with regard to the exercise of due care in selecting a nonadmitted insurer.

(8 Vt. Stat. Ann. § 5023)

Diligent Effort/Diligent Search

Insurance cannot be placed with a nonadmitted insurer unless the full amount of insurance required is not reasonably procurable from admitted insurers actually transacting that kind and class of insurance in Vermont; and the amount of insurance exported shall be only the excess over the amount procurable from admitted insurers actually transacting and insuring that kind and class of insurance.

(8 Vt. Stat. Ann. § 5024(a))

Export List

The commissioner of financial regulation may order eligible for export any class or classes of insurance coverage or risk for which he or she finds there to be an inadequate competitive market among admitted insurers either as to acceptance of the risk, contract terms, or premium or premium rate.

(8 Vt. Stat. Ann. § 5024(b))

A search of the department website did not reveal a list of exportable coverages.

Exempt Commercial Purchasers

Vermont has adopted the NRRA (15 U.S.C. § 8201) definition of exempt commercial purchasers. Coverage for these insureds may be exported to the surplus lines market without making a diligent effort to place the coverage with authorized insurers provided (1) the surplus lines broker has disclosed to the exempt commercial purchaser that coverage may or may not be available from an authorized insurer that may provide greater protection with more regulatory oversight, and (2) such exempt commercial purchaser has subsequently requested such broker, in writing, to procure such policy from an unauthorized insurer.

(8 Vt. Stat. Ann. § 5024(c))

Surplus Lines Broker Filing Requirements

On or before the end of each month next following each calendar quarter, each surplus lines broker shall file with the commissioner, on forms prescribed by him or her, a verified report of all surplus lines insurance transacted during the preceding calendar quarter.

(8 Vt. Stat. Ann. § 5034)

Notices

A surplus line policy must have stamped or written conspicuously in no smaller than ten-point boldface type of a contrasting color upon the first page of the policy and the confirmation of insurance, if any, the following notice:

> The company issuing this policy is a surplus lines insurer and the rates charged have not been approved by the Commissioner of Financial Regulation. Any default on the part of the insurer is not covered by the Vermont Insurance Guaranty Association.

(8 Vt. Stat. Ann. § 5028)

Taxes, Stamping Fees, and Other Government-Imposed Charges

Where Vermont is the home state of the insured, gross premiums charged, less any return premiums, surplus lines tax is 3 percent. At the time of filing his or her quarterly report with the commissioner of taxes, each surplus lines broker shall remit the premium tax due thereon to the commissioner of taxes.

(8 Vt. Stat. Ann. § 5035)

Producer, Policy, Inspection, and Other Fees

A surplus lines broker should not be charging a policy fee for service that is already paid for by the receipt of commission by the broker as part of the sale. In instances where additional services are provided to the insured, a broker can charge a fee that is reasonable in relationship to the service provided. Vermont law requires a broker to obtain a prior written agreement with a client, policyholder, or other member of the public concerning the fees or charges made by that broker for that broker procuring, servicing, or providing advice on insurance contracts.

Per SSAP No. 53, premium is defined as ". . . the contractually determined amount charged by the reporting entity to the policyholder for the effective period of the contract based upon the expectation of risk, policy benefits, and expenses associated with the coverage provided by the terms of the insurance contract."

See "FAQ: Can a Surplus Lines Broker Charge a Fee?" and "FAQ: Are Fees Taxable?" on the department website at https://dfr.vermont.gov/industry/insurance/producer-and-individual-licensing/apply-and-renew-your-license/surplus-lines (last visited Dec. 16, 2020).

Industrial Insured Exemption

Vermont statutes and regulations do not contain an industrial insured exemption with regard to surplus lines insurance.

Independent or Direct Procurement Law

Vermont permits independently procured insurance for any insured whose home state is Vermont. The insured must file a written report with the commissioner of taxes and pay a tax of 3 percent by March 1st of the year after the insurance was procured. The report shall show:

1. The name and address of the insured or insureds;
2. The name and address of the insurer or insurers;
3. The subject of the insurance;
4. A general description of the coverage;
5. The amount of premium currently charged for it;
6. Such additional pertinent information as may be reasonably requested by the commissioner of taxes.

(8 VT. STAT. ANN. § 5036)

VIRGINIA

Virginia State Corporation Commission—Bureau of Insurance
P.O. Box 1157
Richmond, VA 23218-1157
(804) 371-9741
https://www.scc.virginia.gov/boi/

Virginia does not have a stamping office.

Nonadmitted Insurer Eligibility

General Information

Surplus line insurers must meet eligibility standards in order to underwrite risks presented by specially licensed excess line brokers. These insurers are not licensed by the state because of an exception to the insurer licensing requirements.

(VA. CODE ANN. § 38.2-4811)

Foreign

Unlicensed foreign insurers wishing to issue surplus lines coverage may receive such approval upon proving evidence that it is authorized to write the type of insurance in its domiciliary jurisdiction, and proof that it has capital and surplus or its equivalent under the laws of its domiciliary jurisdiction, which equal the greater of (1) the minimum capital and surplus requirement or (2) $15 million.

(VA. CODE ANN. § 38.2-4811 (A–D))

Notwithstanding the capital and surplus requirements, an unlicensed foreign insurer may receive approval upon an affirmative finding of acceptability by the commission.

(VA. CODE ANN. § 38.2-4811 (C))

Alien

An unlicensed alien insurer shall be deemed approved if such insurer is listed on the Quarterly Listing of Alien Insurers maintained by the International Insurers Department of the National Association of Insurance Commissioners.

(VA. CODE ANN. § 38.2-4811 (A–D))

Nonadmitted Insurer Eligibility List

Virginia maintains a list of eligible surplus lines insurers online at https://scc.virginia.gov/boi/ConsumerInquiry/Search.aspx (last visited May 7, 2023). When accessing the site, click "Company" at the top of the page. Then choose Company Type: "Surplus Lines Carrier" then click "Search."

Types of Coverage Permitted or Prohibited

General Information

Under the Virginia Insurance Code, surplus lines insurance means any property and casualty insurance permitted to be placed directly by an insured or through a surplus lines broker with an eligible nonadmitted insurer.

(VA. CODE ANN. § 38.2-4805.2)

"Property and casualty insurance" means the classes of insurance defined in §§ 38.2-109 through 38.2-122.2 and §§ 38.2-124 through 38.2-134.

(VA. CODE ANN. § 38.2-4805.2)

Permitted

Permitted coverage includes accident and sickness, fire, miscellaneous property and casualty, but does not include life and annuities, and title insurance, all of which must be written by a monoline company.

(VA. CODE ANN. § 38.2-135)

Exempt Transactions

The surplus line insurance law does not apply to contracts of insurance on:

1. Vessels or craft, their cargo, freight, marine builders' risk, maritime protection and indemnity, ship repairers' legal liability, towers' liability or other risks commonly insured under ocean marine insurance policies as distinguished from inland marine insurance policies, provided that a property and casualty or limited lines property and casualty agent licensed in this commonwealth sells, solicits, or negotiates these classes of insurance on behalf of any insurer not licensed to transact the business of insurance in this commonwealth; or
2. The rolling stock and operating properties of railroads used in interstate commerce or of any liability or other risks incidental to their ownership, maintenance, or operation.

(VA. CODE ANN. §§ 38.2-1802(C), 38.2-4805.1)

Service of Process

Any act of transacting insurance by any unauthorized insurer constitutes an appointment of the clerk of the commission as attorney of such insurer upon whom may be served all lawful process in any action, suit, or proceeding.
(VA. CODE ANN. § 38.2-801(A))

Limitations on Actions Involving Judicial Proceedings

Before any unlicensed insurer files or causes to be filed any pleading in any action, suit, or proceeding instituted against it, that insurer shall either deposit cash or securities with the clerk of court in which the action, suit, or proceeding is pending, or file with the clerk a bond in any amount to be fixed by the court that shall be sufficient to secure the payment of any final judgment; or procure a certificate of authority and a license to transact the business of insurance in this state.

(VA. CODE ANN. § 38.2-806(A))

Domestic Surplus Lines Insurers

Virginia permits a domestic insurer with at least $15 million minimum capital and surplus to be designated as a domestic surplus lines insurer upon the written approval of the commission.

(VA. CODE ANN. § 38.2-4811.1)

Nonadmitted Insurer Filing Requirements

In order for a foreign surplus lines company to maintain its status as an approved surplus lines carrier in Virginia, a Certificate of Compliance must be filed with the Bureau of Insurance no later than March 1 annually.

There are no annual filing requirements for alien surplus lines companies deemed approved in Virginia.

See https://www.scc.virginia.gov/pages/Company-Licensing-and-Amendments (last visited Aug. 8, 2021). When accessing the site, click "Licensing Applications for Non UCAA Filers" to expand the section and scroll down to the Surplus Lines links.

Surplus Lines Broker Licensing

An individual or business entity who is a resident of another state shall receive a nonresident surplus lines broker license if the applicant presents proof that the applicant is licensed or authorized as a resident surplus lines broker and is in good standing in his home state; the applicant has submitted the proper application, or in lieu thereof has submitted a copy of the application for a Surplus Lines Broker license submitted to the home state, and paid the required fees; and the applicant's home state issues nonresident surplus lines broker licenses to residents of Virginia on the same basis, or will permit a resident of Virginia to act as a surplus lines broker in such state without requiring a license.

(VA. CODE ANN. § 38.2-1857.9(A))

The commission may issue a surplus lines broker's license to any individual or business entity actively licensed as a property and casualty insurance agent for the procuring of insurance in certain classes.

(VA. CODE ANN. § 38.2-1857.1)

Due Care in Selecting Nonadmitted Insurer

Other than determining that an insurer meets the eligibility requirements, Virginia statutes do not set forth any requirements with regard to the exercise of due care in selecting a nonadmitted insurer.

(VA. CODE ANN. § 38.2-1857.1)

Diligent Effort/Diligent Search

The diligent effort requirement that surplus lines brokers attempt to procure insurance from a licensed insurer before placing coverage with a surplus lines insurer was eliminated effective July 1, 2008.

Export List

Virginia does not maintain an list of coverages that may be exported to the surplus lines market without first making a diligent search of licensed insurers.

Exempt Commercial Purchasers

Although the NRRA (15 U.S.C. § 8201) exempts a broker from any applicable diligent search requirements when the insured is an exempt commercial purchaser, Virginia statutes do not address this topic.

Surplus Lines Broker Filing Requirements

Surplus Lines Brokers must file an Annual Surplus Lines Brokers Assessment. The minimum Annual Surplus Lines

Brokers Assessment is $300 and is required even if no business was transacted. Once you have keyed in your Virginia license number, the system will automatically calculate the assessment amount due based on the taxable premium entered. You can print the report and mail it with a check to the address noted on the report, or you can file and pay electronically by selecting the File and Pay Assessment button on the website.

See information and instructions on the Virginia State Corporation Commission website at https://scc.virginia.gov/pages/Surplus-Lines-Brokers (last visited Oct. 28, 2020).

Notices

A notice in a form prescribed by the commission shall be given to the insured by the surplus lines broker procuring the policy or by any duly licensed property and casualty insurance agent placing surplus lines business with the surplus lines broker. The notice shall provide that the policy is being procured from or has been placed with an insurer approved by the commission and that there is no protection under the Virginia Property and Casualty Insurance Guaranty Association against financial loss to claimants or policyholders because of the insolvency of an eligible nonadmitted insurer.

The notice shall also set forth the name, license number, and mailing address of the broker, and shall be given prior to placement of the insurance. In the event that coverage must be placed and become effective within 24 hours after referral of the business to the surplus lines broker, the notice may be given promptly following such a placement. In addition, a copy of the notice shall be affixed to the policy.

(Va. Code Ann. § 38.2-4806)

Taxes, Stamping Fees, and Other Government-Imposed Charges

Every licensed surplus lines broker is subject to the annual taxes, license taxes, and penalties on each policy of insurance procured by him during the preceding calendar year with an eligible nonadmitted insurer. For policies effective on or after July 1, 2011, such payments shall be made based on the direct gross premium income derived from policies for insureds whose home state is Virginia.

Upon the failure of any such surplus lines broker to pay the premium license tax within the time required, there shall be added to such tax a penalty of 10 percent of the amount of the tax and interest at a rate equal to the rate of interest for the period between the due date and the date of full payment.

(VA. CODE ANN. § 38.2-4809(A))

The tax is 2.25 percent and is filed quarterly on April 30, July 30, October 30, and January 30.

(VA. CODE ANN. § 58.1-2501)

See also https://www.tax.virginia.gov/insurance-premiums-license-tax (last visited Dec. 2, 2020) and Form 801, which is available at https://www.tax.virginia.gov/eforms (last visited Dec. 2, 2020).

Producer, Policy, Inspection, and Other Fees

All fees, charges, premiums, or other consideration charged for the insurance or for the procurement of insurance shall be stated in the policy except in the case of fidelity, surety, title, and group insurance and consulting services. Service charges for installment payments of insurance premiums do not need to be stated in the policy if the charges are provided to the insured in writing.

(VA. CODE ANN. § 38.2-310)

Industrial Insured Exemption

Virginia statutes and regulations do not contain an industrial insured exemption with regard to surplus lines insurance.

Independent or Direct Procurement Law

Virginia insurance law permits an insured to acquire insurance coverage "directly" by the insured or through a surplus lines broker with an eligible nonadmitted insurer.

(VA. CODE ANN. § 38.2-4805.2)

WASHINGTON

Insurance Commissioner
5000 Capitol Boulevard SE
Olympia, WA 98512
(800) 562-6900
Alternate Address:
P.O. Box 40255
Olympia, WA 98504-0255
www.insurance.wa.gov/
cap@oic.wa.gov

Washington has a stamping office.

Surplus Line Association of Washington
1710 One Union Square, 600 University Street
Seattle, WA 98101-1129
(206) 682-3409
www.surpluslines.org

Nonadmitted Insurer Eligibility

General Information

The commissioner may waive the financial requirements if it is determined insurance cannot be otherwise procured on risks located in this state.

(WASH. REV. CODE § 48.15.090)

Foreign

Foreign insurers must be authorized to write the insurance in its domiciliary jurisdiction and maintain capital and surplus of at least $15 million.

(WASH. REV. CODE § 48.15.090)

Alien

Alien insurers must be on the Quarterly Listing of Alien Insurers maintained by the International Insurers Department of the National Association of Insurance Commissioners. The broker must obtain a waiver of the solvency requirements from the commissioner if the insurer is not on the Quarterly Listing of Alien Insurers.

(WASH. REV. CODE § 48.15.090)

Nonadmitted Insurer Eligibility List

Washington does not maintain a nonadmitted insurer eligibility list. However, the Surplus Line Association of Washington maintains a list of active surplus lines insurers at http://www.surpluslines.org/carriers/ (last visited July 15, 2020).

Types of Coverage Permitted or Prohibited

General Information

There are no prohibited coverages under Washington law.

Exempt Transactions

The following types of insurance are exempt from the surplus line requirements:

- Reinsurance;
- Ocean marine and foreign trade;
- Insurance on risks located wholly outside of the state of Washington;
- Interstate railroad and their property used in the operations; and
- Insurance of aircraft owned or operated by manufacturers of aircraft, or aircraft operated in scheduled interstate flight, including cargo and liability.

(WASH. REV. CODE § 48.15.160)

Service of Process

Any policy written by an unauthorized insurer must contain a provision appointing the commissioner as the agent for service of process.

(Wash. Rev. Code § 48.15.150)

Limitations on Actions Involving Judicial Proceedings

An unauthorized insurer sued under any contract issued as a surplus line contract has 40 days from the date of the service upon the commissioner within which to plead, answer, or otherwise defend the action. Upon service of process upon the commissioner in accordance with the statute, the court has jurisdiction in personam of the insurer.

(Wash. Rev. Code § 48.15.150)

Domestic Surplus Lines Insurers

Washington statutes have no provision allowing domestic surplus lines insurers.

Nonadmitted Insurer Filing Requirements

The Surplus Line Association of Washington requests that insurers submit annual and quarterly filings to the stamping office.

Surplus Lines Broker Licensing

Resident surplus line applicants must pass an examination before obtaining a surplus line license.

(Wash. Rev. Code § 284-15-010)

Individual and business entities applying for a resident license are required to pay an initial $200 application fee, a $5 filing fee, and a $20 affiliation fee. For individual surplus line brokers not affiliated with a licensed surplus line business entity, the $20 affiliation fee is waived.

See https://www.insurance.wa.gov/surplus-line-broker-indi vidual-resident (last visited Sept. 9, 2020).

Every surplus line broker must maintain two bonds:

1. A bond of $2,500 or 5 percent of premium written with nonadmitted insurers from the prior year up to $100,000; and
2. A $20,000 bond for the people of the state of Washington.

(Wash. Rev. Code § 48.15.070)

Surplus line licenses expire every two years and the licensees are required to pay a $200 renewal fee.

Nonresident surplus line applicants holding a current surplus line license in their home state are exempt from the surplus line examination. Nonresident license terms and fees are the same as for residents. Nonresident surplus line brokers must appoint the commissioner as the surplus line broker's attorney to receive service of legal process issued against the surplus line broker in Washington.

(Wash. Rev. Code § 48.15.073)

See also https://www.insurance.wa.gov/surplus-line-broker -individual-non-resident (last visited Sept. 9, 2020).

Due Care in Selecting Nonadmitted Insurer

Surplus lines brokers are prohibited from knowingly placing insurance with insurers that are not financially sound. They are required to determine the financial condition of an unauthorized insurer before placing the insurance, and maintain written evidence of the fact.

(Wash. Rev. Code § 48.15.090)

Diligent Effort/Diligent Search

If coverage cannot be obtained through authorized insurers, the broker may place the coverage with an unauthorized insurer after a diligent effort has been made to place the risk with a majority of insurers authorized to transact that type of insurance in the state.

At the time of procuring the insurance, the surplus line broker must certify the following:

- The facts supporting the surplus line broker's diligent effort;
- The facts contained in the certification are true and correct (under the penalty of suspension or revocation of the surplus line broker's license); and
- Coverage was not obtained for a lower rate premium.

The certification may be in electronic, digital, or another format as designated by the commissioner and must be filed with the commissioner within 60 days after the insurance is procured.

(WASH. REV. CODE § 48.15.040)

Export List

Washington does not maintain a list of coverages that may be exported to the surplus lines market without first making a diligent search of licensed insurers.

Exempt Commercial Purchasers

Washington has adopted the NRRA (15 U.S.C. § 8201) definition of exempt commercial purchasers. Coverage for these insureds may be exported to the surplus lines market without making a diligent effort to place the coverage with authorized insurers provided (1) the surplus lines broker has disclosed to the exempt commercial purchaser that coverage may or may not be available from an authorized insurer that may provide greater protection with more regulatory oversight, and (2) such exempt commercial purchaser has subsequently requested such broker, in writing, to procure such policy from an unauthorized insurer.

(WASH. REV. CODE § 48.15.043)

Surplus Lines Broker Filing Requirements

Surplus line policies must be filed within 60 days of procurement (WASH. REV. CODE § 48.15.040). Filing is done through the Surplus Line Association of Washington. The following documents must be filed with the Association along with a certification form:

- Policy declaration page, certificate, or cover note
- Supplemental declarations page
- Schedule of forms and endorsements
- Copies of service of suit endorsement

See information on the Association website at http://www.surpluslines.org/filing-information/ (last visited Oct. 28, 2020).

Notices

Every insurance policy written on a surplus line basis must have a statement stamped upon its face and initialed by or include the name of the placing surplus line broker with the following notice:

> This contract is registered and delivered as a surplus line coverage under the insurance code of the state of Washington, Title 48 RCW. It is not protected by any Washington state guaranty association law.

(Wash. Rev. Code § 284-15-030)

Taxes, Stamping Fees, and Other Government-Imposed Charges

The surplus line tax is 2 percent and the stamping fee is .10 percent.

See http://www.surpluslines.org/filing-information/taxes-and-fees/ (last visited Dec. 2, 2020).

On or before the first day of March of each year each surplus line broker must remit a tax on the premiums, exclusive of sums collected to cover federal and state taxes and examination fees, on surplus line insurance transacted during the preceding calendar year as shown by the annual statement filed with the commissioner pursuant to Wash. Rev. Code § 48.15.110, and at the same 2 percent rate as is applicable to the premiums of authorized foreign insurers under Washington Revised Code § 48.14.020.

(WASH. REV. CODE § 48.15.120)

Producer, Policy, Inspection, and Other Fees

The surplus line broker can charge a fee in excess of a commission provided the fee is disclosed to the insured in writing prior to rendering of service and the basis of the fee.

(WASH. ADMIN. CODE § 284-30-750)

Industrial Insured Exemption

Washington statutes and regulations do not contain an industrial insured exemption with regard to surplus lines insurance.

Independent or Direct Procurement Law

Washington does not permit independent or direct procurement. All surplus lines insurance must be obtained from a licensed surplus line broker if the insured's home state is Washington.

(WASH. REV. CODE § 48.15.020)

WEST VIRGINIA

West Virginia Offices of the Insurance Commissioner
West Virginia Lottery Building
900 Pennsylvania Avenue
Charleston, WV 25302
(304) 558-1900
https://www.wvinsurance.gov/

Alternate Address:
PO Box 50540
Charleston, WV 25305-0540
(304) 558-0610
OICWVTaxSection@wv.gov
OICAgentLicensing@wv.gov

West Virginia does not have a stamping office.

Nonadmitted Insurer Eligibility

General Information

A West Virginia "eligible surplus lines insurer" is a nonadmitted insurer with which a surplus lines agent may place surplus lines insurance for an insured whose home state is West Virginia.

A surplus lines agent may not place coverage with a nonadmitted insurer, unless, at the time of placement, the surplus lines agent has determined that the nonadmitted insurer has established satisfactory evidence of good repute and financial integrity and has capital and surplus that equals the greater of the minimum West Virginia capital and surplus requirements or $15 million.

The commissioner may waive the minimum capital and surplus requirements after considering such factors as quality of management, capital, and surplus of any parent company, company underwriting profit and investment income trends, market availability, and company record and reputation within the industry. However, the minimum capital and surplus in all instances is $4.5 million.

In certain instances, a surplus lines agent may place surplus lines insurance with a nonadmitted carrier not on the eligibility list. However, only that portion of a risk eligible for export for which the full amount of coverage is not procurable from listed eligible surplus lines insurers may be placed with any other nonadmitted insurer that does not appear on the eligibility list but nonetheless meets the statutory solvency requirements. The surplus lines licensee seeking to provide coverage through an unlisted nonadmitted insurer shall make a filing specifying the amounts and percentages of each risk to be placed, and naming the nonadmitted insurers with which placement is intended. Within 30 days after placing the coverage, the surplus lines licensee shall also send written notice to the insured that the insurance, or a portion thereof, has been placed with the nonadmitted insurer.

(W. Va. Code § 33-12C(d)(5))

Foreign

Foreign surplus lines insurers must submit evidence of the following to the commissioner to apply for an initial designation as an eligible surplus lines insurer:

1. Complete and file Form SL1, Foreign Insurer Surplus Lines Eligibility Application (SL1).
2. Submit a current certificate from the commissioner of insurance in the insurer's state of domicile showing the insurer is authorized to transact the kinds of insurance proposed to be transacted in the state of West Virginia.
3. Maintain capital and surplus or its equivalent under the laws of its state of domicile of no less than $15 million.
4. File a signed copy of the annual statement jurat page.

5. Submit a description of the products the insurer plans to sell in the state of West Virginia and provide a detailed description of the insurers proposed market plan.
6. Remit a check made payable to the West Virginia Offices of the Insurance Commissioner in the amount of $100 for filing of the annual statement.

(W. Va. Code §§ 33-12C, 33-3-13)

See additional information available at https://www.wvinsurance.gov/company/Forms/Surplus-Lines (last visited May 7, 2023).

Alien

In addition to West Virginia requirements, an insurer not domiciled in the United States or its territories shall be listed on the Quarterly Listing of Alien Insurers maintained by the International Insurers Department of the National Association of Insurance Commissioners.

(W. Va. Code § 33-12C-5)

Alien surplus lines insurers must apply to the commissioner for initial designation as an eligible surplus lines insurer by submitting:

1. Form SL2, Surplus Lines Alien Eligibility Application
2. A current certificate of authority from the insurer's country of domicile
3. A description of products to be sold in the state of West Virginia and proposed market plan
4. A check for $100 for the financial statement filing fee
5. The Surplus Lines Affidavit of Filing and Financial Statement Attestation.

(W. Va. Code §§ 33-12C, 33-3-13)

See additional information available at https://www.wvinsurance.gov/company/Forms/Surplus-Lines (last visited May 7, 2023).

Nonadmitted Insurer Eligibility List

The West Virginia insurance commissioner maintains a mandatory list of insurers that qualify as eligible surplus lines insurers. An eligible surplus lines insurer will appear on the most recent list of eligible surplus lines insurers published by the commissioner. The eligibility list is updated from time to time, at least annually.

(W. Va. Code § 33-12C-5(d)(5))

The list of surplus lines insurers can be accessed online at https://www.wvinsurance.gov/company/ (last visited July 15, 2020). When accessing the site, scroll to the "Quarterly Lists of Licensed/Registered Companies" section and click on "List of Surplus Lines Insurers."

Types of Coverage Permitted or Prohibited

General Information

"Surplus lines insurance" means any property and casualty insurance within West Virginia on properties, risks, or exposures, located or to be performed in West Virginia, permitted to be placed through a surplus lines licensee with a nonadmitted insurer eligible to accept such insurance. The term "excess line" is defined by statute to mean surplus lines insurance.

(W. Va. Code § 33-12C-3)

Workers compensation and personal automobile liability for mandatory minimum coverage may not be written in surplus lines.

(W. Va. Code §§ 23-2C-2(n), 17A, 17D)

Exempt Transactions

The following type of transactions are exempt from West Virginia surplus lines laws:

1. Transactions for which a license to do business is not required of an insurer under the insurance laws of West Virginia;

2. Reinsurance, provided that, unless the commissioner grants a waiver:
   a. The assuming insurer is authorized to do an insurance or reinsurance business by its domiciliary jurisdiction and is authorized to write the type of reinsurance in its domiciliary jurisdiction; and
   b. The assuming insurer satisfies all legal requirements for such reinsurance in the state of domicile of the ceding insurer;
3. The property and operation of railroads or aircraft engaged in interstate or foreign commerce, wet marine, and transportation insurance;
4. Transactions subsequent to issuance of a policy not covering properties, risks, or exposures located, or to be performed in West Virginia at the time of issuance, and lawfully solicited, written, or delivered outside West Virginia.

(W. Va. Code § 33-12C-4)

Service of Process

Any act of transacting insurance by any unauthorized insurer constitutes an appointment of the secretary of state as attorney of such insurer upon whom may be served all lawful process in any action, suit, or proceeding.
(W. Va. Code § 33-12C-20)

Limitations on Actions Involving Judicial Proceedings

West Virginia statutes do not set forth any limitations on actions involving judicial proceedings that apply to the lawful transaction of surplus lines business.

A nonadmitted insurer subject to arbitration or other alternative dispute resolution mechanism arising in West Virginia or relative to property, risks, or exposures located or to be performed in the state under an insurance contract made by it shall conduct the arbitration or other alternative dispute resolution mechanism in West Virginia.

(W. VA. CODE § 33-12C-23)

Domestic Surplus Lines Insurers

West Virginia statutes have no provision allowing domestic surplus lines insurers.

Nonadmitted Insurer Filing Requirements

FOREIGN INSURERS

On or before March 1, complete and file Form SL1, Foreign Insurer Surplus Lines Eligibility Application (SL1).

1. Submit a current certificate from the commissioner of insurance in the insurer's state of domicile showing the insurer is authorized to transact the kinds of insurance proposed to be transacted in the state of West Virginia.
2. File a signed copy of the annual statement jurat page.
3. Submit a description of the products the insurer plans to sell in the state of West Virginia and provide a detailed description of the insurers proposed market plan, if amended or changed from the initial filing.
4. Remit a check made payable to the West Virginia Offices of the Insurance Commissioner in the amount of $100 for filing of the annual statement.

(W. VA. CODE §§ 33-12C, 33-3-13)

ALIEN INSURERS

1. On or before March 1, complete and file Form SL2, Alien Insurer Surplus Lines Eligibility Application (SL2).
2. Insurer's name must appear on the NAIC's most recent quarterly listing of alien insurers.

3. Submit a current certificate from the insurance regulatory authority in the insurer's jurisdiction of domicile showing the insurer is authorized to transact the kinds of insurance proposed to be transacted in the state of West Virginia.
4. File Form SL-Alien Aff., Alien Surplus Lines Insurer Affidavit of Filing and Financial Statement Attestation. The form is available at https://www.wvinsurance.gov/company/Forms/Surplus-Lines (last visited May 7, 2023).
5. Submit a description of the products the insurer plans to sell in West Virginia and provide a detailed description of the insurers proposed market plan, if amended or changed from the initial filing.
6. Remit a check made payable to the West Virginia insurance commissioner in the amount of $100 for filing of the annual statement.

(W. Va. Code §§ 33-12C, 33-3-13)

See https://www.wvinsurance.gov/company/Forms/Surplus-Lines (last visited May 7, 2023). When accessing the site, click on "Surplus lines filing instructions."

Each eligible surplus lines insurer must provide to the commissioner a copy of its current annual statement certified by the insurer and an actuarial opinion as to the adequacy of, and methodology used to determine, the insurer's loss reserves. The statement is due at the same time it is provided to the insurer's domicile, but in no event more than eight months after the close of the period reported upon. The annual statement must be certified as a true and correct copy by an accounting or auditing firm licensed in the jurisdiction of the insurer's domicile and must be certified by a senior officer of the nonadmitted insurer as a true and correct copy of the statement filed with the regulatory authority in the domicile of the nonadmitted insurer.

(W. Va. Code § 33-12C-5(4))

Surplus Lines Broker Licensing

An applicant for a surplus lines licensee's license issued or renewed under the provisions of West Virginia Code § 33-12C-8 must meet the following statutory qualifications:

- Shall be a duly licensed individual insurance producer holding a current and valid license for the type(s) of insurance which the applicant expects and intends to export to the surplus lines market;
- Shall have held for at least three consecutive years immediately preceding the date of application a valid individual insurance producer's license for the type(s) of insurance the applicant expects and intends to export to the surplus lines market, and shall have held a valid West Virginia resident or nonresident individual insurance producer's license for such type(s) of insurance for at least one of those three years, or hold a valid excess or surplus line broker license issued by another state.

The commissioner, in his or her discretion, may waive this requirement if the applicant otherwise demonstrates the necessary trustworthiness and competence by education, experience, or other relevant factors:

- Shall satisfactorily complete an examination administered by the office of the commissioner or its designated agent or hold a valid excess line broker or surplus lines license issued by another state.
- Shall pay the required license fee as established by the provisions of West Virginia Code § 33-12C-8;
- Shall be considered trustworthy for the purpose of conducting insurance business as a surplus lines licensee, as required by the provisions of West Virginia Code § 33-12C-8; and
- Shall satisfy any other criteria reasonably established by the commissioner (West Virginia Code of State Rules § 114-20-3).

The department's website containing further information can be found at https://www.wvinsurance.gov/Divisions/Licensing (last visited Sept. 9, 2020).

Due Care in Selecting Nonadmitted Insurer

A West Virginia surplus lines agent may not knowingly place any coverage in an insolvent insurer.

(W. Va. Code § 33-12C-26)

Prior to placing insurance with an eligible surplus lines insurer, a surplus lines licensee must ascertain that such insurer is in sound financial condition. A surplus lines licensee may not place coverage with a nonadmitted insurer unless, at the time of placement, the surplus lines licensee has determined that the nonadmitted insurer has established satisfactory evidence of good repute and financial integrity and meets the eligibility requirements in the statute.

(W. Va. Code § 33-12C-5(d))

Diligent Effort/Diligent Search

West Virginia surplus lines agents must keep records of an affidavit, on a standardized form promulgated by the commissioner, as to the diligent efforts to place the coverage with admitted insurers and the results of that effort. The affidavit must be open to public inspection.

(W. Va. Code § 33-12C-11(b)(8))

Surplus lines insurance may be placed by a surplus lines licensee if the full amount or line of insurance cannot be obtained from insurers who are admitted to do business in West Virginia. The full amount or type of insurance may be procured from eligible surplus lines insurers, provided that a diligent search is made by the individual insurance producer among the insurers who are admitted to transact and are actually writing the particular type of insurance in West Virginia if any are writing it.

(W. Va. Code § 33-12C-5)

The promulgated form is Due Diligence Form DDF, Revised 8/09) documenting the "due diligence" to place the risk in the admitted market. The form is available at https://www.wvinsurance.gov/Divisions/Financial-Accounting/ItemId/3725 (last visited Sept. 30, 2020). When accessing the site, scroll to the section titled "Taxes—Surplus Lines Licensees" to find the form.

Export List

The commissioner maintains the export list of insurance coverages and classes that may be placed with surplus lines insurers for insureds whose home state is West Virginia.

(W. VA. CODE R. § 114-20-7, West Virginia Code of State Rules § 114-20-7)

Any person may request in writing that, at the next publication of the list, the commissioner add or remove a coverage or class of insurance from the list. The person must provide evidence of market conditions to substantiate the request.

(W. VA. CODE R. § 114-20-7.1, West Virginia Code of State Rules § 114-20-7.1)

The list is available at https://www.wvinsurance.gov/company-home (last visited May 7, 2023). When accessing the site, scroll to the section titled "Quarterly Lists of Licensed/Registered Companies" and look for "West Virginia Surplus Lines Export List."

Exempt Commercial Purchasers

West Virginia has adopted the NRRA (15 U.S.C. § 8201) definition of exempt commercial purchasers. Coverage for these insureds may be exported to the surplus lines market without making a diligent effort to place the coverage with authorized insurers provided (1) the surplus lines broker has disclosed to the exempt commercial purchaser that coverage may or may not be available from an authorized insurer that may provide greater protection with more regulatory oversight, and (2) such exempt commercial purchaser has subsequently requested such broker, in writing, to procure such policy from an unauthorized insurer.

(W. Va. Code §§ 33-12C-5, 33-12C-3; W. Va. Code R. § 114-20-4.A.1)

Surplus Lines Broker Filing Requirements

On or before March 1, each surplus lines licensee must file, on a form prescribed by the commissioner, a report under oath, setting forth facts from which it may be determined whether the statutory requirements have been met with respect to each surplus line policy procured by the surplus lines licensee during the preceding calendar year. The required report includes but is not limited to certain information listed in the statute.

(W. Va. Code § 33-12C-11)

On or before May 1, each surplus lines licensee shall file with the commissioner, on forms prescribed by the commissioner, a verified report in duplicate of all surplus lines insurance transacted during the preceding period showing gross premiums, return premiums, tax remitted to West Virginia, and tax due or remitted to other states for which an allocation is made pursuant to the statute.

(W. Va. Code § 33-12C-17)

Each surplus lines licensee must keep in the state a full and true record of each surplus lines insurance contract placed by or through the licensee. The record of each contract shall be kept open at all reasonable times to examination by the commissioner for a period not less than ten years following termination of the contract.

(W. Va. Code § 33-12C-16)

Notices

Each surplus lines insurance policy or evidence of insurance shall have printed or stamped in contrasting color on the front page the following statement:

> THIS COMPANY IS NOT LICENSED TO DO BUSINESS IN WEST VIRGINIA AND IS NOT SUBJECT TO THE WEST VIRGINIA INSURANCE GUARANTY ACT.

West Virginia surplus lines agents must keep a record of an affidavit on a standardized form promulgated by the commissioner, as to the diligent efforts to place the coverage with admitted insurers and the results of that effort. The affidavit shall be open to public inspection.

The affidavit shall affirm that the insured was expressly advised in writing prior to placement of the insurance that:

a. The surplus lines insurer with whom the insurance was to be placed is not licensed in West Virginia and is not subject to its supervision; and
b. In the event of the insolvency of the surplus lines insurer, losses will not be paid by the state insurance guaranty fund.

(W. Va. Code § 33-12C-11(b)(8))

The surplus lines licensee shall give the following consumer notice to every person applying for insurance with a nonadmitted insurer not on the eligibility list.

Notice:

1. An insurer that is not licensed in West Virginia is issuing the insurance policy that you have applied to purchase. These companies are called "nonadmitted" or "surplus lines" insurers.
2. The insurer is not subject to the financial solvency regulation and enforcement that applies to licensed insurers in West Virginia.
3. These insurers generally do not participate in insurance guaranty funds created by state law. These guaranty funds will not pay your claims or protect your assets if the insurer becomes insolvent and is unable to make payments as promised.
4. Some states maintain lists of approved or eligible surplus lines insurers, and surplus lines brokers may use only insurers on the lists. Some states issue orders that particular surplus lines insurers cannot be used.
5. For additional information about the preceding matters and about the insurer, you should ask questions of your

insurance agent or surplus lines licensee. You may also contact your insurance commission consumer help line.

(W. VA. CODE § 33-12C-12)

The notice shall be printed in 16-point type on a separate document affixed to the application. The applicant shall sign and date a copy of the notice to acknowledge receiving it. The surplus lines licensee shall maintain the signed notice in its file for a period of ten years from expiration of the policy. The surplus lines licensee shall tender a copy of the signed notice to the insured at the time of delivery of each policy the licensee transacts with a nonadmitted insurer. The copy shall be a separate document affixed to the policy.

(W. VA. CODE § 33-12C-12)

No contract of insurance placed by a surplus lines licensee in West Virginia is binding upon the insured and no premium or fee charged is due and payable until the surplus lines licensee has notified the insured in writing, in a form acceptable to the commissioner, a copy of which shall be maintained by the licensee with the records of the contract and available for possible examination, that:

- The insurer with which the licensee places the insurance is not licensed by West Virginia and is not subject to its supervision; and
- In the event of the insolvency of the surplus lines insurer, losses will not be paid by the state insurance guaranty fund.
- Nothing herein contained shall nullify any agreement by any insurer to provide insurance.

(W. VA. CODE § 33-12C-13)

Taxes, Stamping Fees, and Other Government-Imposed Charges

Any surplus lines licensee subject to insurance premium taxes or surcharge in a given taxable year must file a tax statement for that year, even if the surplus lines licensee has no tax liability.

The surplus lines tax rate is 4.55 percent of the gross premiums and gross fees charged, less any return premiums.

(W. VA. CODE § 33-43-6(a))

The surplus lines tax rate is 4.55 percent of the gross premiums and gross fees charged, less any return premiums. The individual insurance producer may not pay any portion of the tax or rebate any part of the tax or commission.

(W. VA. CODE § 33-12C-7)

Producer, Policy, Inspection, and Other Fees

Gross fees are included with gross premiums when calculating surplus lines premium tax. The surplus lines licensee may charge the prospective policyholder a fee for the cost of underwriting, issuing, processing, inspecting, service, or auditing the policy for placement with the surplus lines insurer if:

1. The service is required by the surplus lines insurer;
2. The service is actually provided by the individual insurance producer or the cost of the service is actually incurred by the surplus lines licensee; and
3. The provision or cost of the service is reasonable, documented, and verifiable.

The surplus lines licensee shall also make a clear and conspicuous written disclosure to the policyholder of:

1. The total amount of premium for the policy;
2. Any fee charged;
3. The total amount of any fee charged; and
4. The total amount of tax on the premium and fee.

(W. VA. CODE § 33-12C-7)

Industrial Insured Exemption

West Virginia statutes and regulations do not contain an industrial insured exemption with regard to surplus lines insurance.

Independent or Direct Procurement Law

West Virginia statutes and regulations do not contain provisions addressing independently procured insurance.

WISCONSIN

Wisconsin Office of the Commissioner of Insurance (OCI)
125 South Webster Street
Madison, WI 53703
(608) 266-3585

Alternate Address:
PO Box 7873
Madison, WI 53707-7873
https://oci.wi.gov

Wisconsin does not have a stamping office.

Nonadmitted Insurer Eligibility

General Information

Wisconsin has adopted the NRRA (15 U.S.C. § 8201) eligibility requirements, with some modifications.
(WIS. STAT. § 618.416)

Foreign

For an insurer domiciled in the United States to be eligible to write in Wisconsin, it must be licensed in its domiciliary jurisdiction to write the type of insurance and must capital and surplus of at least the minimum capital and surplus requirements under the laws of Wisconsin or $15 million, whichever is greater. An insurer that does not meet these requirements can be eligible upon an affirmative finding of the commissioner, provided the capital and surplus are at least $4.5 million.
(WIS. STAT. § 618.416(1))

Alien

For an alien insurer, it must be listed on the Quarterly Listing of Alien Insurers maintained by the International Insurers Department of the National Association of Insurance Commissioners and must meet any additional requirements established by the commissioner.

(WIS. STAT. § 618.416(2))

Nonadmitted Insurer Eligibility List

Wisconsin does not maintain a nonadmitted insurer eligibility list. Although such a list is contemplated in Wisconsin Statutes § 618.41(6)(d) and was previously in effect, the commissioner stopped creating the list and reviewing surplus lines insurer financial statements effective March 31, 2004.

See OCI website: https://oci.wi.gov/Pages/Companies/SrplsLnsIns.aspx (last visited July 15, 2020).

Types of Coverage Permitted or Prohibited

Prohibited

Wisconsin regulations prohibit the placement of title insurance, mortgage guaranty insurance, and worker's compensation insurance with unauthorized insurers.

(WIS. ADMIN. CODE Ins. § 6.17(2)(a))

The commissioner may by rule prohibit surplus lines placement in a specified class of insurance if authorized insurers provide an established market for the class in this state that is adequate and reasonably competitive with reputable unauthorized insurers. The commissioner may by rule place restrictions and limitations on and create special procedures for surplus line insurance for a specified class of insurance if there have been abuses of placements in the class or if the policyholders in the class, because of limited financial resources, business experience, or knowledge, cannot be expected to protect their own interests adequately.

(WIS. STAT. § 618.41)

Exempt Transactions

Wisconsin statutes do not set forth any transactions exempt from surplus lines laws.

Service of Process

Any act of transacting insurance by any unauthorized insurer constitutes an appointment of the commissioner and Department of Financial Institutions as attorneys of such insurer upon whom may be served all lawful process in any action, suit, or proceeding.

(WIS. STAT. § 601.72(2))

Limitations on Actions Involving Judicial Proceedings

Before any unauthorized insurer files any pleading in any court action, they must post a bond or obtain a certificate of authority. However, this does not prevent an unauthorized insurer from filing a motion to quash a writ or to set aside service on the ground that he or she has not done an insurance business in this state.

(WIS. STAT. § 618.47(1))

Domestic Surplus Lines Insurers

Wisconsin permits a domestic insurer with at least $15 million minimum capital and surplus to be designated as a domestic surplus lines insurer upon the written approval of the commissioner.

(WIS. STAT. § 618.41(13))

Nonadmitted Insurer Filing Requirements

Wisconsin statutes do not set forth periodic filing requirements for nonadmitted insurers.

Surplus Lines Broker Licensing

The commissioner may issue a license as an agent or broker authorized to place surplus lines business. The commissioner may by rule require a bond not larger than $100,000.
(WIS. STAT. § 628.04(2))

Residents must hold an active property and casualty license, apply via www.nipr.com, and pay an initial license fee of $100. Nonresidents must hold an active surplus lines license in their resident state, apply via www.nipr.com, and pay an initial license fee of $100. Surplus lines licenses renew annually on the last day of the agent's birth month. Surplus lines renewals are available to renew 60 days prior the license expiration date.

See OCI website at https://oci.wi.gov/Pages/Agents/Surplus Lines.aspx (last visited Sept. 9, 2020).

Due Care in Selecting Nonadmitted Insurer

Other than determining that an insurer meets the eligibility requirements, Wisconsin statutes do not set forth any requirements with regard to the exercise of due care in selecting a nonadmitted insurer.

(WIS. STAT. § 618.416)

Diligent Effort/Diligent Search

Wisconsin statutes do not set forth a diligent effort/diligent search requirement for surplus lines brokers.

Export List

Wisconsin does not maintain a list of coverages that may be exported to the surplus lines market without first making a diligent search of licensed insurers.

Exempt Commercial Purchasers

Although the NRRA (15 U.S.C. § 8201) exempts a broker from any applicable diligent search requirements when the insured is an exempt commercial purchaser, Wisconsin statutes do not address this topic.

Surplus Lines Broker Filing Requirements

All premium tax collected by the surplus lines agent shall be reported and forwarded to the commissioner on or before March 1, for all insurance procured, renewed, or continued during the preceding calendar year with unauthorized insurers (Wis. Admin. Code Ins. § 6.17(5)). While the regulation prescribes a specific form, the OCI has changed to using OPTIns for reporting forms and payment of surplus lines taxes.

See information on OCI website at https://oci.wi.gov/Pages/Companies/SrplsLnsIns.aspx (last visited Oct. 28, 2020).

Notices

Surplus line proposals must be in a form substantially similar to Appendix 1 of Wisconsin Administrative Code Insurance § 6.17, which includes policyholder notice wording. Appendix 1 can be found at https://docs.legis.wisconsin.gov/code/admin_code/ins/6/17 (last visited Nov. 11, 2020).

Surplus lines policies must bear the name and address of the insurance agent or broker who procured it and shall have stamped or affixed upon it the following:

> This insurance contract is with an insurer which has not obtained a certificate of authority to transact a regular insurance business in the state of Wisconsin, and is issued and delivered as a surplus line coverage pursuant to s. 618.41 of the Wisconsin Statutes. Section 618.43 (1), Wisconsin Statutes, requires payment by the policyholder of 3 percent tax on gross premium.
>
> (Wis. Stat. § 618.41(9)(a))

Domestic surplus lines insurer policies must bear the name and address of the insurance agent or broker who procured it and shall have stamped or affixed upon it the following:

> This insurance contract is issued and delivered as a surplus line coverage pursuant to s. 618.41 of the Wisconsin Statutes. Section 618.43 (1), Wisconsin Statutes, requires payment by the policyholder of 3 percent tax on gross premium. If the insurer that issued and delivered this policy becomes insolvent, insureds or claimants will not be eligible for Wisconsin Insurance Security Fund protection under chapter 646 of the Wisconsin Statutes.
>
> (Wis. Stat. § 618.41(9)(c))

Taxes, Stamping Fees, and Other Government-Imposed Charges

The Wisconsin surplus line tax rate is 3 percent.
(Wis. Stat. § 618.43(1)(a))
Surplus lines tax payments are due annually on March 1.
(Wis. Admin. Code Ins. § 6.17(5))
The surplus lines payments may now be submitted online using the NAIC OPTins Premium Tax Payment system for producers/agents filing in 2017 and later.

See "Bulletin, November 15, 2016, Change in Submission and Payment for Surplus Lines Taxes to OPTins" on the OCI website at https://oci.wi.gov/Pages/Regulation/Bulletin20161115SurplusLinesTaxes.aspx (last visited Dec. 2, 2020).

With regard to premium taxes on surplus lines business, there are no tax exemptions for any policyholder or risk, except for Indian Tribes and federally chartered credit unions.

See OCI website at https://oci.wi.gov/Pages/Consumers/PI-026.aspx (last visited Dec. 2, 2020). When accessing the site, click on "Is surplus lines business subject to Wisconsin tax?" to expand the section.

Producer, Policy, Inspection, and Other Fees

Surplus lines premium tax is based on any payment made as consideration for an insurance contract for such insurance, including premium deposits, assessments, registration fees, and any other compensation given in consideration for a contract of insurance.

(Wis. Stat. § 618.40)

Industrial Insured Exemption

Wisconsin statutes and regulations do not contain an industrial insured exemption with regard to surplus lines insurance.

Independent or Direct Procurement Law

Wisconsin allows independent procurement with unauthorized insurers if negotiations occur primarily outside the state. Independently procured insurance must be reported to the commissioner within 60 days after the insurance was procured or renewed and the tax must be paid. Insureds may not independently procure insurance from unauthorized insurance for any insurance on personal property sold on the installment plan or under a conditional sales contract for which a charge is made to the buyer, or for any compulsory insurance required by Wisconsin law.

(Wis. Stat. § 618.42)

Premium tax for independently procured policies is 3 percent.

(Wis. Stat. § 618.43(1)(a)(1))

WYOMING

Wyoming Department of Insurance
106 E. 6th Street
Cheyenne, WY 82011
(307) 777-7401
http://doi.wyo.gov/

Wyoming does not have a stamping office.

Nonadmitted Insurer Eligibility

General Information

A surplus lines broker may not place coverage with a nonadmitted insurer unless the broker determines that the nonadmitted insurer is eligible to place surplus lines insurance.
(Wyo. Stat. § 26-11-107(e))

Foreign

A U.S.-domiciled insurer is eligible to write nonadmitted insurance in Wyoming for risks whose home state is Wyoming if:

- It is eligible in its state of domicile to write the kinds of insurance that it intends to write in Wyoming; and
- It maintains minimum capital and surplus (or equivalent) requirements in the amount of $15 million or the minimum requirements of Wyoming Statutes §§ 26-11-101 *et seq.*, whichever requirements are greater. These requirements may be reduced, but not below $4.5 million, for an insurer as a result of an affirmative finding of acceptability by the commissioner based upon such factors as quality of management, capital, and surplus of any parent company, company underwriting profit and investment

income trends, market availability, and company record and reputation within the industry.

(WYO. STAT. § 26-11-107)

Alien

A surplus line broker may not place insurance with an alien insurer unless the insurer is listed on the Quarterly Listing of Alien Insurers maintained by the International Insurers Department of the National Association of Insurance Commissioners.

(WYO. STAT. § 26-11-107(f)(iv))

Nonadmitted Insurer Eligibility List

The Wyoming Department of Insurance is authorized, but not required, to maintain an insurer eligibility list.

(WYO. STAT. § 26-11-107(d))

The department currently does not maintain an eligibility list.

Types of Coverage Permitted or Prohibited

General Information

There are no prohibited coverages under Wyoming law.

Exempt Transactions

The following transactions by nonadmitted insurers are exempt from Wyoming's surplus lines laws:

- Wet marine and transportation insurance;
- Insurance on subjects located, resident, or to be performed wholly outside of Wyoming, or on vehicles or aircraft owned and principally garaged outside of Wyoming;
- Insurance on operations of railroads and their property; and
- Insurance on aircraft owned or operated by manufacturers of aircraft, or on aircraft operated in commercial

interstate flight, or cargo of that aircraft, or against liability, other than worker's compensation and employer's liability, arising out of the ownership, maintenance, or use of that aircraft.

(WYO. STAT. § 26-11-102(a))

Service of Process

An unauthorized insurer issuing a policy is deemed to have consented to service of process upon the commissioner.
(WYO. STAT. § 26-11-120)

Limitations on Actions Involving Judicial Proceedings

Wyoming statutes do not set forth any limitations on actions involving judicial proceedings that apply to the lawful transaction of surplus lines business.

Domestic Surplus Lines Insurers

Wyoming statutes have no provision allowing domestic surplus lines insurers.

Nonadmitted Insurer Filing Requirements

Wyoming statutes do not set forth periodic filing requirements for nonadmitted insurers.

Surplus Lines Broker Licensing

An individual who holds a current Wyoming property and casualty insurance broker license may receive a resident surplus lines insurance broker license by remitting the application and fee to the commissioner, currently $100, passing a written exam, and establishing and maintaining an office in Wyoming.
(WYO. STAT. §§ 26-11-112(f), 26-4-101(a)(viii))

An individual who holds a current surplus lines broker license in his or her home state other than Wyoming may receive a nonresident surplus lines broker license through the same procedures as a Wyoming resident if the individual's home state licenses Wyoming residents on the same basis.

(WYO. STAT. § 26-9-209(d))

The application fee for nonresidents is currently $150.

(WYO. STAT. § 26-4-101(a)(viii))

A resident or nonresident business entity acting as a surplus lines broker must obtain a surplus lines broker license in the same manner as a resident or nonresident individual, except that, in addition, the business entity must designate a licensed surplus lines broker responsible for the business entity's compliance with Wyoming's insurance laws, rules, and regulations.

(WYO. STAT. § 26-11-112(h))

Due Care in Selecting Nonadmitted Insurer

Other than determining that an insurer meets the eligibility requirements, Wyoming statutes do not set forth any requirements with regard to the exercise of due care in selecting a nonadmitted insurer.

(WYO. STAT. § 26-11-107)

Diligent Effort/Diligent Search

Surplus lines coverage may be procured from nonadmitted insurers if the full amount or kind of insurance is not procurable from authorized insurers and a diligent search to procure the coverage from at least three authorized insurers has been made, as attested by the surplus lines broker.

(WYO. STAT. § 26-11-104(a))

Export List

The commissioner may declare certain classes of insurance coverage or risk eligible for export generally, and such classes of insurance are exempt from the diligent effort requirement and the "not exported for the purpose of securing advantages" requirement.

(Wyo. Stat. § 26-11-106(a))

The list of classes of insurance coverage or risk the commissioner has declared eligible for export generally is available on the Wyoming Department of Insurance's website at https://doi.wyo.gov/companies/surplus-lines (last visited May 7, 2023). When accessing the site, scroll to the Frequently Asked Questions and click on "Does Wyoming Have an Export List?"

Exempt Commercial Purchasers

Wyoming has adopted the NRRA (15 U.S.C. § 8201) definition of exempt commercial purchasers. Coverage for these insureds may be exported to the surplus lines market without making a diligent effort to place the coverage with authorized insurers provided (i) the surplus lines broker has disclosed to the exempt commercial purchaser that coverage may or may not be available from an authorized insurer that may provide greater protection with more regulatory oversight, and (ii) such exempt commercial purchaser has subsequently requested such broker, in writing, to procure such policy from an unauthorized insurer.

(Wyo. Stat. § 26-11-104)

Surplus Lines Broker Filing Requirements

Within 45 days of placing surplus lines insurance, a surplus lines broker must execute and file a confidential report with the commissioner. The report must be on a form prescribed by the commissioner and must contain:

1. The name and address of the insured;
2. The identity of the insurer(s);
3. A description of the subject and location of the risk;
4. The amount of premium charged;
5. Tax allocation information detailing the portion of the premium attributable to properties, risks, or exposures located in each state; and
6. Any other information required by the commissioner.

(Wyo. Stat. § 26-11-105(a))

Each surplus lines broker, on or before February 15, May 15, August 15, and November 15 of each year, if applicable, shall file with the commissioner an affidavit report verifying that all surplus lines insurance transacted during the preceding calendar quarter has been submitted as required by the commissioner. The report shall be in the form and manner the commissioner prescribes and shall include a statement as to the diligent efforts made to place the coverage with admitted insurers.

(Wyo. Stat. § 26-11-117)

Filing is accomplished using the SLAS Clearinghouse. Information and directions are available on the DOI website at http://doi.wyo.gov/companies/surplus-lines (last visited May 7, 2023). When accessing the site, scroll down and click on "Surplus Lines Forms" to expand the section.

Notices

Any insurance procured as surplus lines coverage must have stamped or printed on it, in at least ten-point bold type font, the name and address of the surplus lines broker who procured the coverage and the following language:

> This insurance contract is issued pursuant to the Wyoming Insurance Laws by an insurer neither licensed by nor under the jurisdiction of the Wyoming Insurance Department. In the event of insolvency of the surplus lines insurer, losses will not be paid by the Wyoming Insurance Guaranty Association.

No contract of insurance placed by a surplus lines broker shall be binding upon the insured and no premium charged shall be due and payable until the surplus lines broker notifies the insured in writing, in a form acceptable to the commissioner, that (1) the insurer with which the surplus lines broker places the insurance is not licensed by this state and is not subject to its supervision; and (2) in the event of the insolvency of the surplus lines insurer, losses will not be paid by the state insurance guaranty association.

(Wyo. Stat. § 26-11-109)

Taxes, Stamping Fees, and Other Government-Imposed Charges

Wyoming imposes a premium tax on surplus lines insurance of 3.0 percent of gross premiums, which the surplus lines broker is required to collect and pay. Surplus lines brokers are prohibited from rebating any part of the premium tax.

(Wyo. Stat. § 26-11-118)

Premium includes any assessment, membership, policy, survey, inspection, service of similar fee, or other charge in consideration for an insurance contract, and such fees are therefore subject to the premium tax.

(Wyo. Stat. § 26-1-102(a)(xxii))

Producer, Policy, Inspection, and Other Fees

Surplus lines premium tax is based on any payment made as consideration for an insurance contract for such insurance, including premium deposits, assessments, registration fees, and any other compensation given in consideration for a contract of insurance.

(Wyo. Stat. § 26-11-103(a)(xv))

Industrial Insured Exemption

Wyoming permits an insured that meets the definition of an industrial insured to acquire insurance coverage directly from an insurer not authorized to do an insurance business in the state.

(Wyo. Stat. § 26-12-102(b)(v))

An "industrial insured" means an insured:

1. Which procures the insurance of any risk other than life and annuity contracts through the services of a full-time employee acting as an insurance manager or buyer or the services of a regularly and continuously retained qualified insurance consultant; and

2. Whose aggregate annual premiums for insurance on all risks total at least $25,000; and
3. Which has at least 25 full-time employees.

(WYO. STAT. § 26-12-101)

Independent or Direct Procurement Law

"Independently procured insurance" means insurance procured directly by an insured from an eligible nonadmitted insurer.

(WYO. STAT. § 26-11-103(a)(xii))

Each insured who independently procured insurance must, within 45 days after the insurance was procured, file a report with the commissioner showing the name and address of the insured(s), name and address of the insurer, the subject of insurance, a general description of the coverage, the amount of premium currently charged, and additional information requested by the commissioner. At the time of filing the report, the insured is subject to the same tax payment requirements applicable to surplus lines brokers.

(WYO. STAT. § 26-11-124)